"Thinking about money is an activity which can send one into a state that borders on anything from a slight uneasiness to terror."

from *Bread Upon the Waters*
by Irwin Shaw
Delacorte Press

To Loraine Grover Wallace, whose need gave me the idea for the book. To Mike Dworken, Certified Public Accountant, who lent ideas and support to the project. And to my children, Valerie and Eric.

YOUR PERSONAL
FINANCIAL
FITNESS PROGRAM

1997–98 Edition

YOUR PERSONAL FINANCIAL FITNESS PROGRAM

1997–98 Edition

Elizabeth S. Lewin, CFP

Facts On File, Inc.

Your Personal Financial Fitness Program 1997–98 Edition
Copyright © 1997 by Elizabeth S. Lewin

Facts On File, Inc.
11 Penn Plaza
New York NY 10001

Library of Congress Cataloging-in-Publication Data

Lewin, Elizabeth.
    Your personal financial fitness program / Elizabeth S. Lewin.—
1997–98 ed.
      p.   cm.
    Includes index.
    ISBN 0-8160-3575-X
    1. Finance, Personal.   I. Title.
HG179.L48 1997
332.024—dc20   90-49087

Facts On File books are available at special discounts when purchased in bulk
quantities for businesses, associations, institutions or sales promotions. Please call
our Special Sales Department in New York at 212/967-8800 or 800/322-8755.

Cover design by Semadar Megged

This book is printed on acid-free paper.

Printed in the United States of America

VB FOF 9 8 7 6 5 4 3 2 1

ACKNOWLEDGMENTS

o   o   o

This book would not have been possible without the assistance of Bernard Ryan Jr. I also wish to thank Jill E. Hill, Hewitt Associates, Lincolnshire, Ill.; Charlotte Rush, Vice President Public Affairs, MasterCard International; Linda L. Stanier, Senior Vice President, The Rowland Company, New York, N.Y.; Richard Fulljames, Wyatt & Company, Stamford, Conn.; and the late Harold Schifreen and Anita Greenhut, both of whom helped with the first edition.

CONTENTS

o   o   o

WHY I WROTE
THIS BOOK

○   ○   ○   ○

If you have ever made the discovery that money doesn't stretch as far as you expect it to . . . if you have ever hoped or prayed for a way to eliminate the frustration that arises from financial turmoil . . . this book is for you.

It is for singles, for couples starting out in marriage and couples in midstream with large or small families, for the widowed, the divorced and the retired—and especially for those who are in transition from one such stage to another. It is for anyone who needs practical, instructive ways to control his or her own finances.

My Total Financial Fitness Program grew out of the many seminars I have given. Their purpose is to build confidence and create a sense of security about handling money in much the same way a physical fitness program builds confidence and security about your weight, muscle tone and health. When your body is out of shape, you know you need a physical fitness program. When handling money gets out of control, you need this Financial Fitness Program.

That's why I wrote this book—to help you meet that need. And to help you see that even if you are in a crunch, you don't need a lot of money to get out of it.

I urge you to use this book in a very direct way. Study the sample worksheets. Get acquainted with the three typical families (one from each of three generations) that show you how financial situations are linked directly to life situations. Then start filling out your own individual worksheets. Use a pencil with a good eraser, and don't be afraid to use the eraser end, too! Feel free to photocopy the worksheets for your personal use.

Above all, take your time. Like a physical fitness program, my Total Financial Fitness Program cannot be done in one sitting. If you try to cram it all together, you will gain frustrations—not control.

Finally—and also like physical fitness—remember that the more you work and gain control, the better you will feel and the more fun you will have.

Elizabeth Lewin

YOUR PERSONAL FINANCIAL FITNESS PROGRAM

1997–98 Edition

WHY MANAGE MONEY?

○   ○   ○   ○

"How come my money runs out before the month runs out?"
"There's another call from somebody who wants to get paid!"
"Oh, dear—where did I put that insurance policy?"

○   ○   ○

Sooner or later, almost everyone gets in a quandary over money matters. Most people feel they need help, but they don't always know where to begin. When people come to my Personal Financial Fitness seminars, they are usually surprised to discover that they don't have to drown in a flood of papers, or stew about unpaid bills, or feel embarrassed because they can't seem to manage.

It is my job to help people understand their money needs, and to help them realize that they have feelings about money—just as they have feelings about every other subject that is vital to them. These feelings are an integral part of their attitudes and abilities where handling money is concerned. At the same time, it is my job to help them become financially fit by learning to manage their money—both for the immediate future and for the years ahead.

The goal: control your money

The only way to be financially fit is to get control of your own finances. That is the purpose of this book—to help *you* get control of your money. Just like a physical fitness program, it requires some exercises. But instead of calisthenics, you'll be doing your exercises with a pencil or computer. If you stay on the program, you'll be as financially fit as anyone could desire.

If you are confused, or think you are confused, about money, you are certainly not alone. There is plenty to get confused about, from continuing changes in tax laws, inflation, fluctuations in interest rates, and new ways to invest, to the buy-now pay-later world of the credit card.

You may feel standoffish or inadequate when it comes to money matters. Most people do. Most people don't even like to think about money and are afraid to look at their own situation. It is always out of control, they feel. Their incomes are too small for long-range planning or even for immediate planning. Besides, planning takes too much time. How could it be worth it?

That is the key to Financial Fitness. Planning *is* worth it. No matter how large or small your income, planning can put you fully in charge of it. Planning can make you the boss of your financial destiny. And you do not have to be a financial wizard to plan how to handle your money and make educated decisions.

Planning answers the "what ifs"

Planning can get you ready to answer the "what if" questions that are so important in life:

"What if I buy a new car now?"
"What if I take out another loan—can my lifestyle stand it?"
"What if we sell the house now?"

"What if we have our first baby this year?"
"What if I lost my job?"

All of the "what if" questions (and you may be able to think of dozens more) fall into one of the five main categories of financial planning:

1. Coping with an emergency
2. Saving for future expenses
3. Maintaining adequate insurance
4. Providing the income for retirement
5. Preserving and maximizing an estate for survivors.

Planning is also important to your emotional security. With financial planning under control, you reduce risks, avoid anxiety over spending, and manage to increase savings. You are ready to cope with unexpected and unplanned expenses that can adversely affect your resources, such as a relocation, a divorce, the death of a spouse or a parent, disability, loss of a job, even the arrival of a child.

While many people hope and wish that nothing would ever change, life is change and change affects finances. Let's look at just three major changes that affect most people:

1. *Living alone.* More than 80 percent of today's women will live alone during some period of their lives, probably because of divorce or widowhood. Many divorced women must exist on less money than they have become accustomed to. And many find themselves having to manage money for the first time. Simply learning to balance the checkbook, let alone planning several years of higher education for their children, can be traumatic for women with no financial experience. Widows often feel intellectually ill-equipped to handle their own money and make financial decisions, even in situations where retirement and estate planning have been carefully considered beforehand.

2. *Debt.* Consumer debt is now over $1 trillion. Many couples have kept up with the Joneses via a spending spree three decades long—and find themselves bogged deeply in debt. Today's income no longer covers yesterday's excesses and a terrible double drain occurs: While a large proportion of income must be paid out to reduce debt, inflation raises the cost of basic expenses. The result? Some people borrow to cover basic living expenses—a near-suicidal lifestyle.

3. *Retirement.* The retirement years are supposed to be sun-filled with time for travel, leisure and hobbies—but only if finances are in place. Sadly, income from Social Security and pensions is inadequate for most people. Today, many retirees worry about paying for food and other basic necessities. They are reevaluating their assets and studying alternative ways to make

the money they have saved contribute to their total income. Savings must begin years ahead of retirement if income is to be adequate for those golden years. In addition, economic changes and corporate restructuring are forcing millions of Americans to reevaluate their careers and their futures. Downsizing is commonplace as companies try to stay competitive. People need to think seriously about retirement, no matter how far off it is in the future.

You will be surprised how much frustration can be eliminated from your life by becoming and staying financially fit. And you will be especially thankful when a crisis or major change occurs, as one inevitably will, and you find that you have come through it with financial matters under control.

Only you can do it

One other point: Like physical exercise, no one can do it for you. You cannot leave money matters to fate, for fate can be cruel. You cannot leave them until some future time, for they will not go away. And you cannot, over the long haul, leave them to someone else, for ultimately management of your money will become your business and yours alone. Leaving financial matters to fate, the future, or others will simply create more problems for you.

Once you've gotten used to managing your money, though, you can relax. Financial Fitness will become part of day-to-day living, as much a part of your routine as shopping for groceries or getting the laundry done.

No one plans to fail. But most of us fail to plan. The first and most essential step in planning is to get your thinking and your record-keeping organized. One will increase the effectiveness of the other.

The next two chapters deal with these aspects of Financial Fitness: thinking about where you want to go and the kind of record-keeping that will help you decide whether you are on the right road.

○   ○   ○

INTRODUCING THREE VERY SPECIAL FAMILIES . . .

Say hello to three generations of one family: the Youngs, the Mids, and the Elders. Each is a typical family of today who will turn up now and then in these pages to illustrate how some of the principles and advice in this book can be used to apply to those who are just starting out, those who have well-established homes and families, and those who have reached retirement age.

Dolly and James Young

The Youngs have been married for six years. They are now in their late twenties and have a baby a little over a year old.

The Youngs met in college and were married soon after they graduated. Jim, with a B.S. in software engineering, went to work for the Madison Ice Cream Company as a computer programmer. After marrying Dolly, Jim went to night school and earned a master's degree in computer science. He now works for a larger firm, tracking inventory, orders, sales, and other aspects of nationwide distribution. The new job requires some travel around the country.

The Youngs rented a two-bedroom apartment. Their immediate goal was to furnish the apartment and save for a house or condominium. Along with the furnishings came a large-screen TV and a new car for Dolly—plus a new kind of lifestyle in order to keep up with their friends. This included eating out a great deal, which was much more convenient with both of them working.

A year before Dolly became pregnant, they took a good, hard look at their finances. The bottom line was: debt, and plenty of it. They had almost no cash on hand. Nearly everything they bought went on credit cards, so big payments had to be met every month.

Planning on starting their family, they decided to get tough on themselves. They cut back on dining out, skipped buying CDs, vacationed around the house, parked the credit cards deep in a desk drawer, "bare-boned it" wherever they could. With hard-nosed determination, they started a savings program so they could buy a house. By the time the baby arrived, they were out of debt.

Dolly took four months of maternity leave but is now back working full time for a small public relations firm that is close to home and to the baby's day-care facility. An office manager, she earns $32,000, while Jim's salary is $45,000. He gets good benefits at his company, including major medical and dental plans. But the company does not provide life insurance. Neither Jim's nor Dolly's company offers traditional pension plans, but both provide pre-tax retirement 401(k) savings plans. The couple contribute through automatic payroll deductions, but neither is taking out the maximum allowed.

The Youngs' situation is this: Jim expects to change jobs when economic conditions improve. He figures that the only way to get ahead is to make a job change when an opportunity comes up. He remembers how his father and his father-in-law both stayed put all their working lives, counting on their companies to keep increasing their pay and responsibilities and take care of them later on. That world, he says, no longer exists.

Dolly and Jim, with their big load of debt behind them, a toddler chasing them hard, and serious saving for a house under way (not to mention interest rates being uncertain), hope and expect to buy a home of their own soon. And, luckily, they both have parents who have promised to help provide some of the down payment.

Mary and Marty Mid

Marty was born in 1941, Mary a year later. Marty remembers the emphasis his parents placed on education. His father worked in the construction business, building houses in the boom after World War II and getting top overtime pay, yet he always worried that the busy days would end and his earning power would drop. Marty's mother always wanted him to get a college education so he would have the job security his father never had.

Marty did get his college education and married Mary, his high school sweetheart, at the end of his sophomore year. Mary worked as a secretary during Marty's last two years of college before their first child, a daughter, was born.

After graduating, Marty worked for a series of firms. Then in 1968 he joined the accounting department of the company where he now works. The Mids lived first in apartments. In 1971, after their third child was born, they bought their first house. They sold it in 1976 to buy their present, $60,000 house.

The Mids' goal when they were first married was to buy their own home. When their daughter was born, Mary stayed home to raise her, and she remained at home after the births of the Mids' next two children. The Mids' long-term goal was to save substantially, especially for their children's educations—a top priority. Marty's salary increased steadily and the Mids managed to live comfortably, to take family vacations, to furnish their home as they wanted. They used credit only for car payments and an occasional home improvement loan; otherwise they waited until they could afford any major purchase, for they wanted to avoid being caught as their parents had been.

As the children approached college age, however, the Mids realized that they could not pay for their educations with just their savings and the income from one salary. So Mary went back to college while the kids were in high school, earning a graduate degree. Then, by the time her first child entered college, Mary had a full-time job as a junior high school teacher. She allocated her income with two goals in mind: paying the kids' college costs and contributing as much as possible (though never quite the maximum) to her payroll deduction 401(k) plan. Marty was contributing to his 401(k) at the same time.

The Mids have now completed payments on their children's educations (the youngest graduated two years ago). Now they are investing for retirement. Both have increased their contributions to their 401(k) plans, and have set up Individual Retirement Accounts (IRAs). They are trying to sock away as much as they can now, for they sense tough times ahead: Marty's company has been downsizing. Mary knows that, much as she had hoped to cut back on her teaching schedule, she won't be able to if Marty retires early. Marty is thinking about what he can do with the computer skills he has picked up to augment his accounting experience. He figures he will look for part-time work for small companies if he is forced into early retirement, and maybe set up his own office.

Gertrude and Frank Elder

The Elders came to America as children, with their parents. Frank went to technical school and became a skilled mechanic. Gertrude worked in a factory. They married in 1936, and during the Depression one of them was usually working. They had one child and lived in half of a two-family house on a quiet side street.

World War II found Frank Elder still young enough to serve, but his skills as a mechanic kept him deferred from the military. He worked long overtime hours, earning good money that he and his wife were able to save.

Gertrude did volunteer work during the war. Afterward she stayed home as a housewife and the Elders put their savings into a new home. Both worked steadily at landscaping and improving their property.

Until he retired at 65, Frank Elder was always employed. However, he worked at a number of different places. Luckily, he stayed long enough with his last job to qualify for a small pension. Frank also invested in America's future by buying "blue chip" stocks. The Elders lived simply. They saved. They invested. They were ready if ever another depression came along.

Sometimes the Elders took carefully budgeted vacations. One such trip found them in the sunny Southwest. Deciding they liked the steady warm climate, they bought a small lot.

A year after they retired, Frank and Gertrude sold their home for $40,000. They bought a new car and paid cash, so as not to incur any debt at this time. The car had all the extras that would allow them to travel comfortably to the Southwest. They put a prefabricated house on their lot, and added drapes and carpeting and some new furniture. After moving expenses were paid, they had $12,000 in cash left over plus savings and a small stock portfolio.

Things have not gone as expected for the Elders. Frank gets $950 a month from Social Security. This includes all benefit increases that have occurred since he retired. Gertrude started taking Social Security benefits at age 65, and she gets $475 a month.

Expenses have soared since the Elders moved to the Southwest. Electricity and water are way up; in fact, utility costs have quadrupled. Gasoline has skyrocketed. Since they bought a lot far out of town, purposely to get away from the kind of built-up neighborhood they were used to, the Elders use their car a great deal. When it reached high mileage and needed frequent repair five years ago, they traded it for a good used car.

Many of the auto trips to town are for medical care: a seemingly never-ending saga that includes unreimbursed office visits, new glasses, drugs, dental work, an operation, and other expenses. "The bills are killing us," says Frank. "We keep shelling out for insurance but it doesn't pick up so many of the bills. We're living from hand to mouth."

The Elders had planned to travel the Southwest, to dine out frequently, to get back East now and then to see family and old friends. They do some traveling with other senior citizens in the Southwest, but they do not dine out as much as they would like or get back to see Marty and the grandchildren and great-grandchildren very often. They rely on the telephone for visits back home, but try to keep a watchful eye on the phone bill. When they can save a bit from their Social Security income, the money goes into a rainy-day account. Potential medical expenses continue to be their chief worry.

Frank Elder sums it up: "We sit here among the other angry senior citizens, spending our savings for necessities—not for fun."

○   ○   ○

SETTING YOUR FINANCIAL FITNESS GOALS

○   ○   ○   ○

Most of us don't like to face up to the needs of the future. Education for the kids? A new house? Retirement and travel? Who knows?

Only *you* know. And only you can put your goals on paper and so design your Financial Fitness Program to reach them.

Realistic financial goals do several things:

- They establish a framework for financial stability.
- They help you to utilize your income to best advantage.
- They help you to accept the reality of your particular situation so you can learn not to spend against a dream.

How do you establish your own goals?

Start by asking yourself, "What's important to me?" Your goals reflect your value system—usually the attitudes you were raised with. For most of us, values are based on what is desirable and worthy. And, for most of us, value systems aren't usually very flexible. If you're old enough to be working with this book, chances are your attitudes have been pretty much set for quite some time now.

Within the framework of goals, based on your values and attitudes, you'll have priorities—goals that are most important.

Values dictate behavior

Now comes the catch: How do you actually behave when it comes to finances? If your behavior is not consistent with your values, attitudes, and goals, you are off base.

Say you've been raised with a value system which holds that education is of prime importance: College is therefore a must for your children, a goal that may dictate saving $100 a month. But say your behavior is not consistent with your goal. You decide you cannot afford to save $100 a month for education, or you put some other goal first. Your behavior shows that your goal of college for your children is of lower priority.

Most people need to establish priorities among their financial goals because their desires often exceed their resources.

Take a good, hard look at your goals and your behavior. Is your behavior helping you to achieve your goals, or hindering you?

Conflict: A couple or an individual may have two goals which cannot both be satisfied because achieving one prevents achieving the other.

Short-, mid-, and long-range goals

A *short-range goal* is something you want to do next year. Pay off a loan, say. Or plan Christmas shopping money in advance, instead of paying off bills through winter and spring. Or buy a vacation in advance, so you can really enjoy it, instead of moaning as the Visa and MasterCard charges mount up.

A *middle-range goal* is something you want to do in, say, three to five years. Buy a second home, perhaps, or a better car, or take a trip abroad. Maybe you want to plan on having another child (yes, at today's projected costs of approximately $200,000 from age 0 to 18, a child is a middle-range goal).

A *long-range goal* covers such items as education and retirement.

Agreement on goals

Goals have another dimension besides time: family commitment. Certainly you and your wife or husband must talk freely, openly, and at length about goals. But also include your children in discussions. If you and your spouse and your children communicate your individual financial objectives and reach an understanding about them, you can all avoid many arguments and financial crises. Many, many misunderstandings about money develop simply because people haven't let their goals be known.

Remember that the primary objective of a viable plan is the accumulation of money, or capital. Everything else in your financial plan is directed to achieving this goal.

Thus you must not only define your goals but follow through on the details. If your children's education is a top goal, take the time now to estimate what it will cost. Use today's dollars, then update the figure once a year, just as you update the grocery budget to meet inflation.

What you are trying to avoid, of course, is waking up one day to find that you have to borrow to meet a goal such as education.

Goals and needs keep changing. They should be checked every year. Never feel that you must stay locked into a specific goal. But, by the same token, never use the money set aside for a medium- or long-term goal to pay for something you want now.

Important: List your goals. Give each one a dollar amount and a time frame.

o   o   o

MARY AND MARTY MID HAVE THREE BASIC GOALS . . .

First, with two college educations paid for, they are tackling home-improvement projects that they put off for many years. Their *immediate short-range goal* is to get these completed within the next year—updating the kitchen, rebuilding the porch to make it a sun room, general painting.

Their *mid-range goal* is to give themselves the long vacation they have delayed for several years while the kids were going through college.

Third is their *long-range* goal: to plan a retirement that maintains the lifestyle they are accustomed to. Although the numbers seem daunting, the Mids feel that their contributions to their 401(k)s and IRAs, along with matching contributions from their employers, should be sufficient to cover their savings requirement. This is a major concern, as they realize that the Elders are not having the kind of retirement they expected.

o   o   o

Worksheet I: Mr. & Mrs. Mid
SAVING FOR A SPECIFIC GOAL

A.	GOAL	RETIREMENT
B.	DATE NEEDED	12/30/05
C.	NUMBER OF YEARS TILL GOAL	8
D.	AMOUNT NEEDED	$300,000
E.	MONEY ALREADY SET ASIDE	$97,024
F.	AMOUNT MONEY SET ASIDE WILL GROW TO AT __5__% (see Exhibit 2)	$143,595
G.	AMOUNT STILL NEEDED	$156,405
H.	AMOUNT TO BE SAVED PER YEAR AT __5__% INTEREST (see Exhibit 3)	$16,266

Worksheet I: Yours
SAVING FOR A SPECIFIC GOAL

A. GOAL _____

B. DATE NEEDED _____

C. NUMBER OF YEARS TILL GOAL _____

D. AMOUNT NEEDED _____

E. MONEY ALREADY SET ASIDE _____

F. AMOUNT MONEY SET ASIDE
   WILL GROW TO AT _____%
   (see Exhibit 2) _____

G. AMOUNT STILL NEEDED _____

H. AMOUNT TO BE SAVED PER
   YEAR AT _____% INTEREST
   (see Exhibit 3) _____

Setting goals accomplishes several things. It forces you and your family to examine your values and clarify them. It enables you to devise ways to use your available resources to attain your goals. And it puts you in charge, makes you take control of your life and your money.

Exhibit 1
INFLATION FACTOR TABLE

YEARS BEFORE GOAL IS MET	3% INFLATION	5% INFLATION	7% INFLATION
1	1.03	1.05	1.07
2	1.06	1.10	1.14
3	1.09	1.16	1.23
4	1.13	1.22	1.31
5	1.16	1.28	1.40
6	1.19	1.30	1.50
7	1.23	1.41	1.61
8	1.27	1.48	1.72
9	1.30	1.55	1.84
10	1.34	1.63	1.97
11	1.38	1.71	2.10
12	1.43	1.80	2.25
13	1.47	1.89	2.40
14	1.51	1.98	2.58
15	1.56	2.08	2.76

Exhibit 2
ASSUMED RATES OF RETURN
(less estimated inflation)

ESTIMATED RATE OF RETURN LESS INFLATION	Years to Goal						
	5	8	10	12	15	20	25
2%	1.10	1.17	1.22	1.27	1.35	1.49	1.63
3%	1.16	1.27	1.34	1.43	1.56	1.81	2.10
4%	1.22	1.37	1.48	1.60	1.80	2.19	2.66
5%	1.28	1.48	1.63	1.80	2.08	2.65	3.39
6%	1.34	1.59	1.79	2.01	2.40	3.21	4.30

Exhibit 3
ASSUMED DISCOUNT FACTOR

DISCOUNT RATE FACTOR	Years to Goal						
	5	8	10	12	15	20	25
2%	.192	.116	.091	.074	.057	.041	.031
3%	.188	.112	.087	.070	.053	.037	.027
4%	.184	.108	.083	.066	.049	.033	.023
5%	.180	.104	.079	.062	.046	.030	.020
6%	.177	.101	.075	.059	.042	.027	.018

On page 6 you will find the first Financial Fitness worksheet. Each time you come to a worksheet you'll find at least one completed as an example and a blank one for you to fill out. The first worksheet is **Saving for a Specific Goal.** Let's look together at how the Mids have filled it out. They have established the goal as their retirement. To maintain the lifestyle they are accustomed to, they will want to have $70,070 in income (70 percent of their present income). But by the year 2005 (if we assume a 3 percent annual rate of inflation) they will need about $88,989—in their first year of retirement—$70,070 times the inflation factor of 1.27 (see Exhibit 1). The Mids have seen what inflation has done to the Elders. It has affected their purchasing power, savings, and investments. The Mids have figured out that Social Security and Mr. Mid's pension will not begin to cover their retirement needs. So they must accumulate $300,000 to meet that goal. The figure in line F is the amount their money that is already saved will grow to (see Exhibit 2). The Mids know they can get an 8 percent

rate of return but adjust that figure for inflation. Thus the $97,024 will grow to $143,595 ($97,024 times 1.48). The amount still needed ($156,405) is multiplied by the assumed discount factor of .104 (see Exhibit 3) to show the amount they need to save each year for the next eight years. Now decide what your saving goal is and fill out the worksheet on page 7.

Whatever your age, establishing your own goals should also make you aware of the goals of others who are younger or older. Goals for the recently married are quite different from those of their parents or grandparents. Most young couples don't need two cars. Most parents of teenage children—or of schoolchildren of any age, in many cases—need a second car. A retired couple usually needs but one car.

Keep your behavior in mind, and under control. Your Financial Fitness Program must be compatible and consistent with your goals—otherwise you're headed for conflict and trouble.

THE FOUNDATION
OF FINANCIAL
FITNESS: YOUR
RECORD SYSTEM

○   ○   ○   ○

Every night at 10 P.M. a New York television station used to ask its audience, "Do you know where your children are?": a sensible reminder of parental responsibility.

The station would be performing another valuable public service if it occasionally asked, "Do you know where your life insurance policies are?" or "Do you know where the certificate of title to your automobile is ?"

A good record-keeping system is an important part of Financial Fitness. Financial Fitness means being able to prove what you spent, where you spent it, what you spent it for, and how it improved or failed to improve your financial situation. What you need for all this is *records*: not a mountain of paper but a practical system for keeping track of financial matters, and important papers related to them, over a long period of time.

You should begin keeping records from your first job on through retirement. The record-keeping itself can be a simple file system of various papers, some items being permanent, some semi-permanent, others temporary. For instance, obviously you keep a life insurance policy as long as it is in force. You keep automobile papers as long as you own the car. You keep home improvement receipts until you sell the house and want to prove how much extra capital you have put into it over the years. You keep ordinary sales receipts and other income tax records for three years, until the statute of limitations runs out: An audit by the Internal Revenue Service (IRS) may go back no more than three years. However, you should keep your final IRS tax return for each year in a permanent file. It makes an excellent financial history.

A costly failing

Not having a good system of record-keeping can be not only embarrassing but costly. The newly widowed woman who cannot find her husband's life insurance policies suffers embarrassment as well as grief. The widow who has a very good offer for her husband's classic automobile but cannot find the certificate of title may wait weeks for the molasses-like motor vehicle department to issue a new one—and thus lose the sale. The difference between the first offer and the next to come along may be $500 or more. The widow who was never told by her ex-GI husband that he had a paid-up service insurance policy put away somewhere goes without the proceeds for which she is eligible.

Exhibit 4
UNCLAIMED BANK ACCOUNT NOTICE

RE: 1031520   Balance 167.24

Dear Customers:

According to our records, we have a savings account in your name that has been inactive for more than 10 years. State laws regarding abandoned property require banks to remit the balance of accounts 10 years or more inactive to the Treasurer of the State of Connecticut.

In order to activate your account, please mail or present your passbook to us to be updated. Please notify us if your passbook has been lost. Enclosed is a bank-by-mail envelope for your convenience.

If we do not hear from you within ten days from receipt of this letter, the account will automatically be remitted to the State of Connecticut.

Very truly yours,

Enc.

You don't have to be newly widowed to lose money in another way. Banks regularly take out local newspaper advertisements to list the names and last known addresses of thousands of customers who have left accounts inactive for a specified period of time.

The fact is that billions of dollars from bank accounts are held in state treasuries simply because no one can trace the assets to their rightful owners. If a bank account is totally inactive for a certain number of years (the period varies from state to state), and if the bank fails to locate the owner after placing an advertisement listing the last known address, the unclaimed money goes to the state.

By the same token, if you own a piece of property, move away, forget to tell the tax assessor where you have gone and then fail to pay the taxes (every year it is astonishing how many people can and do forget such things), the town may auction that parcel of land to the highest bidder—and keep the proceeds.

Some states exact a personal property tax on cars and boats. In this computer age, any motor vehicle department can make a quick check on whether tax has been paid on an automobile and will refuse to renew a car's registration if it has not. One of my clients sold his boat and did not save the bill of sale. Months later the state demanded tax due on the boat. To prove that the boat

had been sold and that he owed no tax, my client had to trace the boat dealer to Florida and get another receipt.

Ever try to reconstruct the history of an illness a year or more after you got well? Many have—all because they didn't make medical records promptly and hang onto them. With most doctors' offices asking for payment at the time of your visit and leaving it up to you to handle major medical and other insurance claims, it is important to make a habit of getting a photocopy of all receipts and claim forms and of filing all claims promptly.

If your doctor (or hospital or lab) was not paid at the time of your visit and you are reimbursed by an insurance company, it is important that you immediately pay the bill rather than spend the money and say, "Oh, I'll take care of the doctor [or hospital or lab] later."

Many records can be replaced, but it takes time, effort, and postage to replace them. Take stock certificates. If you own more than one or two, you should have an accurate list by name, number of shares, purchase price, and date of purchase. Compiling such a list after your certificates have been lost, stolen, or destroyed can be a horrendous task, and the result may be incomplete. Before any company will issue a replacement certificate, you will have to sign an affidavit that the certificate was destroyed and put up a surety bond, which can cost as much as 3 percent of the current market price.

What goes to the bank, what stays home

Where should you keep important papers and records? You should keep some in a safe deposit box in a bank, and others at home in a safe and sensible file.

Best kept in a safe deposit box are those papers that are difficult to replace, including:

Birth certificates
Stock certificates
Marriage certificate
Citizenship papers
Bonds
Certificate of title for an automobile
Real estate deeds
Copy of will (but not the original)
Divorce decree
Death certificates
Passports
Discharge from military service
Veterans Administration papers
Adoption papers
Contracts
Household inventory (with photographs for
     appraisal purposes)

Why don't life insurance policies and the original copy of your will go into the safe deposit box? Because in most states when the owner, or joint owner, of a safe deposit box dies, the bank seals the box until all tax and legal matters are taken care of. Access is granted only when the bank receives legal permission, and then in the presence of an authorized person. A life insurance company will not pay a claim until the policy is surrendered. The probation of a will cannot begin until the last will is presented to the probate court. Thus, everything is held up if legal permission to open a safe deposit box must be obtained.

The best place to keep your life insurance policies is at home. The best place to keep your will is in the files of the attorney who drew it up.

After reading the examples for Mr. and Mrs. Mid, fill out the worksheets at the end of this chapter on **Personal Information** (II), **Personal Contacts** (III), **Record-Keeping** (IV), and **Location of Other Important Papers** (V). Detail is important; better to jot down too much than too little.

Some of these details may seem obvious. Some may look like a nuisance to get hold of. Just remember they will not seem obvious to anyone who must track down all this information if you're not around to supply it. And lawyers can tell you how much they are paid to take care of "nuisance" details you could easily have had ready in a file.

When you have filled out these sheets, get duplicates made. Give a set to someone else to keep for you, someone who will understand the method of your madness.

File—and throw out

Your filing system? It can be an elaborate, decorated file cabinet or a collection of shoe boxes. What counts is not what it looks like but how well you have organized it. The key is to get into the habit of filing those papers that are important and *throwing out* those that are not.

Your permanent home file should include:

Annuities
Automobile insurance
Bankbooks and statements
Children's records
Credit histories
Disability insurance policy
Educational records (for each family member)
Employment history
Federal income tax returns
Gift tax returns
Gifts
Health insurance coverage and policies
Health records
Home improvements
Homeowner's insurance
Household inventory (with receipts and
     appraisals)
Inheritances
Insurance policies (if not filed under subject
     headings, such as auto, medical, and so on)
IRA (individual retirement account)
Keogh plan
Life insurance policies
List of important advisers
Loan applications
Loans
Medical insurance
Medicare
Money market funds
Mutual funds
Paid bills
Pension and profit-sharing plans
Property tax bills and receipts
Real estate investments
Social Security earnings records
Social Security numbers
State income tax returns
Stock options

Stock and bond record book
Warranties and guarantees
Wills (file signed original with attorney)

A word about records of stock and bond transactions and home improvements. This is strictly a matter of keeping good records for tax purposes.

If you use a stock and bond record book, use a differently colored pen for each year in which you have stock transactions. If you are using blue ink for this year, for instance, you will know that all blue ink items that are sold must be included in this year's tax return.

It is important to have a record of when you bought a particular stock, and at what price. When you sell it, it will be necessary to figure out the gain or loss on the sale. Many years may have passed between the purchase and the sale, and you will have to pay a tax on the profit.

The same is true of your house or condominium. When you sell, you will pay a tax on the profit (that is, the difference between the original purchase price and the sale price). But every permanent improvement made over the years may be deducted from the profit: landscaping, for instance, or converting a garage to a playroom, installing insulation and other energy-saving devices, the addition of a building, swimming pool, deck, or patio, or doing anything else that added value to the house. An accurate record of bills paid and canceled checks will be invaluable when the house is sold.

Before moving out, take pictures in and around the house. When you prepare your tax return, they will help jog your memory. You'll be surprised at how many deductible improvements you will see in these photographs.

o   o   o

SUPPOSE MR. AND MRS. MID DECIDE TO SELL THEIR HOUSE . . .

They find that with appreciation over the years (mostly due to inflation) since they bought it in 1976, their split-level purchased for $60,000 can now be sold for over $150,000. If they sell it for $150,000 before they are 55 years old, they must pay a capital gains tax on $74,500 of the price. (Those over 55 benefit from a once-in-a-lifetime exemption of $125,000 when selling a house.) But the Mids' well-kept records can cut down the tax bite:

House purchased 1976		$60,000
Permanent		
improvements:		
landscaping	3,000	
insulation	1,000	
carpeting	1,500	
garage converted		
to playroom	8,000	
new driveway	2,000	
	$15,500	$15,500
		$75,500
Selling price		$150,000
Less costs of improvements plus		
original purchase price		$ 75,500
Capital gains tax is calculated on		$ 74,500

o   o   o

For your annual income tax return, a continuing file is vital. If the IRS decides to audit your return, the burden of proof will be on you. By the same token, an accordian file of canceled checks, organized by categories, will help you with budget planning as well as tax returns. Categories include such items as:

Automobile expenses
Bills from specific stores
Children's expenses
Clothing
Contributions
Education
Entertainment and recreation
Household expenses (maintenance)
Household purchases (major)
Insurance premiums
Medical and dental expenses
Mortgage payments
Taxes (real estate and personal property)
Utilities

With this file at your fingertips, you can tackle a new year's budgeting and your end-of-year tax return with confidence in your accuracy. Many bills can then be thrown out (yes, this is worth repeating, because it is so hard to get people to realize that "throw out" means what it says). Only those bills needed as evidence for tax purposes need be saved.

If the IRS audits you

A cardinal rule: Always remember that the IRS does not understand the words "I can't find it." If you want to prove something, such as an expenditure, you must show up with the proof in your hand.

In fact, the IRS considers you guilty until you prove yourself innocent. It is permitted by law to audit you for three years from the date you file a return. For example, if your 1996 return was filed on April 15, 1997, you may be audited on it at any time until April 15, 2000, but no later. (Exception: The IRS is legally entitled to audit you at a later date if it expects to charge you with fraud or gross negligence.) Once the three

Worksheet II: Mr. & Mrs. Mid
RECORD-KEEPING
personal information

Yourself:
1. Name _Martin Mid_ Address _846 Tower Ct._
City/State _Iowa City, Iowa 52240_ Telephone Number _(319) 555-1212_
Place of Birth _Chicago, Ill._ Date of Birth _12/3/41_
Social Security # _987-65-4320_ Marital Status _Married_

2. Spouse's Name _Mary Elder Mid_ Address _846 Tower Ct._
City/State _Iowa City, Iowa 52240_ Telephone # _(319) 555-1212_
Place of Birth _Chicago, Ill._ Date of Birth _2/11/42_
Social Security # _045-30-5867_

3. Children:

Name	1 Dolly Young	2 John Mid	3 Sally Mid	4
Address	1482 North St.	800 Park St.	550 Sycamore St.	
City/State	Denver, Colo.	Boston, Mass.	Ann Arbor, Michigan	
Telephone	(303)555-3671	(617)555-5600	(313)555-8800	
Place of Birth	Chicago, Ill.	Iowa City	Iowa City	
Date of Birth	5/5/68	4/25/70	3/15/73	
Social Security #	042-68-1505	999-41-3841	888-11-9876	
Marital Status	married	single	single	

4. Parents
Names _deceased_ Address _____
City/State _____ Telephone # _____
Place of Birth _____ Date of Birth _____
Mother's maiden name _____

5. Spouse's Parents
Names _Gertrude & Frank Elder_ Address _41 Sun Drive_
City/State _Desert City, Arizona_ Telephone _(602) 555-4615_
Place of Birth _mother Hungary father Germany_ Date of Birth _mother 6/15/13 father 8/20/15_
Mother's Maiden Name _Gosborg_

Next of Kin:
Name _James Mid_ Relationship _brother_
Address _Peach Drive, Atlanta, Ga._ Telephone # _(404) 555-3054_

Neighbor or Close Friend
Name _Elaine & John Wilson_ Address _2100 Tower Ct._
City/State _Iowa City, Iowa 52240_ Telephone _(319) 555-1000_

Worksheet III: Mr. & Mrs. Mid
RECORD-KEEPING
personal contacts

	NAME	ADDRESS	TELEPHONE NUMBER
Attorney	J. P. Brown	State Bank Building	(319) 555-6157
Accountant	P. W. Smith	State Bank Building	(319) 555-4100
Clergyman	Rev. Ray Ernest	First Church	(319) 555-6600
Stockbroker	none		
Physician	Dr. J. Green	University Hospital	(319) 555-7000
Trust Officer	none		
Banker	Ms. Mary Jones	State Bank	(319) 555-1234
Life Insurance Agent	John L. Long	83 Madison St.	(319) 555-4111
Other Insurance Agents			
Homeowner	Helen Blank	M. Horn & Co.	(319) 555-1111
Automobile	Helen Blank	M. Horn & Co.	(319) 555-1111
Medical	at work		
Disability	at work		
Executor of Estate	James Young		(303) 555-3671
Financial Planner	Elizabeth Lewin, CFP	Main St., Chicago, Ill.	(312) 555-7000
Others			

years have passed, you should *throw out* most of your canceled checks and documentation, keeping only those items that have to do with possible future capital gains tax information, such as home improvements or purchase of collectibles and stocks and bonds.

A word about IRS audits. Being called in for an audit evokes horror in most people's minds, equivalent to the feeling produced by the words "root canal" at the dentist's. What can you do?

Be prepared is the answer. Your notice from the IRS will indicate the sections of your tax return that it wants to check on. The letter will tell you to call for an appointment, probably at the nearest IRS office. If your return was prepared by an accountant, contact him or her and see if the accountant will go in your place; it's best to check if there will be an additional fee for this service. If you decide to make an appearance yourself, take with you all the bills and canceled checks relating to the particular items the IRS has said it wants to check on.

Important: Keep your eyes and ears open and your mouth closed as much as possible in an IRS meeting. Answer only the questions you are asked. Do not chitchat. Control the natural tendency to babble in nervous situations. Concentrate on counting the holes in the ceiling tiles, if you must, but fight the urge to blurt out something you may regret. Let out your primal scream when you get out of the office.

There are indeed emotional aspects to record-keeping. Being able to put your hands on the right piece of paper, at the moment you need it, is the greatest relief ever devised for an anxiety attack. If you have taken the precaution of letting someone else in on the secret of your method, you will be in much better shape during an unexpected period of transition or emotional turmoil.

1. CHECKING ACCOUNTS, SAVINGS ACCOUNTS, CREDIT UNION ACCOUNTS, OTHER CASH ACCOUNTS

Name of Institution	Type and # of Account	Interest Rate	Current Balance	Owned By	Location of Checkbook or Passbooks
State Bank	checking 23098	0	$2,000.	joint	pocket book
State Bank	money market 784432	varies	$20,000	joint	desk file

2. MONEY MARKET FUNDS, CERTIFICATES OF DEPOSIT, TREASURY BILLS AND NOTES

Name of Institution	Type and # of Account	Maturity Date	Amount Invested	Interest Rate	Owned by	Location of Passbooks

TOTAL

3. SECURITIES

Stocks & Mutual Funds:

Number of Shares	Company	Date Purchased	Total Cost	Current Market Value	Owned By	Location of Stock Certificate	Annual Income

TOTAL:

Bonds: Corporate & Municipal

Face Amount	Company	Purchase Date	Maturity Date	Total Cost	Interest Rate	Current Market Value	Owned by	Location of Book	Annual Income

4. REAL ESTATE (RESIDENCE, RECREATIONAL, INCOME PROPERTY)

	1.	2.	3.
Location:	846 Tower Ct.		
Date Purchased	7/1/76		
Cost	$60,000		
Current Market Value	$150,000		

5. LIFE INSURANCE

	1.	2.	3.	4.
Insured	Marty	Marty	Marty	
Company	May Ins. Co.	XXZ Ins. Co.	ABC Ins. Co.	
Type of Policy	Whole	Whole	Term	
Number of Policy	46381460	53964105	14680014	
Face Amount	$50,000	$25,000	$50,000	
Owner	Marty	Marty	Marty	
Beneficiary	Mary	Mary	Mary	
Case Value		$2,000		
Amount Borrowed Out		$10,000		
Location of Policy	desk file	desk file	desk file	

6. ANNUITIES, PENSIONS, PROFIT SHARING PLANS, INDIVIDUAL RETIREMENT ACCOUNTS

Description	Participant	Company or Institution	Benefits	Present Value
pension plan	Marty	Big-Little Co.	retirement	$185,000
IRA's	Marty	ABC Fund	retirement	$12,600
IRA's	Mary	ABC Fund	retirement	$9,700
401 K	Marty	Big-Little Co.	retirement	$46,124
403 (b)	Mary	Board of Ed.	retirement	$28,600

7. BUSINESS INTERESTS

Company Name	Type of Business	Percentage of Ownership	Value of Your Interest

8. CREDIT OBLIGATIONS

Real Estate (Residence, Recreational, Income Property)

	1.	2.	3.
Mortgage Holder	First Bank		
Mortgage Balance	$26,145		
Interest Rate	8%		
Monthly Payment	$270		

Other Debt Obligations (automobile loans, education loans, life insurance loans, home improvement loans, etc.)

Lender	Type of Loan	Interest Rate	Balance Due	Monthly Payment	Co-signer
State Bank	Auto	12.5%	$5,500	$155	
First Bank	home improve.	8%	$4,560	$95	

Credit Cards

Name of Card	Number of card	Balance Due
Mastercard	838457	$75.
VISA	596922	$75.
American Express	77004210	$ 50.

Worksheet V: Mr. & Mrs. Mid
LOCATION OF OTHER IMPORTANT PAPERS

Homeowner's Insurance _in desk file_

    Name of Company _World Insurance_   Policy Number _0989-02-82_

Automobile Insurance _in desk file_

    Name of Company _World Insurance_   Policy Number _7450-20-221879_

Medical Insurance _at work_

    Name of Company _The Blue_   Policy Number _000B638919_

    Type of Policy _Major Medical_

    Location of card _wallet_   Group Number _45106_

Disability Insurance _at work_

    Name of Company _American_   Policy Number _369847_

Last Will _at Lawyer's_

Codicils

Birth Certificates _safe deposit box_

Mortgage Papers or Lease _safe deposit box_

Deeds to Real Estate _safe deposit box_

Titles to Automobiles _safe deposit box_

Military Discharge Papers _safe deposit box_

Citizenship Papers

Divorce Decree

Social Security Cards _wallet_

Income Tax Returns _desk file_

Power of Attorney

Living Will

Yourself:

1. Name_____ Address_____

   City/State_____ Telephone Number_____

   Place of Birth_____ Date of Birth_____

   Social Security #_____ Marital Status_____

2. Spouse's Name_____ Address_____

   City/State_____ Telephone #_____

   Place of Birth_____ Date of Birth_____

   Social Security #_____

3. Children:

Name	1_____	2_____	3_____	4_____
Address	_____	_____	_____	_____
City/State	_____	_____	_____	_____
Telephone	_____	_____	_____	_____
Place of Birth	_____	_____	_____	_____
Date of Birth	_____	_____	_____	_____
Social Security #	_____	_____	_____	_____
Marital Status	_____	_____	_____	_____

4. Parents

   Name_____ Address_____

   City/State_____ Telephone #_____

   Place of Birth_____ Date of Birth_____

   Mother's maiden name_____

5. Spouse's Parents

   Names_____ Address_____

   City/State_____ Telephone_____

   Place of Birth_____ Date of Birth_____

   Mother's Maiden Name_____

   Next of Kin:

   Name_____ Relationship_____

   Address_____ Telephone #_____

   Neighbor or Close Friend

   Name_____ Address_____

   City/State_____ Telephone_____

Worksheet III: Yours
RECORD-KEEPING
personal contacts

NAME	ADDRESS	TELEPHONE NUMBER
Attorney		
Accountant		
Clergyman		
Stockbroker		
Physician		
Trust Officer		
Banker		
Life Insurance Agent		
Other Insurance Agents		
Homeowner		
Automobile		
Medical		
Disability		
Executor of Estate		
Financial Planner		
Others		

1. CHECKING ACCOUNTS, SAVINGS ACCOUNTS, CREDIT UNION ACCOUNTS, OTHER CASH ACCOUNTS

Name of Institution	Type and # of Account	Interest Rate	Current Balance	Owned By	Location of Checkbook or Passbooks
_____	_____	_____	_____	_____	_____
_____	_____	_____	_____	_____	_____
_____	_____	_____	_____	_____	_____
_____	_____	_____	_____	_____	_____

2. MONEY MARKET FUNDS, CERTIFICATES OF DEPOSIT, TREASURY BILLS AND NOTES

Name of Institution	Type and # of Account	Maturity Date	Amount Invested	Interest Rate	Owned by	Location of Passbooks
_____	_____	_____	_____	_____	_____	_____
_____	_____	_____	_____	_____	_____	_____
_____	_____	_____	_____	_____	_____	_____
_____	_____	_____	_____	_____	_____	_____
_____	_____	_____	_____	_____	_____	_____

TOTAL

3. SECURITIES

Stocks & Mutual Funds:

Number of Shares	Company	Date Purchased	Total Cost	Current Market Value	Owned By	Location of Stock Certificate	Annual Income
_____	_____	_____	_____	_____	_____	_____	_____
_____	_____	_____	_____	_____	_____	_____	_____
_____	_____	_____	_____	_____	_____	_____	_____
_____	_____	_____	_____	_____	_____	_____	_____
_____	_____	_____	_____	_____	_____	_____	_____
_____	_____	_____	_____	_____	_____	_____	_____

TOTAL:

Bonds: Corporate & Municipal

Face Amount	Company	Purchase Date	Maturity Date	Total Cost	Interest Rate	Current Market Value	Owned by	Location of Book	Annual Income
_____	_____	_____	_____	_____	_____	_____	_____	_____	_____
_____	_____	_____	_____	_____	_____	_____	_____	_____	_____
_____	_____	_____	_____	_____	_____	_____	_____	_____	_____
_____	_____	_____	_____	_____	_____	_____	_____	_____	_____

4. REAL ESTATE (RESIDENCE, RECREATIONAL, INCOME PROPERTY)

	1.	2.	3.
Location:	_____	_____	_____
Date Purchased	_____	_____	_____
Cost	_____	_____	_____
Current Market Value	_____	_____	_____

5. LIFE INSURANCE

	1.	2.	3.	4.
Insured				
Company				
Type of Policy				
Number of Policy				
Face Amount				
Owner				
Beneficiary				
Case Value				
Amount Borrowed Out				
Location of Policy				

6. ANNUITIES, PENSIONS, PROFIT SHARING PLANS, INDIVIDUAL RETIREMENT ACCOUNTS

Description	Participant	Company or Institution	Benefits	Present Value

7. BUSINESS INTERESTS

Company Name	Type of Business	Percentage of Ownership	Value of Your Interest

8. CREDIT OBLIGATIONS

Real Estate (Residence, Recreational, Income Property)

	1.	2.	3.
Mortgage Holder			
Mortgage Balance			
Interest Rate			
Monthly Payment			

Other Debt Obligations (automobile loans, education loans, life insurance loans, home improvement loans, etc.)

Lender	Type of Loan	Interest Rate	Balance Due	Monthly Payment	Co-signer

Credit Cards

Name of Card	Number of card	Balance Due
_____	_____	_____
_____	_____	_____
_____	_____	_____
_____	_____	_____
_____	_____	_____

Worksheet V: Yours
LOCATION OF OTHER IMPORTANT PAPERS

Homeowner's Insurance_____
    Name of Company_____ Policy Number_____

Automobile Insurance_____
    Name of Company_____ Policy Number_____

Medical Insurance_____
    Name of Company_____ Policy Number_____
    Type of Policy_____
    Location of card_____ Group Number_____

Disability Insurance_____
    Name of Company_____ Policy Number_____

Last Will_____

Codicils_____

Birth Certificates_____

Mortgage Papers or Lease_____

Deeds to Real Estate_____

Titles to Automobiles_____

Military Discharge Papers_____

Citizenship Papers_____

Divorce Decree_____

Social Security Cards_____

Income Tax Returns_____

Power of Attorney_____

Living Will_____

THE BAROMETER OF FINANCIAL FITNESS: YOUR NET WORTH STATEMENT

○   ○   ○   ○

If you will now look at the financial worksheets on pages 25–32, you will find a framework in which to work. It gives you a way of looking realistically at where you are now and a way to plan your Financial Fitness Program for the future.

Here are some tough questions. You can find the answers by filling out the worksheet headed **Net Worth Statement** on page 31.

- How much will you have to pass on to your heirs?
- Will it produce enough income for them to survive?
- Are you accumulating enough assets to help support yourself during retirement?
- Should your investments be producing income now or in the future?
- Are you carrying too much debt?
- What about inflation: Are you keeping ahead of it, are you even keeping up with it?

Your Net Worth Statement can tell you where you stand financially at any given point in time. It's like weighing and measuring yourself before you start a physical fitness program. The definition of net worth? It's the difference between your assets, what you own that has monetary value, and your debts, or what you owe. In short, it's an inventory of everything you own that has any monetary value.

Why go to all this trouble, calculating your net worth? Because it is essential for estate planning, retirement planning, and for any sound investment strategy. Knowing your net worth can give you security both now and in the future. It is also your only way of estimating how much you will have available to pass on to your heirs.

If your Net Worth Statement reveals some negatives —if your net worth is not increasing, if you have taken on more debt than you can handle, if your investments have not kept up with inflation—you can assess what is going on and do something about it. Financial needs do change, remember. Your Net Worth Statement can help you get over the hurdles imposed by change.

How much are things worth?
Now it's time to be objective. As accurately as possible, write down the actual market value of your property, be

it your home, your great-aunt's heirloom diamonds, or your automobile. Not what you think your property might be worth, mind, but what it would actually fetch if you were putting it up for sale.

How do you find out what things are worth? Your best bet is to get a dealer or appraiser who knows houses, diamonds, or automobiles—or rare coins, antique dolls, or whatever else you own that is of real value—and have an estimate made.

Talk with a real estate broker about the current market value of your home. And check your local newspaper for advertisements for comparable houses.

It can be tough to get accurate values on personal property. Clothing and furniture and other household furnishings may have depreciated since you purchased them. Silver, gold, stamps, antiques, and coins have probably risen in value since you bought them or inherited them. In some cases, such as coins or antiques, a reputable specialized magazine may include listings you can depend on.

Go back to your record-keeping worksheets for a guide to items to list. The first is cash on hand, in saving or checking accounts. Certificates of deposit due within the coming year, money market funds, stocks, and bonds should all be itemized. A daily newspaper listing will tell you today's market value of stocks, bonds, and mutual funds.

Don't forget the hidden assets:

- Your employee benefits
- Your pension or profit-sharing plan (list present values)
- Life insurance (cash values of whole policies should be listed)
- Your interest in a business partnership or similar venture (list the price you would receive if you sold your share; this is often one's largest asset and the most difficult to appraise)

A pension plan that can be received only in the form of an annuity should not be listed here.

How much do you owe?

Now for the liabilities. Start with current bills. List everything you have been billed for but have not yet paid, as of today. List any taxes that are unpaid, including all taxes that have not been deducted from your paycheck, federal or state income tax, capital gains tax, real estate taxes, personal property taxes.

Next list the unpaid balance on the mortgage on your home or condominium or vacation house. Itemize installment debts: everything you owe to MasterCard, Visa, American Express, other rotating charge accounts, and your cash reserve account at the bank. Add up unpaid balances on a car loan, home improvement loan, education loan, or life insurance loan.

Got the form filled out? Please check it again. Anything you forgot to list under assets? Any missing liabilities?

Total the assets column, then the liabilities column. Now subtract your liabilities from your assets. The result is your net worth as of right now.

If your liabilities turn out to be greater than your assets, you have a "negative net worth" at the moment. The exercise has been doubly worthwhile for you, for it has drawn your attention to a precarious situation that needs immediate attention.

○　　○　　○

NET WORTH OF YOUNGS, MIDS, AND ELDERS . . .

Now that they have paid off their sizable debts, the Youngs can see real improvement in their financial situation. Until they went to work on reducing debt, their Net Worth Statement showed that they owed more than they had. They are still carrying an auto loan, but they have begun to build up savings. They will be able to have their own house soon.

Their parents, the Mids, have built up their assets by saving. Their home, purchased a number of years ago, has appreciated greatly in value. Compared with many in their situation, they have few large obligations, though they are still paying on their mortgage and have some outstanding credit obligations. The Mids were able to use some of their assets to finance their children's educations.

The Elders have assets in their home, on which mortgage payments have been completed, and in securities. They have almost no liabilities.

○　　○　　○

Assets and liabilities change continually, of course, almost on a daily basis. You need not redo your Net Worth Statement to reflect weekly or monthly fluctuations. But as your major needs and situations change, the emphasis on assets and liabilities will vary and it will be important to keep an eye on your net worth.

What kinds of major needs and situations are important enough to make you revise your Net Worth Statement? I'd say the following: buying a larger house; inheriting securities; becoming vested in an employee profit-sharing plan; signing for a car or boat or second-home loan; putting savings into an Individual Retirement Account (IRA) or 401(k).

Review your Net Worth Statement at least once a year. It is a barometer of your financial situation. When you are weighing needs, a look at your assets and at your net worth can help you make a sound decision.

Worksheet VI: Example One—Mr. & Mrs. Young
NET WORTH STATEMENT
DATE___3 / 1 / 97___

When filling out this form, refer back to Chapter 3, Worksheet IV, Record-keeping.

ASSETS	MONETARY VALUE	OWNER OF ASSET

Current Assets (see 1. Current Balance, 2, Amount Invested)

Checking Account___$150.___   ___joint___

Savings Account___$1,500___   ___joint___

Credit Union Accounts___   ___

Money Market Funds___   ___

CDs___   ___

Treasury Bills___   ___

Treasury Notes___   ___

Securities (see 3. Current Market Values)

Stocks___   ___

Bonds___   ___

Mutual Funds___   ___

Real Estate (see 4. Current Market Value)

Residence___   ___

Recreational Property___   ___

Income Property___   ___

Long Term (see 5. Cash Value, 6. Present Value, 7. Value of Your Interest)

Insurance___   ___

Annuities___   ___

Pensions___   ___

Profit Sharing Plans___   ___

401(k)___$9,400___   ___husband___

401(k)___$3,000___   ___wife___

Individual Retirement Accounts___   ___

PERSONAL PROPERTY	MONETARY VALUE	OWNER OF ASSET
Home Furnishings	$5,000	joint
Automobiles	$7,000	joint
Clothing & Furs		
Jewelry		
Antiques		
Stamp Collection		
Coins		
Fine Art		
Other		
TOTAL ASSETS	$35,250	

LIABILITIES OR CREDIT OBLIGATIONS

CURRENT LIABILITIES:	AMOUNT DUE	OBLIGATOR
Medical & Dental		
Current Bills	$460.	joint
Charge Accounts		

Unpaid Taxes

Capital Gains		
Federal		
State		
Local		

Real Estate (see 8).

Residence		
Recreational		
Income Property		

Other Debt or Installment Debt (see 8.)

Automobile Loans	$4,100	joint
Home Improvement Loans		
Education Loans		
Life Insurance Loans		
Margin Accounts		
Bank Loans		
Credit Cards	$150	joint
TOTAL ASSETS	$35,250	
TOTAL LIABILITIES	$4,710	
NET WORTH	$30,540	

Worksheet VI: Example Two—Mr. & Mrs. Mid
NET WORTH STATEMENT
Date   3 / 1 / 97

When filling out this form, refer back to Chapter 3, Worksheet IV, Record-keeping.

ASSETS	MONETARY VALUE	OWNER OF ASSET
Current Assets (see 1. Current Balance, 2, Amount Invested)		
Checking Account	$2,000	joint
Savings Account	$2,500	joint
Credit Union Accounts		
Money Market Funds	$20,000	joint
CDs		
Treasury Bills		
Treasury Notes		
Securities (see 3. Current Market Values)		
Stocks		
Bonds		
Mutual Funds		
Real Estate (see 4. Current Market Value)		
Residence	$150,000	joint
Recreational Property		
Income Property		
Long Term (see 5. Cash Value, 6. Present Value, 7. Value of Your Interest)		
Insurance	$2,000	husband
Annuities		
Pensions		
Profit Sharing Plans		
401(k)	$46,124	husband
401(k)	$28,600	wife
Individual Retirement Accounts	$12,600	husband
	$9,700	wife

PERSONAL PROPERTY	MONETARY VALUE	OWNER OF ASSET
Home Furnishings	$ 30,000	joint
Automobiles	$ 11,000	joint
Clothing & Furs	$ 5,000	joint
Jewelry	$ 10,000	Wife
Antiques		
Stamp Collection		
Coins		
Fine Art		
Other	$ 5,000	husband
TOTAL ASSETS	$ 334,524	

LIABILITIES OR CREDIT OBLIGATIONS

CURRENT LIABILITIES:	AMOUNT DUE	OBLIGATOR
Medical & Dental	$ 100	joint
Current Bills	$ 600	joint
Charge Accounts	$ 200	joint

Unpaid Taxes

Capital Gains		
Federal		
State		
Local		

Real Estate (see 8).

Residence	$ 26,145	joint
Recreational		
Income Property		

Other Debt or Installment Debt (see 8.)

Automobile Loans	$ 5,500	joint
Home Improvement Loans	$ 4,560	joint
Education Loans		
Life Insurance Loans		
Margin Accounts		
Bank Loans		
Credit Cards	$ 150	joint
TOTAL ASSETS	$ 334,524	
TOTAL LIABILITIES	$ 37,255	
NET WORTH	$ 297,269	

Worksheet VI: Example Three—Mr. & Mrs. Elder
NET WORTH STATEMENT
Date 3 / 1 / 97

When filling out this form, refer back to Chapter 3, Worksheet IV, Record-keeping.

ASSETS	MONETARY VALUE	OWNER OF ASSET

Current Assets (see 1. Current Balance, 2, Amount Invested)

Checking Account	$ 500	joint
Savings Account		
Credit Union Accounts		
Money Market Funds	$ 5,000	joint
CDs	$ 36,000	joint
Treasury Bills		
Treasury Notes		

Securities (see 3. Current Market Values)

Stocks	$29,795	husband
Bonds		
Mutual Funds		

Real Estate (see 4. Current Market Value)

Residence	$ 40,000	joint
Recreational Property		
Income Property		

Long Term (see 5. Cash Value, 6. Present Value, 7. Value of Your Interest)

Insurance		
Annuities		
Pensions		
Profit Sharing Plans		
401(k)		
401(k)		
Individual Retirement Accounts		

PERSONAL PROPERTY	MONETARY VALUE	OWNER OF ASSET
Home Furnishings	$10,000	
Automobiles	$2,000	
Clothing & Furs	$10,000	
Jewelry		
Antiques		
Stamp Collection		
Coins		
Fine Art		
Other		
TOTAL ASSETS	$133,295	

LIABILITIES OR CREDIT OBLIGATIONS

CURRENT LIABILITIES:	AMOUNT DUE	OBLIGATOR
Medical & Dental	$500	
Current Bills	$450	
Charge Accounts	0	

Unpaid Taxes

Capital Gains		
Federal		
State		
Local		

Real Estate (see 8).

Residence		
Recreational		
Income Property		

Other Debt or Installment Debt (see 8.)

Automobile Loans		
Home Improvement Loans		
Education Loans		
Life Insurance Loans		
Margin Accounts		
Bank Loans		
Credit Cards		
TOTAL ASSETS	$133,295	
TOTAL LIABILITIES	$950	
NET WORTH	$132,345	

Worksheet VI: Yours
NET WORTH STATEMENT
Date_____

When filling out this form, refer back to Chapter 3, Worksheet IV, Record-keeping.

ASSETS	MONETARY VALUE	OWNER OF ASSET

Current Assets (see 1. Current Balance, 2, Amount Invested)

Checking Account_____ _____

Savings Account_____ _____

Credit Union Accounts_____ _____

Money Market Funds_____ _____

CDs_____ _____

Treasury Bills_____ _____

Treasury Notes_____ _____

Securities (see 3. Current Market Values)

Stocks_____ _____

Bonds_____ _____

Mutual Funds_____ _____

Real Estate (see 4. Current Market Value)

Residence_____ _____

Recreational Property_____ _____

Income Property_____ _____

Long Term (see 5. Cash Value, 6. Present Value, 7. Value of Your Interest)

Insurance_____ _____

Annuities_____ _____

Pensions_____ _____

Profit Sharing Plans_____ _____

401(k)_____ _____

401(k)_____ _____

Individual Retirement Accounts_____ _____

PERSONAL PROPERTY	MONETARY VALUE	OWNER OF ASSET
Home Furnishings	_____	_____
Automobiles	_____	_____
Clothing & Furs	_____	_____
Jewelry	_____	_____
Antiques	_____	_____
Stamp Collection	_____	_____
Coins	_____	_____
Fine Art	_____	_____
Other	_____	_____

TOTAL ASSETS _____

LIABILITIES OR CREDIT OBLIGATIONS

CURRENT LIABILITIES:	AMOUNT DUE	OBLIGATOR
Medical & Dental	_____	_____
Current Bills	_____	_____
Charge Accounts	_____	_____

Unpaid Taxes

Capital Gains	_____	_____
Federal	_____	_____
State	_____	_____
Local	_____	_____

Real Estate (see 8).

Residence	_____	_____
Recreational	_____	_____
Income Property	_____	_____

Other Debt or Installment Debt (see 8.)

Automobile Loans	_____	_____
Home Improvement Loans	_____	_____
Education Loans	_____	_____
Life Insurance Loans	_____	_____
Margin Accounts	_____	_____
Bank Loans	_____	_____
Credit Cards	_____	_____

TOTAL ASSETS _____

TOTAL LIABILITIES _____

NET WORTH _____

B U D G E T   Y O U R
W A Y   T O
F I N A N C I A L   F I T N E S S

○   ○   ○   ○

"Budget" is a forbidding word, even frightening to some people. They see it written down or, worse yet, actually say it and their palms begin to sweat.

"Budget." The word does seem to reach down into you, twisting and tightening, just as the word "homework" used to and perhaps "dentist" still does today.

But you can make friends with a budget. It doesn't have to be something you dread. You can draw it to you, make it a part of your life—so much so that the day will come when you will feel lost without it, when you will knock down anyone who tries to take your budget away from you, when it will be as simple and practical and valuable a tool as your checkbook or shopping list.

A budget is a worksheet. A budget is a road map. A budget is a resume. It describes your lifestyle. It tells you who you are and where you are and where you want to be.

Today your standard of living is called your lifestyle. But whatever you want to call it, it is simply how you live—the goods and services you spend your money on. Your budget is to Your Financial Fitness Program what your diet is to your physical fitness program.

There are no fixed rules that apply to everyone when it comes to budgeting. One man's hamburger is another man's steak. Variations are endless. Some put their money into cars while their homes fall apart. Some eat well but wear threadbare clothes.

Some achieve a nice balance among home, cars, clothing, food, and education for their children. But no one can tell anyone else how to spend his or her money. All of us have to decide for ourselves just what our priorities are, for no two individuals, no two families, no two budgets are quite alike. Your budget is your own: your picture of your lifestyle. So you must create it and nurture it.

The budget as a road map

Think of your budget as a road map. Its purpose is to show you where you are going and how to get there. But like any road map, it can also show you where you can sensibly get off the road, and then get safely back on again without losing direction or missing your destination. That is important. Sometimes you do have to change your route, in order to cope with an emergency or a change in plans that may entail delay in reaching your destination. Nothing wrong with that if you have your map to guide you and remind you of your goal and the route you structured to reach it.

Your budget is the key to knowing how much credit you can safely afford to carry. Often inflation, with its threat of higher prices tomorrow if you don't buy today, has encouraged people not to wait until they can afford to buy. But, for many people, the day of reckoning is at hand. With paychecks stretched to the breaking point, there is no more room for impulsive buying while still paying for yesterday's excesses. And so each of us faces a risk when we want to take on a new credit obligation: Can we really afford the payments? Only a well-tended budget can provide an answer to that question.

o   o   o

THE TIGHT BUDGET OF DOLLY AND JIM YOUNG . . .

Four years ago the Youngs' fixed expenses were higher than they are today—nearly half of them going to reduce debt. For a little over a year they cut down on some expenses, making do with the clothes they had and slashing their entertainment expenses. Jim also cut down his lunch cost by brown-bagging. Since the debt has been paid off, they are still watching expenses, and saving now comes off the top. They pay themselves first for a house that will be a reality within the next year.

o   o   o

The Gemini budget: getting and spending

All budgets have two sides. One covers revenue, or what comes in. The other covers expenses, or what goes out. These two sides, income and outgo, are basic to every budget ever created, whether it is that of a single person or a giant corporation with world-wide production, employees, and sales.

Let's start with your revenue budget. See Worksheet VII headed **Sources of Income** on page 49. On this sheet,

write down *all* your income for yourself and your spouse by category: what you earn as wages or salary; extra money you take in from part-time work, moonlighting, hobbies, or whatever; interest you get from savings accounts; dividends from investments; rent from property you own or from roomers or boarders; gifts and contributions from family members or others; Social Security or other pension payments; payments from disability or unemployment insurance; tax refunds.

Be honest with yourself. Don't count any unhatched chickens. The raise you've been promised is not income until you see it in your paycheck. Your budget should reflect what is happening right *now* and never what might be.

Expenditures are of two kinds: fixed and flexible.

Fixed expenses are those that you cannot escape or change to any great degree: the mortgage or rent payment, for instance. Insurance premiums, taxes, monthly credit obligations, and utilities also come under this heading. (You can, of course, reduce utility bills somewhat by being careful about telephone usage, turning out lights, and lowering the thermostat.)

Handling fixed expenses

Your most important fixed expense is the toughest to make. It is a payment to yourself for an emergency fund. More about that in a moment.

The second most important expense is payment to a "fixed expenses" account. Many people set up a separate checking account for this purpose. To determine how

Worksheet VII: Example One—Mr. & Mrs. Young
BUDGET
SOURCES OF INCOME (Yearly)

EARNED INCOME	HUSBAND	WIFE	JOINT	TOTAL	MONTHLY
Wages/Salary	45,000	32,000		77,000	6,417
Self-Employment Income				0	0
Bonus				0	0
INVESTMENT INCOME					
Interest/Savings					
Interest/Bonds				750	63
Capital Gains				0	0
Dividends				0	0
Rental Income				0	0
Trust Income				0	0

EARNED INCOME	HUSBAND	WIFE	JOINT	TOTAL	MONTHLY
RETIREMENT INCOME					
Social Security					
Employer's Pension					
Private Pension					
Other					
OTHER INCOME					
Family Contributions					
Gifts					
Unemployment, Disability Insurance					
Alimony/Child Support					
GROSS INCOME	45,000	32,000	0	77,750	6,479

DEDUCTIONS	HUSBAND	WIFE	JOINT	TOTAL	MONTHLY
Social Security	3,443	2,448		5,891	491
Federal Taxes				12,700	1,058
State Taxes				1,900	158
Local Taxes				0	0
Benefits	500			500	42
401(k) Contributions	1,350	960		2,310	193
Other				0	0
TOTAL DEDUCTIONS	5,293	3,408	0	23,301	1,942
NET INCOME	39,707	28,592	0	54,449	4,537

much to put into this account every month, line up all your fixed expenses for the year. Worksheet VIII headed **Fixed & Flexible Expenses** will help you to work out the details outlined here: Note that you have to pay some expenses every month (rent or mortgage, for example); some quarterly (insurance premiums, probably); some semi-annually (real estate taxes); and some annually (motor vehicle licenses, for example).

Total each category and figure out its monthly average. Then total the monthly averages of all the categories to see how much must go into your fixed-expenses account each month. Hard as it will be—*at first*—you must start immediately to put in that amount every

month. (If possible, put it in an interest-bearing account.) And you must resist with every fiber in your body the urge to take that fixed-expenses account checkbook to the supermarket or to a sale. Once you have set the habit, though, it will be easy to maintain. And with the account established and functioning well, you will always be able to pay the tax bill or the insurance premium when it comes due.

An emergency fund is not the same as a fixed-expenses account. Your emergency fund should contain the equivalent of from three to six months' net income. If you and your spouse are young and both working, if car and appliances and house are new and not likely to

Worksheet VIII: Example One—Mr. & Mrs. Young
FIXED & FLEXIBLE EXPENSES

	FIXED EXPENSES	JAN	FEB	MAR	APR	MAY	JUNE	JULY	AUG	SEPT	OCT	NOV	DEC	TOTAL
1	Rent/Mortgage	675	675	675	675	675	675	675	675	675	675	675	675	8,100
2	Fuel													
3	Electricity	40	40	45	33	55	40	85	90	75	55	45	40	643
4	Telephone	75	50	55	60	55	45	50	60	55	55	65	75	700
5	Water													
6	Homeowner's Insurance				175						175			350
7	Automobile Insurance		300			300			300			300		1,200
8	Disability Insurance													
9	Life Insurance													
10	Personal Property Tax													
11	Real Estate Tax													
12	Estimated Income tax													
13	Automobile Loan	275	275	275	275	275	275	275	275	275	275	275	275	3,300
14	Loan Repayment													
15	Loan Repayment													
16	Other Debt													
17	Emergency Fund													
18	Savings/Investing (IRAs)													
19	Other													
20														
21	TOTAL FIXED EXPENSES	1,065	1,340	1,050	1,218	1,360	1,035	1,085	1,400	1,080	1,235	1,360	1,065	14,293
22	MONTHLY AVERAGE	1,191	1,191	1,191	1,191	1,191	1,191	1,191	1,191	1,191	1,191	1,191	1,191	
23	DIFFERENCE	126	-149	141	-27	-169	156	106	-209	111	-44	-169	126	

Mr. & Mrs. Young
FIXED & FLEXIBLE EXPENSES

	FLEXIBLE EXPENSES	JAN	FEB	MAR	APR	MAY	JUNE	JULY	AUG	SEPT	OCT	NOV	DEC	TOTAL
24	**Food**	575	575	575	575	575	575	575	575	575	575	575	575	6,900
25	Food/Beverages	150	150	150	150	150	150	150	150	150	150	150	150	1,800
26	Take-Home Food	75	75	75	75	75	75	75	75	75	75	75	75	900
27	Dining Out	200	200	200	200	200	200	200	200	200	200	200	200	2,400
28	Lunches at Work													
29														
30	**Clothing**	400	250		200		250	150	300	200	150		300	2,200
31	Clothing/Shoes	35	35	35	35	35	35	35	35	35	35	35	35	420
32	Laundry/Dry Cleaning		75				45			65			55	240
33	Alterations													
34				125	75		125				150		1,000	1,475
35	**Gifts**													
36	Animals	35		55	40	50	75	45		45			75	420
37	Personal Care/Toiletries	25	25	25	25	25	25	25	25	25	25	25	25	300
38	Periodicals/Books													
39														
40	**Entertainment**													
41	Recreation							1,500						1,500
42	Travel/Vacations	25	25	25	25	25	25	25	25	25	25	25	25	300
43	Movies/Theater Tickets		75				85							160
44	Sporting Events													
45														
46	**Household Expenses**													
47	Lawn/Snow Removal													
48	Maid													
49	Garbage													
50	Repairs		300		85		150				350		400	1,285
51	Home Furnishings					200								
52	Major Appliances			75					95					
53														
54	**Transportation**	90	120	95	115	95	125	150	95	95	95	95	120	1,290
55	Gas/Oil		200			200			95			80		575
56	Repairs			75										75
57	Licenses/Registration													
58	Commutation, Parking													
59														
60	**Children's Expenses**													
61	Allowances													
62	Lessons													
63	Camp	700	700	700	700	700	700	700	700	700	700	700	700	8,400
64	Babysitting/Child Care													
65	Recreation/Sports													

Mr. & Mrs. Young
FIXED & FLEXIBLE EXPENSES

		JAN	FEB	MAR	APR	MAY	JUNE	JULY	AUG	SEPT	OCT	NOV	DEC	TOTAL
66	**Education**													
67	Tuition													
68	Room/Board													
69	Books/Supplies													
70	Travel													
71														
72	**Medical Expenses**													
73	Doctor													
74	Dentist		75				75			75		85		310
75	Drugs	20	20	20	20	20	20	20	20	20	20	20	20	240
76														
77	**Contributions**													
78	Church/Synagogue	75	75	75	75	75	75	75	75	75	75	75	75	900
79	Other Charity	25	25	25	25	25	25	25	25	25	25	25	25	300
80														
81														
82														
83	**TOTAL FLEXIBLE EXPENSES**	2,430	3,000	2,255	2,420	2,250	2,835	3,750	2,395	2,385	2,650	2,165	3,855	32,390
84	**TOTAL FIXED EXPENSES**	1,065	1,340	1,050	1,218	1,360	1,035	1,085	1,400	1,080	1,235	1,360	1,065	14,293
85	**TOTAL EXPENSES**	3,495	4,340	3,305	3,638	3,610	3,870	4,835	3,795	3,465	3,885	3,525	4,920	46,683
86	**NET INCOME**													54,449
87	**PROFIT (LOSS)**													7,766
88														
89														

cry for major repairs soon, it is safe to have a minimum of three months' income stashed away. If you are older, have a large family and many obligations, you will feel a lot more comfortable when you maintain a six-month cushion for emergencies.

This cash reserve is intended for emergencies only, such as a major medical expense not covered by insurance, a major auto or household repair, a stretch of unemployment. Such emergencies, without the reserves ready to pay for them, could send you off to sign for a loan. That in turn would add to your fixed obligations each month, giving you more to pay, more to worry about, and less to have for flexible expenses and discretionary spending.

(If your self-discipline is really strong, you can easily keep your emergency fund in your separate fixed-expenses account; even better, however, is to put it into a separate savings account.)

> *Important*: Think about your emergency fund before you think about an investment program. It takes precedence.

Handling flexible expenses

What are flexible expenses? They are payments you make regularly but which vary in amount depending on what you're doing, how you're feeling, what you need. Food is a major item, of course. Other expenses include clothing; medical care; transportation; entertainment and recreation; household maintenance, such as cleaning services, reupholstering, redecorat-ing or recarpeting; laundry and dry-cleaning; and magazine subscriptions. Worksheet VIII will help you to categorize all these items and more.

○   ○   ○

THE MIDS: BUDGET UNDER CONTROL . . .

Mr. and Mrs. Mid have a combined *gross income* of $101,600, including both their salaries and interest on savings. But for budget purposes they must look at their *net income*, which is $62,937. Here's how payroll deductions based on their itemized deductions and personal exemptions reduce their income:

$19,026	Federal income taxes (IRS)
4,362	State income taxes
7,643	FICA (Social Security) (7.65% on maximum of $65,400)
+7,632	payroll savings plan
$38,663	total deducted from paychecks

$101,600	gross income to Mr. and Mrs. Mid
-38,663	payroll deductions
$62,937	net income

Some people have more payroll deductions than the Mids, such as contributions to a pension plan, union dues, premiums for Blue Cross, major medical, life insurance, and so on, depending on the particular situation.

Worksheet VII: Example Two—Mr. & Mrs. Mid
BUDGET
SOURCES OF INCOME (Yearly)

EARNED INCOME	HUSBAND	WIFE	JOINT	TOTAL	MONTHLY
Wages/Salary	65,600	34,500		100,100	8,342
Self-Employment Income					
Bonus					
INVESTMENT INCOME					
Interest/Savings			1,550	1,550	129
Interest/Bonds					
Capital Gains					
Dividends					
Rental Income					
Trust Income					

EARNED INCOME	HUSBAND	WIFE	JOINT	TOTAL	MONTHLY
RETIREMENT INCOME					
Social Security					
Employer's Pension					
Private Pension					
Other					
OTHER INCOME					
Family Contributions					
Gifts					
Unemployment, Disability Insurance					
Alimony/Child Support					
GROSS INCOME	65,600	34,500	1,550	101,650	8,471

DEDUCTIONS	HUSBAND	WIFE	JOINT	TOTAL	MONTHLY
Social Security	5,003	2,640		7,643	637
Federal Taxes			16,300	19,026	1,586
State Taxes			4,362	4,362	363
Local Taxes					
Benefits					
401(k) Contributions	4,592	3,040		7,632	636
Other					
TOTAL DEDUCTIONS	10,207	5,680	20,800	39,413	3,284
NET INCOME	55,393	28,820		62,937	5,245

The Mids' largest expense up to two years ago was for college education for their children. Mary's salary paid for educational expenses. Now that they are finished with those expenses, they have begun the long-delayed home improvement projects that were put off and are increasing their savings for retirement. For the first time in many years they are seeing a positive cash flow.

The Mids bought their home in 1976 for $60,000, paying $15,000 down. Their 25-year mortgage on the $45,000 balance demands a monthly payment of $270 for principal and interest. In addition, they pay $2,400 in real estate taxes each year. When Marty reaches retirement age at 65, the house will be free and clear.

o   o   o

THE STRAINED BUDGET OF THE ELDERS

Things have not gone as expected for the Elders. They had thought that their retirement income from Social Security, interest, and dividends would stretch further in the sunny Southwest. However, expenses have soared since they made the move. Their fixed expenses seem low compared to the Youngs' and the Mids'. Yet, over half of these expenses go to pay ever-increasing utility bills and insurance premiums. Food, transportation, and unreimbursed medical expenses cut into over half of their

Worksheet VIII: Example Two—Mr. & Mrs. Mid
FIXED & FLEXIBLE EXPENSES

	FIXED EXPENSES	JAN	FEB	MAR	APR	MAY	JUNE	JULY	AUG	SEPT	OCT	NOV	DEC	TOTAL
1	Rent/Mortgage	270	270	270	270	270	270	270	270	270	270	270	270	3,240
2	Fuel	90	90	90	90	90	90	90	90	90	90	90	90	1,080
3	Electricity	65	75	65	55	55	50	125	150	85	55	65	65	910
4	Telephone	65	65	65	65	65	65	65	65	65	65	65	65	780
5	Water	55			60			85			85			285
6	Homeowner's Insurance	320						320						640
7	Automobile Insurance	600						600						1,200
8	Disability Insurance													
9	Life Insurance		200						200					400
10	Personal Property Tax													
11	Real Estate Tax										75			75
12	Estimated Income tax				1,200						1,200			2,400
13	Automobile Loan	155	155	155	155	155	155	155	155	155	155	155	155	1,860
14	Loan Repayment	95	95	95	95	95	95	95	95	95	95	95	95	1,140
15	Loan Repayment													
16	Other Debt													
17	Emergency Fund													
18	Savings/Investing (IRAs)				4,000									4,000
19	Other													
20														
21	TOTAL FIXED EXPENSES	1,715	950	740	5,990	730	725	1,085	1,025	760	2,090	740	740	18,010
22	MONTHLY AVERAGE	1,501	1,501	1,501	1,501	1,501	1,501	1,501	1,501	1,501	1,501	1,501	1,501	
23	DIFFERENCE		551	761		771	776		478	741		761	761	

Mr. & Mrs. Mid
FIXED & FLEXIBLE EXPENSES

	FLEXIBLE EXPENSES	JAN	FEB	MAR	APR	MAY	JUNE	JULY	AUG	SEPT	OCT	NOV	DEC	TOTAL
24	**Food**	300	300	300	300	300	300	300	300	300	300	300	300	3,600
25	Food/Beverages	80	80	80	80	80	80	80	80	80	80	80	80	960
26	Take-Home Food	150	150	150	150	150	150	150	150	150	150	150	150	1,800
27	Dining Out	125	125	125	125	125	125	125	125	125	125	125	125	1,500
28	Lunches at Work													
29														
30	**Clothing**	200	500	150	100	300			300	200		300	600	2,650
31	Clothing/Shoes	50	50	50	50	50	50	50	50	50	50	50	50	600
32	Laundry/Dry Cleaning	15				75			50				60	200
33	Alterations													
34														
35	**Gifts**		250		200		400		150		300		2,500	3,800
36	Animals	60	60	60	60	60	60	60	60	60	60	60	60	720
37	Personal Care/Toiletries	75		125		45		60			65		65	435
38	Periodicals/Books	50	50	50	50	50	50	50	50	50	50	50	50	600
39														
40	**Entertainment**													
41	Recreation		1,500					2,000						3,500
42	Travel/Vacations	125	125	125	125	125	125	125	125	125	125	125	125	1,500
43	Movies/Theater Tickets		75				80		90					245
44	Sporting Events													
45														
46	**Household Expenses**	75		35			85	85	85	85	250			700
47	Lawn/Snow Removal													
48	Maid	22	22	22	22	22	22	22	22	22	22	22	22	264
49	Garbage		250				75			125			400	850
50	Repairs				3,500		240			2,000				5,740
51	Home Furnishings				1,500									1,500
52	Major Appliances													
53														
54	**Transportation**	125	85	125	125	85	95	110	120	125	80	75	110	1,260
55	Gas/Oil		250			150				600		200		1,200
56	Repairs				140									140
57	Licenses/Registration	25	25	25	25	25	25	25	25	25	25	25	25	300
58	Commutation, Parking													
59														
60	**Children's Expenses**													
61	Allowances													
62	Lessons													
63	Camp													
64	Babysitting/Child Care													
65	Recreation/Sports													

Mr. & Mrs. Mid
FIXED & FLEXIBLE EXPENSES

		JAN	FEB	MAR	APR	MAY	JUNE	JULY	AUG	SEPT	OCT	NOV	DEC	TOTAL
66	**Education**													
67	Tuition													
68	Room/Board													
69	Books/Supplies													
70	Travel													
71														
72	**Medical Expenses**													
73	Doctor	75			80			90			125			370
74	Dentist		130			80			130			75		415
75	Drugs	30	30	30	30	30	30	30	30	30	30	30	30	360
76														
77	**Contributions**													
78	Church/Synagogue	250	250	250	250	250	250	250	250	250	250	250	250	3,000
79	Other Charity	125	75	200			250	75	100	200	150		300	1,475
80														
81														
82														
83	**TOTAL FLEXIBLE EXPENSES**	1,957	4,382	1,902	6,912	2,002	2,492	3,687	2,292	4,602	2,237	1,917	5,302	39,684
84	**TOTAL FIXED EXPENSES**	1,715	950	740	5,990	730	725	1,805	1,025	760	2,090	740	740	18,010
85	**TOTAL EXPENSES**	3,672	5,332	2,642	12,902	2,732	3,217	5,492	3,317	5,362	4,327	2,657	6,042	57,694
86	**NET INCOME**													62,237
87	**PROFIT (LOSS)**													4,543
88														
89														

flexible expenses. Little is left for vacations, dining out, and a little fun. They are going to have to take a look at their assets to see if they can make ends meet.

○   ○   ○

Your best guide to how much money you will need each month to meet these flexible expenses is last year's spending record. If you have no records for last year, start *today* to keep records for the future.

How do you pay for things?

You pay for each expense in one of several ways: with cash, by check at the time of purchase, by charge account, debit card, or electronically.

Cash. Cash is nice. But it moves fast. If you cannot break the habit of carrying cash, try to control the habit of spending it. Keep a pocket notebook. Jot down every expenditure, rounding figures up or down, so you can enter accurate figures in your spending plan.

Check. Paying by check is better than paying cash. Just about any store will take your check if you provide identification—most just want to see your driver's license, some want a look at your MasterCard or Visa card, too. Writing checks gives you accurate records. When you pay by check, be sure your checkbook stub notes what the purchase was for and for whom it was made (always write the stub first).

Credit cards. Credit cards are here to stay, at least until the cash card becomes so universal it puts them out of business. Collect your credit-card receipts and use them to verify your monthly billing from the credit-card company and to keep your spending plan on track. Each month, categorize on your charge accounts what is actually charged, not what you are paying on your charge bills, as you may be paying it off in installments.

Cash cards. The cash card is here. It is your automated teller machine (ATM) card. With it, you can now shop in millions of stores and restaurants in the United States and around the world. Originally, you will recall, the ATM card gave you access to your checking and savings accounts only at machines owned by your own bank or credit union. Then came regional networks. Next you discovered access to your accounts from any machine anywhere—at home or abroad.

Now the ATM card has been enhanced so you can shop with it at all kinds of participating merchants, from supermarkets to gas stations, from high-class department stores to mass-market discount outlets. When you buy with the card, your purchase amount is immediately deducted from your account. The seller is paid then and there.

How does it work?

1. You slide your card through a slot that reads the information contained on the magnetic strip on the back.
2. The cashier enters the amount of your purchase.
3. On a keyboard, you punch in your Personal Identification Number (PIN) or secret code. You may (or may not) be asked to sign for the purchase, as you do with a regular credit card.

Worksheet VII: Example Three—Mr. & Mrs. Elder
BUDGET
SOURCES OF INCOME (Yearly)

EARNED INCOME	HUSBAND	WIFE	JOINT	TOTAL	MONTHLY
Wages/Salary					
Self-Employment Income					
Bonus					
INVESTMENT INCOME					
Interest/Savings			1,950	1,950	163
Interest/Bonds					
Capital Gains					
Dividends	1,554			1,554	130
Rental Income					
Trust Income					

EARNED INCOME	HUSBAND	WIFE	JOINT	TOTAL	MONTHLY
RETIREMENT INCOME					
Social Security	11,410	5,710		17,120	1,427
Employer's Pension	4,500			4,500	375
Private Pension					
Other					
OTHER INCOME					
Family Contributions					
Gifts					
Unemployment, Disability Insurance					
Alimony/Child Support					
GROSS INCOME	17,464	5,710	1,950	25,124	2,094

DEDUCTIONS	HUSBAND	WIFE	JOINT	TOTAL	MONTHLY
Social Security					
Federal Taxes					
State Taxes					
Local Taxes					
Benefits					
401(k) Contributions					
Other					
TOTAL DEDUCTIONS					
NET INCOME	17,464	5,710	1,950	25,124	2,094

4. The cashier presses a key that initiates an automatic phone call to your bank or credit union to confirm that your account has enough money available.
5. Your bank or credit card then automatically deducts the amount from your account, just as when it processes a check.
6. You receive a receipt of the transaction.

The cash card works more easily than writing a check, and is safer than carrying cash. You don't need to show various forms of identification. A store will accept it more readily than an out-of-town check. But caution: Be sure to keep your records straight, recording your purchases immediately in your checkbook. This makes sure you always know how much money is in your account and prevents you from overdrawing.

Computer. If your computer has a modem and the Windows program, and if you subscribe to an online service such as CompuServe, you can probably pay many bills—telephone, utilities, credit cards, and stores—via your keyboard, telling your bank how much to pay to whom without human hands touching cash or checks, envelopes, or stamps. You will need a program like Microsoft's Money or Intuit's Quicken. If you maintain a sufficient balance, which can include your IRAs and CDs, there should be no cost involved.

Worksheet VIII: Example Three—Mr. & Mrs. Elder
FIXED & FLEXIBLE EXPENSES

	FIXED EXPENSES	JAN	FEB	MAR	APR	MAY	JUNE	JULY	AUG	SEPT	OCT	NOV	DEC	TOTAL
1	Rent/Mortgage													
2	Fuel	75	125	125							75	60	75	535
3	Electricity	50	40	50	75	120	130	120	150	110	85	75	55	1,060
4	Telephone	75	65	125	65	85	45	65	60	55	65	65	80	850
5	Water		85			100			85			75		345
6	Homeowner's Insurance							240						240
7	Automobile Insurance		200			200			200			200		800
8	Medical Insurance	175	175	175	175	175	175	175	175	175	175	175	175	2,100
9	Life Insurance													
10	Personal Property Tax													
11	Real Estate Tax	150			150			150			150			600
12	Estimated Income tax													
13	Automobile Loan													
14	Loan Repayment													
15	Loan Repayment													
16	Other Debt													
17	Emergency Fund													
18	Savings/Investing (IRAs)													
19	Other													
20														
21	TOTAL FIXED EXPENSES	525	690	475	465	680	350	750	670	340	550	650	385	6,530
22	MONTHLY AVERAGE													
23	DIFFERENCE													

Mr. & Mrs. Elder
FIXED & FLEXIBLE EXPENSES

#	FLEXIBLE EXPENSES	JAN	FEB	MAR	APR	MAY	JUNE	JULY	AUG	SEPT	OCT	NOV	DEC	TOTAL
24	**Food**													
25	Food/Beverages	350	350	350	350	350	350	350	350	350	350	350	350	4,200
26	Take-Home Food													
27	Dining Out	50	50	50	50	50	50	50	50	50	50	50	50	600
28	Lunches at Work													
29														
30	**Clothing**													
31	Clothing/Shoes	125		45		65	45	125	55	65	75	40	75	715
32	Laundry/Dry Cleaning				35			45						80
33	Alterations													
34														
35	**Gifts**		125			85					125		625	960
36	Animals	25	25	25	25	25	25	25	25	25	25	25	25	300
37	Personal Care/Toiletries		40		25		35	40	35		35		50	225
38	Periodicals/Books	25	25	25	25	25	25	25	25	25	25	25	25	300
39														
40	**Entertainment**													
41	Recreation													
42	Travel/Vacations				800					750				1,550
43	Movies/Theater Tickets	25		30		15			35			20		125
44	Sporting Events													
45														
46	**Household Expenses**													
47	Lawn/Snow Removal													
48	Maid													
49	Garbage													
50	Repairs			150			75				125		65	415
51	Home Furnishings		60		85			250		100				495
52	Major Appliances													
53														
54	**Transportation**													
55	Gas/Oil	125	100	85	150	85	75	85	65	175	85	85	85	1,200
56	Repairs		85			450			150					685
57	Licenses/Registration				75									75
58	Commutation, Parking													
59														
60	**Children's Expenses**													
61	Allowances													
62	Lessons													
63	Camp													
64	Babysitting/Child Care													
65	Recreation/Sports													

Mr. & Mrs. Elder
FIXED & FLEXIBLE EXPENSES

		JAN	FEB	MAR	APR	MAY	JUNE	JULY	AUG	SEPT	OCT	NOV	DEC	TOTAL
66	**Education**													
67	Tuition													
68	Room/Board													
69	Books/Supplies													
70	Travel													
71														
72	**Medical Expenses**													
73	Doctor	55	250	150	125		300		95	250	185	400	250	2,060
74	Dentist	75	125	150	150	75			300		100	75		1,050
75	Drugs	125	145	90	90	65	150	125	65	130	95	85	125	1,290
76														
77	**Contributions**													
78	Church/Synagogue	50	50	50	50	50	50	50	50	50	50	50	50	600
79	Other Charity													
80														
81														
82														
83	**TOTAL FLEXIBLE EXPENSES**	1,030	1,430	1,200	2,035	1,340	1,180	1,170	1,265	1,970	1,325	1,205	1,775	16,925
84	**TOTAL FIXED EXPENSES**	525	690	475	465	680	350	750	670	340	550	650	385	6,530
85	**TOTAL EXPENSES**	1,555	2,120	1,675	2,500	2,020	1,530	1,920	1,935	2,310	1,875	1,855	2,160	23,455
86	**NET INCOME**													25,124
87	**PROFIT (LOSS)**													1,669
88														
89														

Phone. An easy way to pay many bills, even if you do not have a computer, is by telephone. Most banks, utilities, major stores, and credit cards are networked so you can call your bank and tell them whom to pay, how much, and when.

Receipts are valuable. Always get one, whether you are paying cash or by cash card or check or credit card. If you cannot get a receipt or a cash-register tape, make your own note of the date, item, and amount. Put all your receipts on a spindle at home, or in large envelopes, filed chronologically. Keep charge receipts on a spindle or in the envelopes, too. When you pay by check, be sure your checkbook stub notes what the purchase was and for whom it was made. Each month, categorize on your charge accounts what is actually charged, not what you are paying on your charge bill as you may be paying it off in installments.

Now add up all the columns. Are your total expenditures higher than your income? Don't be discouraged if they are. Overspending prods you into making a cash flow analysis—the way being overweight forces you to diet. Here are some questions to ask yourself.

- Do we need all these magazines we subscribe to? Are we reading them all?
- Should we eat out as often as we do?
- Does the dog (or the cat, or the bird) really need gourmet food?

IMPORTANT BUDGETING DON'TS

- Don't be dictatorial. Work out the budget by agreement with other family members.
- Don't be in a hurry. You can't do it in an hour or a single sitting. It takes time.
- Don't go by what others spend (that is, don't keep up with the Joneses).
- Don't expect miracles. A budget is a tool to help you manage more effectively. By itself, it will not give you more money or cut your spending.
- Don't nickel and dime it. Round figures up or down to the nearest dollar, and big figures to the nearest ten dollars.
- Don't overdo the paper work. Report the essentials, that's all.
- Don't be inflexible. Remember that a budget must have room for give and take: Circumstances change. The kids will grow, demands will shift, income as well as outgo will change. Be ready to review, evaluate, revise, and adjust as your lifestyle changes.

- Can we buy in larger quantities, storing extra supplies of nonperishables that we can buy on sale or at a discount, and thus reduce unit costs?
- How much can we save if we cut back on recreation and entertainment?

Worksheet VII: Yours
BUDGET
SOURCES OF INCOME

EARNED INCOME	HUSBAND	WIFE	JOINT	TOTAL	MONTHLY
Wages/Salary					
Self-Employment Income					
Bonus					
INVESTMENT INCOME					
Interest/Savings					
Interest/Bonds					
Capital Gains					
Dividends					
Rental Income					
Trust Income					

EARNED INCOME	HUSBAND	WIFE	JOINT	TOTAL	MONTHLY
RETIREMENT INCOME					
Social Security					
Employer's Pension					
Private Pension					
Other					
OTHER INCOME					
Family Contributions					
Gifts					
Unemployment, Disability Insurance					
Alimony/Child Support					
GROSS INCOME					

DEDUCTIONS	HUSBAND	WIFE	JOINT	TOTAL	MONTHLY
Social Security					
Federal Taxes					
State Taxes					
Local Taxes					
Benefits					
401(k) Contributions					
Other					
TOTAL DEDUCTIONS					
NET INCOME					

A close look at cash flow and overspending can change your lifestyle. So can the births of children or their reaching school age or going off to college. If both husband and wife work after a child arrives, the budget must include child care. If private schooling is preferred, the budget must be adapted. New interests —travel, hobbies, golf or tennis or swim clubs—can change the budget, too. So never think of your budget, or your lifestyle, as set in concrete.

One of the biggest budgetary traumas is suffered by the recently married couple, living to the hilt on two incomes, who suddenly realize that a family will put a severe strain on their spending habits.

Do you really need it?

When you want to buy something, ask yourself the question: "Do I really need this?" What the experts call "purchase analysis," the question tends to put the clamp on impulse buying, for, having taken a good hard look at your priorities as you analyze your cash flow, you find yourself distinguishing between buying for pleasure and buying for need. Unless you make this distinction every time you make a significant expenditure—and only you know what's significant for you—you are *not* financially fit.

There's a good way to test whether you really need to buy something. Instead of buying it, first write out a

Worksheet VIII: Yours
FIXED & FLEXIBLE EXPENSES

	FIXED EXPENSES	JAN	FEB	MAR	APR	MAY	JUNE	JULY	AUG	SEPT	OCT	NOV	DEC	TOTAL
1	Rent/Mortgage													
2	Fuel													
3	Electricity													
4	Telephone													
5	Water													
6	Homeowner's Insurance													
7	Automobile Insurance													
8	Medical Insurance													
9	Life Insurance													
10	Personal Property Tax													
11	Real Estate Tax													
12	Estimated Income tax													
13	Automobile Loan													
14	Loan Repayment													
15	Loan Repayment													
16	Other Debt													
17	Emergency Fund													
18	Savings/Investing (IRAs)													
19	Other													
20														
21	TOTAL FIXED EXPENSES													
22	MONTHLY AVERAGE													
23	DIFFERENCE													

FIXED & FLEXIBLE EXPENSES

	FLEXIBLE EXPENSES	JAN	FEB	MAR	APR	MAY	JUNE	JULY	AUG	SEPT	OCT	NOV	DEC	TOTAL
24	**Food**													
25	Food/Beverages													
26	Take-Home Food													
27	Dining Out													
28	Lunches at Work													
29														
30	**Clothing**													
31	Clothing/Shoes													
32	Laundry/Dry Cleaning													
33	Alterations													
34														
35	**Gifts**													
36	**Animals**													
37	**Personal Care/Toiletries**													
38	**Periodicals/Books**													
39														
40	**Entertainment**													
41	Recreation													
42	Travel/Vacations													
43	Movies/Theater Tickets													
44	Sporting Events													
45														
46	**Household Expenses**													
47	Lawn/Snow Removal													
48	Maid													
49	Garbage													
50	Repairs													
51	Home Furnishings													
52	Major Appliances													
53														
54	**Transportation**													
55	Gas/Oil													
56	Repairs													
57	Licenses/Registration													
58	Commutation, Parking													
59														
60	**Children's Expenses**													
61	Allowances													
62	Lessons													
63	Camp													
64	Babysitting/Child Care													
65	Recreation/Sports													

FIXED & FLEXIBLE EXPENSES

		JAN	FEB	MAR	APR	MAY	JUNE	JULY	AUG	SEPT	OCT	NOV	DEC	TOTAL
66	**Education**													
67	Tuition													
68	Room/Board													
69	Books/Supplies													
70	Travel													
71														
72	**Medical Expenses**													
73	Doctor													
74	Dentist													
75	Drugs													
76														
77	**Contributions**													
78	Church/Synagogue													
79	Other Charity													
80														
81														
82														
83	**TOTAL FLEXIBLE EXPENSES**													
84	**TOTAL FIXED EXPENSES**													
85	**TOTAL EXPENSES**													
86	**NET INCOME**													
87	**PROFIT (LOSS)**													
88														
89														

FOR THE COMPUTER LITERATE

Your computer can help make budgeting easy. Check out programs like Quicken, Managing Your Money, and Microsoft Money, which are compatible with DOS, Windows, and the Macintosh. They help you categorize your income and expenses.

How do you do this? On the programs, you set up an account that duplicates your own checkbook. The programs give you an on-screen register on which you record any and all transactions that affect the balance in your account. Each is categorized. To set up your budget and then follow it, the programs use the data that you have entered into your account register.

The programs come with categories for income (such as salary, dividends, interest, and Social Security) and for expenses (such as telephone, groceries, and clothing). But you can tailor them to your own situation by adding any categories not already listed. From this you can produce reports that show you where your money is coming from, where it is going, and how your budgeted amounts compare to the actual amounts you are spending.

One excellent feature is that of splitting any single payment made into any number of budget categories. Say you are recording your credit card payments. Each credit card statement is likely to include your purchases in any number of different categories. You can make the programs sort them into your budget categories.

What about cash transactions? You set up a cash account, then transfer money from your checking account into the cash account. If, for example, you transfer $100 weekly, be sure to keep all receipts as well as a notebook in which you jot daily expenses. Then enter these in the cash account once a week.

Your budget program lets you set up a goal for how much you want to spend in a particular category—for example, $150 a month for dining out. You can also enter estimated amounts for income and expenses, then track them against your plan. Special graphs and other reports enhance the picture of how well you are—or are not—keeping to your budget.

---

check to yourself for its purchase price. Look at the check. Do you need that amount in order to buy groceries or pay a department store bill? If you do, you don't need that item now. Can you make up the amount by skipping several trips to the movies, by putting off buying that special book, by postponing a holiday trip? Better to do so than to find that you cannot pay for basic flexible expenses, or that you are dipping into money you need for fixed expenses (not so likely to happen if you have set up a fixed-expenses account and are leaving *that* checkbook in the desk when you go shopping).

What about cost effectiveness?

Another good habit of the financially fit: Figure out the cost effectiveness of the goods or services you are buying. These days there is no need to purchase items that you use only rarely, for you can rent almost anything —cars, appliances, furniture, special clothing, camping gear, ski equipment, party dishes, and tableware.

Smart grandparents whose grandchildren live too far away to visit more often than a few times a year are better off renting a crib or high chair when they are needed. Smart couples now think twice about owning two cars. With today's gasoline, insurance, and maintenance costs, alternatives such as car pooling, riding public transportation, or renting a second car only when necessary can make excellent sense.

By carefully controlling your expenditures, you can actually increase the amount of money you have available to invest for intermediate and long-range objectives. Think of this as profit—the difference between income and the cost of doing business.

To summarize: "Budget" will not be a dreaded word if you let yourself think positively and practically about your lifestyle—what you want to be and how you want to live—and how much money you have available to provide that style. Recognize that financial fitness can be achieved only by tracking your spending habits and knowing where the money goes. Formulate judgments about what is important and how you may want to shift your priorities. Create your own road map that shows how you are going to reach your destination. Stick to it unless there is good reason to detour.

There will come times when you must detour in order to pick up assistance, when you must ask for credit. "Credit" is a pleasant, friendly word. One of its synonyms, though, is "debt": a dreaded word. The next chapter will tell you about debt—how to get into it and how to get out again safely and successfully.

HOW TO GET
INTO DEBT
(THE RIGHT WAY)
AND
OUT AGAIN

○   ○   ○   ○

"If I wait until I can afford it, the price will be even higher."

"Fly now. Pay later."

"No money down. No payment for 90 days."

"Dear Mrs. _____ : With the convenience of cash reserve banking, you can write a check even when you have no money in your account . . ."

○   ○   ○

Sound familiar? These phrases are symptomatic of the easy-credit world we have lived in for the past 30 years.

Credit has been so easy, in fact, that its abuse has become a major problem in the last few years and one of the principal reasons why so few of us are financially fit. Buying has become excessive, and impulsive, as Mr. and Mrs. America (not to mention Ms. America) have enjoyed an incredible spending spree.

Paychecks have been stretched—and stretched again—to and beyond the breaking point. Spending habits have been established, reinforced, and expanded until buying has become such second nature that it can scarcely be brought under control.

Credit is nothing new. Shakespeare knew creditors so well he brought Shylock to life for all time. (Debt is older than Dickens, who depicted debtor's prison well over a century ago.) But *consumer credit*, as we know it, did not really come about in this country until 1856, when Isaac Singer hit upon the idea of time payments ($5 down and $5 a month) to sell his $125 sewing machines at a time when the average American's annual income was $525.

Singer's idea generated sales that never could have been achieved if people had been forced to pay cash. It took a few generations for the idea to become commonplace, but eventually buying big-ticket items "on time" and paying for them while you used them became an American standard. (It also created an industry—bank loan departments, credit unions, General Motors Acceptance Corporation, loan sharks, and myriad others —with millions of employees.)

By the way, credit, as discussed in this chapter, means credit as handled by the kinds of organizations mentioned above. Mortgages are not involved.

Then came the all-purpose credit cards. Diners Club was the first. When it started in 1950 the total outstanding debt of the American consumer stood at $21.5 billion. Forty-five years later—with American Express, Visa, MasterCard, and many others vying with Diners Club—the figure had reached over $1 trillion.

Renting money

What is credit? It is a means of renting money when you need it, and for as long as you need it. It is just as easy as renting a trailer or a floor sander or extra tables and chairs for a party. Rental firms charge you a rental fee. Credit institutions charge you interest. When interest rates rise, you pay the lender more for the money you borrow—just as you would pay more for the trailer or sander if the rental company raised its rates.

o   o   o

THE YOUNGS WERE IN OVER THEIR HEADS . . .

Four years ago, here's what the Youngs' credit situation looked like. With too much debt piled up, they were paying off $730 a month. That meant they used 19 percent of their net income for debt reduction—too high a ratio for them, especially when they were trying to save to buy a house. (See Worksheet X on page 63.) They went to work to get the debt level down.

The Youngs looked at it this way: When they had the furniture store paid off 10 months after they started "bare-boning it," they could easily have begun using the $248 formerly paid monthly for furniture as money available for ordinary living expense. But they figured that if they kept their debt reduction at the $730-per-month level for 14 months, they would pay it all off and start a solid saving plan.

That's what they did. When the $248 was no longer needed to pay the furniture store, they disciplined themselves to apply it to reducing their Visa and MasterCard accounts.

o   o   o

Getting credit—and using it

If you have never borrowed money or bought anything on credit, how do you get credit in the first place?

It's a catch-22 situation. You can't get credit until you prove you can be depended on to pay your debts, and you can't prove you can pay your debts until someone takes the risk of extending credit to you.

If you are a young couple applying for your first credit card, or a woman who has always relied on her husband's credit, you may have a tough time at first. A lender will probably ask you to fill out an application form that is very much like the **Net Worth Statement** (Worksheet VI) and **Sources of Income** statement

(Worksheet VII) in this book. The creditor is looking for three things:

1. Do you have the ability to repay? What is your present total income, including such sources as alimony, child support payments, investments, and part-time employment?
2. What are your assets? Again, your Net Worth Statement lists them and their value.
3. Do you have the willingness to pay? If you have no previous history of repayments, this is the catch-22.

If you have no credit history, the lender may insist on a cosigner. Recently I requested a credit card for my daughter, in her own name. She does not yet have enough income to qualify for the card, so I was asked to be a cosigner for her. My income and credit history were used, in effect, to enable her to qualify. This means that I am as liable for payments on her account as she is, but the card is in her name and will be reported as such. Thus she will begin to establish a credit identity of her own.

If you are refused credit on your own the first time you apply, and cannot find a cosigner, what can you do? Try these suggestions:

- Open a checking account at a local bank in your own name. Be sure not to get overdrawn. Get to know your banker. Let him or her get to know you.
- Apply for a charge account at a local store. Pay it promptly.
- Apply for a small bank loan, even if you don't need it. Put the money in a savings account. Withdraw enough each month to make the payments on the loan.
- Establish an installment loan at a local store, purchasing something on time (as distinguished from simply charging).
- Try obtaining a credit card (MasterCard or Visa) through the bank where you have established your checking account and where the banker now knows you and knows you are trustworthy.

Look at the situation from the point of view of the lending institution—the bank, store, American Express, Diners Club, whatever. It is concerned with its own risk. It is taking a chance on you, based on your current income and circumstances. (By the way, your loan application should not show income that is based on overtime pay or moonlighting. What if that income ceased? Also, do you have enough emergency funds to carry you and pay your debts if you are laid off? What about a contingency for a large medical expense? All

Exhibit 5 page 1
UPDATED CREDIT PROFILE

Subscriber   Applicant's   Current
Number   Name   Address

Previous   Social   Year   Type,
Addresses   Security   of   Terms
           Number   Birth   and
                         Amount   Employment

Updated Credit Profile   TRW

TCA1   INQUIRY INFORMATION

RTS 3122250X1J CONSUMER JOHN .S., 10655 B 91502,

P-6613 S 92708,235 E 74202, S-548603388, Y-1944, T-18010005,

E-AJAX HARDWARE/2035 BROADWAY/LOS ANGELES CA 90019

PAGE	DATE	TIME	PORT	H/V		
1	09-30-87	11:23:45	HP26	A60	CONSUMER	TCA1 ③

7-87 JOHN Q CONSUMER   3-87 AJAX HARDWARE
① 10655 BIRCH ST   ② 2035 BROADWAY
     BURBANK CA 91502   LOS ANGELES CA 90019

ACCOUNT PROFILE POS NON NEG	SUBSCRIBER NAME/COURT NAME / STATUS COMMENT	STATUS DATE	DATE OPENED	SUBSCRIBER #/COURT CODE TYPE	ASSN CODE TERMS	AMOUNT	BALANCE	ACCOUNT NUMBER/DOCKET BALANCE DATE	AMOUNT PAST DUE	PAYMENT PROFILE NUMBER OF MONTHS PRIOR TO BALANCE DATE 1 2 3 4 5 6 7 8 9 10 11 12
≫≫≫	CHECKPOINT ≫≫ SS# NOT ISSUED AS OF 08/87									
A	MOUNTAIN BK / CURWAS30-2	1-87	8-84	1139999 SEC	2 60	ORIGL $43000 SCH MONTH PAY	$19330 $956	3562401973 8-26-87 LASTPAY 7-30-87		CCCCCCC1C1CC
A	HILLSIDE BK / CURR ACCT	7-87	11-86	3149999 AUT	5 48	ORIGL $6300 SCH MONTH PAY	$3748 $155	29144508119 7-30-87 LASTPAY 7-01-87		CCCCCCCC
A	HEMLOCKS / TOO NEW RT	9-87	7-87	3309999 CHG	2 REV	HIBAL $600 SCH MONTH PAY	$437 $44	986543184026 9-05-87		CC
A	BAY CO / CUR WAS 60	3-87	10-Y	3339999 CHG	1 REV	LIMIT $1500	$0	46812391013 8-21-87 LASTPAY 3-15-87		CCCCC2CCCCCC
M	BOWERS / CHARGE OFF	3-86	6-80	3369999 CHG	2 REV	C/OAM $200		212250		
A	GARDEN FIN / DELINQ 120	8-87	8-86	3509999 UNS	2 24	ORIGL $2200 SCH MONTH PAY	$1400 $100	24187010 8-17-87 LASTPAY 4-05-87	$325	321CCCCCCCCC
A	WISTERIA FIN / PD SATIS	10-86	9-85	8549999 SEC	2 12	$500		5238610		
A	HILLSIDE BK / INQUIRY	10-18-86		3149999 AUT	48	$6300				
M	CO SPR CT SANTA ANA / JUDGMENT	9-19-85		3019999		$1200		07505853 ALLIED CO		
≫≫≫	CHECKPOINT ≫≫ SS# IS 524479971/OTHER FILE IDENT:MID INIT IS Q/ STREET INIT IS S, ZIP IS 92708									
	JOH Q CONSUMER / 6613 S 92708									
A	WYATT FIN / REPO	12-84	6-82	3519999 AUT	1 36	$7500		29416413		
M	GROVE CREDIT UNION / INQUIRY	3-09-87		3789999 H/I	12	$5000				
- - - - -	END — TRW INFORMATION SERVICES									

Confidential

© TRW Inc 1971, 1987
TRW is the name and
mark of TRW Inc

Exhibit 5 page 2
GUIDE TO UPDATED CREDIT PROFILE REPORT

(1) Name and address as recorded on automated subscriber tapes, including date of most recent update.

(2) Employment name and address as reported by a subscriber through an inquiry on the date shown.

(3) A code designating the TRW or Credit Bureau office nearest the consumer's current address, for your use in consumer referrals.

(4) Three columns indicating positive, nonevaluated, and negative status comments.

(5) A (Automated) and M (Instant Update or Manual Form) indicate the method by which the credit grantor reports information to TRW.

(6) Name and number of reporting subscriber.

(7) Association code describing the legal relationship to the account.

(8) Account or docket number.

(9) Status comment reflecting the payment condition of the account as of the status date.

(10) Date the account was opened.

(11) Scheduled monthly payment amount.

(12) Date last payment was made.

(13) Type and terms of the account.

(14) The applicant's payment history during the past 12 months. The code reflects the status of the account for each month, displayed for balance reporting subscribers only.

C	—	Current
1	—	30 days past due
2	—	60 days past due
3	—	90 days past due
4	—	120 days past due
5	—	150 days past due
6	—	180 days past due
— (Dash) —		No history reported for that month.
Blank	—	No history maintained; see status comment.

(15) The original loan amount (ORIGL), credit limit (LIMIT), historical high balance (HIBAL), or original amount charged to loss (C/OAM), represented in dollar amounts.

(16) Balance owing, balance date, and amount past due, if applicable.

(17) Inquiries indicate a request for the applicant's credit information — inquiring subscriber, date of inquiry, and type, terms and amount, if available.

(18) Public Record: Court name, court code, docket number, type of public record, filing date, amount, and judgment creditor. This information may include bankruptcies, liens and/or judgments against the applicant.

(19) Profile report messages alert the subscriber about a credit applicant's social security number, name, address, generation, or year of birth.

these are factors you should be thinking about when you apply for credit.)

Once you have acquired credit, remember that it is an obligation. You have agreed to pay back the money, and credit must not be abused. Your monthly obligation to repay the debt should be listed as a fixed expense on your budget sheet. Repay it just as you pay your rent or your utilities.

You are now building up a credit record. Next time you seek credit, the lender may obtain a "credit report" on you from a credit bureau. (See Exhibit 5.) The report lists all your accounts, noting whether payments have been made on time and are current. It may also include civil suits, judgments against you that were awarded to creditors, and other information that might affect the lender's opinion of you as a credit risk. Note that credit bureaus do not make judgments. They do not rate any consumer's credit history or ability to repay. They only provide information that banks, department stores, gasoline companies, and other companies use to help determine whether the applicant is worthy of credit.

The credit report also shows whether there is a billing problem—from the seller's point of view. For example, if you are disputing a charge by a store and have refused to pay until the matter is settled, or if a former spouse fails to pay his or her own debts, the credit report may show such items as unpaid debts. You are permitted to add up to 150 words to the report to tell your side of the story. This becomes part of your permanent credit record. (Your record is maintained as "permanent" for seven years; bankruptcies, however, are kept on the record for ten years.)

Under the law, you are entitled to see any credit report on you that has been prepared by a credit bureau and to challenge any items in the report that seem incorrect. The credit bureau is obligated to make an investigation and correct any errors. This is especially important if the information or evidence is misleading.

Any time you are denied credit by any organization to which you have applied, you are entitled to receive a copy of your credit history free of charge. If you simply want to check into what a local credit bureau has on you in its files, the bureau may charge a fee for issuing a copy of your report. Usually the fee is less than $10.

○   ○   ○

THE MIDS—AND CREDIT . . .

Mary and Marty Mid never got into the "buy now, pay later" syndrome. Both were raised with conservative ideas about money. Over the years, they have borrowed only to buy automobiles and to build the addition to their home, so they are carrying less than 10 percent of take-home pay in credit obligations. The result is that they have no monthly juggling act to see who gets paid next, they do not have to debate whether they can afford to go out to dinner or a movie, and finding education funds for their children has never produced headaches.

○   ○   ○

Budget: key to credit

To use credit without setting up a working budget is foolhardy. Your budget tells you how much credit you can safely afford. People get into trouble when they don't check to see how much they can carry each month in credit repayments. They get overextended. Then when they run out of money they use credit cards or charge accounts to continue buying items that should be included in regular living expenses.

The scenario goes like this. Checking account balance—zero. Cash in wallets and purses—zero. Need to buy something—use credit. Balance in charge account and on credit cards—rising monthly. Payment each month—a minimum part of the total bill. Balance reaches approved limit—apply for additional credit (in the case of charge cards) or go to other stores and open new accounts.

Eventually the minimum payments plus the finance charges on a number of accounts get to be a major expense, cutting even further into each month's available cash. A monthly payment or two is missed. You start paying each account less than the minimum due. Or you start to juggle, paying this account this month and that account next month. Past due notices begin to come in the mail. Finally a collection agency sends a notice or calls. (See Exhibit 6.)

This scenario produces knotted tummies, tense nerves, headaches, ulcers—and a bad credit report. Sometimes it produces total indebtedness that is equal to or greater than your annual income.

The problem crosses all economic and social lines. A $25,000-a-year secretary may owe $25,000. A $150,000-a-year executive may have $150,000 in unpaid debts.

Figuring out your debt ratio

Turn to Worksheets IX and X, **List of Debts** and **Personal Debt Ratio.** Fill in all debts that are current. The total amount of indebtedness is on the Net Worth Statement. Monthly obligations are included under credit repayment on the Fixed Expenses Worksheet.

Now use the Personal Debt Ratio sheet to figure out a ratio for yourself, based on your total take-home pay and your installment obligations. Your debt ratio is a percentage of your take-home pay (the net income you figured out on your budget sheet after all payroll deductions) that is committed to the repayment of debts.

Exhibit 6
COLLECTION AGENCY NOTICE

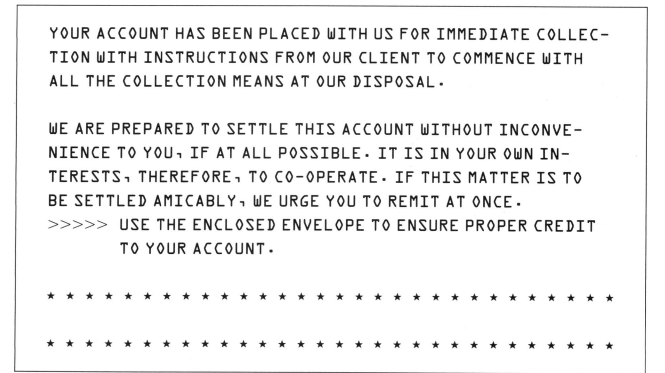

YOUR ACCOUNT HAS BEEN PLACED WITH US FOR IMMEDIATE COLLEC-
TION WITH INSTRUCTIONS FROM OUR CLIENT TO COMMENCE WITH
ALL THE COLLECTION MEANS AT OUR DISPOSAL.

WE ARE PREPARED TO SETTLE THIS ACCOUNT WITHOUT INCONVE-
NIENCE TO YOU, IF AT ALL POSSIBLE. IT IS IN YOUR OWN IN-
TERESTS, THEREFORE, TO CO-OPERATE. IF THIS MATTER IS TO
BE SETTLED AMICABLY, WE URGE YOU TO REMIT AT ONCE.
>>>>> USE THE ENCLOSED ENVELOPE TO ENSURE PROPER CREDIT
        TO YOUR ACCOUNT.

★ ★

★ ★

Most people find that they are in danger if more than 15 to 20 percent of net income is committed to repaying debts. If the ratio goes higher, one is usually robbing Peter to pay Paul: borrowing to meet daily expenses, lengthening the time between payments, charging items that will have a life span less than the time it takes to pay for them.

Here's one good standard to apply: Can all your debts be paid off in 18 to 24 months? If not, your debt ratio is too high.

You should know the ratio of all your debts at any one time. It will change, of course, when you pay off a loan. You can then judge whether it is safe to borrow again, and how much it makes sense to borrow.

Caution: It is easy, when you have just paid off a loan with an obligation of $50 a month, say, to take on another loan with a $65 monthly payment. You think, what's another $15 a month? But if your non-credit expenses are rising along with inflation, that added $15 can be disastrous. Repeatedly adding a new debt that is larger than the one just paid off will slowly but surely put you into a higher and more dangerous debt ratio. Keeping debt within your means, on the other hand, will give you more income for your own security and pleasure. When you are not paying out a large amount for interest, you have more spendable dollars.

Kicking the spending habit: The crash fitness program

When your budget, your cash flow analysis, and your debt ratio all show that it is time to cut back on expenses in order to pay off debts, you may have to spend a year or so repaying current debts and being scrupulously careful not to add any new ones.

Credit offers many benefits. It allows you to do things and purchase products that you might never be able to do or get otherwise, or that would have taken years to save for. Yet it can be a bane as well. To determine the amount of credit you can comfortably afford to carry, budgeting is a valuable tool. It is the only way to control credit abuse and, if abuse occurs, to take charge and get it back under control.

Either you control credit or credit controls you. It's your choice whether you want to be financially fit.

If you really want to kick the spending habit, your best way to do it is cold turkey. It's tough, but you can do it. Sign an agreement with yourself. Then take all your charge cards and put them in a friend's safe deposit box; or cut them in half and return them to the creditors, with a note of explanation. Look steely-eyed at your budget. Cut out every living expense that is not an absolute necessity and stick to it. Open a separate bank account and put in a certain amount every payday. Use the money in this account for debt reduction and debt reduction only.

Worksheet IX: Mr. & Mrs. Young
LISTS OF DEBTS
Date____1993____

CREDITOR'S NAME	TYPE OF LOAN	DATE OF LAST PAYMENT	MATURITY DATE	MONTHLY PAYMENT From Budget	TOTAL AMOUNT DUE From Net Worth Statement
1. State bank	auto	2/1/88	1 YEAR	$162	$1,950
2. Midtown bank	auto	3/1/88	1½ YEARS	$200	$3,600
3. Main St. Furniture		up-to-date	10 mo.	$248	$2,480
4. Mastercard				$55	$1,000
5. VISA				$65	$1,000

TOTAL MONTHLY PAYMENTS $

_____

TOTAL AMOUNT OWED $

A CREDIT CARD FITNESS TIP

If you have more than one multipurpose card (Visa, MasterCard, American Express, Diners Club), it is better to put all large items you charge onto one card. Say you know you are going to pay for a stereo, for instance, over a long time. Why put small items like a shirt or cosmetics on the same card and pay a monthly finance charge on these as well as the stereo? Two multipurpose cards can be helpful: one for large items not to be paid in full and another for small items that you do pay in full each month. But be careful not to charge large items on the one you intend to pay in full regularly. And be sure that you do pay it in full each month. Otherwise—trouble.

If you put yourself on this strict regimen, you will achieve Personal Financial Fitness by managing on the amount of money you actually *have*.

Here are some good points to remember on *how to stay out of credit trouble*:

1. Bear in mind that paying a loan is a fixed expense; debt must be paid off.
2. Ask yourself: Would I buy this if I were paying cash? Deferred spending often turns into avoided spending.
3. For smaller purchases, if you can't afford to pay cash, the chances are you can't afford to buy it on credit.
4. Before you decide on a loan, shop around.
5. Avoid impulse shopping or buying something to "lift your spirits."
6. Never use credit for everyday expenses.
7. Keep careful track of credit card purchases, lest you be surprised by an unexpected or unnoticed bill. Everyone in the household who uses credit

Worksheet IX: Yours
LIST OF DEBTS
Date_____

CREDITOR'S NAME	TYPE OF LOAN	DATE OF LAST PAYMENT	MATURITY DATE	MONTHLY PAYMENT From Budget	TOTAL AMOUNT DUE From Net Worth Statement

TOTAL MONTHLY PAYMENTS $ _____

TOTAL AMOUNT OWED $ _____

cards should put the slips in one place immediately after each purchase. Nothing is worse than opening a monthly credit card bill to discover that your spouse has added a large purchase (especially if you happen to think it was an unnecessary one) that you had not anticipated.

Some lending institutions offer to help you by consolidating all your debts. They lend you enough to pay everyone you owe. You then pay them back over an extended period of time.

This type of loan may involve a substantial amount of interest. But it does usually give you a lower monthly payment for debt reduction—lower than the total of paying all those separate accounts. What you have to watch out for is the simple act of starting to use the plastic cards again while you are still paying off that big loan. If you do start charging, you start the cycle all over again. Almost inevitably, within a few months or a year or two, you will be signing another consolidation loan. The pattern will repeat. This is the path to bankruptcy.

Congress passed the Bankruptcy Reform Act of 1978 to ease the burdens of going bankrupt and to facilitate repayment of a substantial portion of one's debt. The law recognizes the fact that people get themselves into economic situations that are often beyond their control, for the ripple effect of our inflationary economy is especially hard on those who are extended beyond any safety margin. The act has resulted in a tremendous increase in the amount of personal bankruptcy. In 1995, American creditors lost nearly $10 billion through some one million personal bankruptcies.

Before you decide to declare personal bankruptcy, talk with a lawyer. Find out about the various "chapters" of the Bankruptcy Act. You'll learn that petitions have to be filled out, that Chapter 7 covers a "straight bankruptcy" in which the court collects, sells and distributes debtor's assets, with certain exemptions, while Chapter 13 encourages debtors to repay their loans. Chapter 13, the so-called "wage earner plan," allows you to consolidate debts and repay a court-approved percentage of them over three years. Creditors must suspend interest

Worksheet X: Mr. & Mrs. Young
PERSONAL DEBT RATIO

Your ratio is based on take-home pay. You have figured out the amount of debt that you owe for installment loans. Is this too much for you?

		MONTHLY	YEARLY
1.	Your total take-home pay	$ 3,750	$ 45,000
2.	Use 20% (maximum for most consumers). Divide income by 5. If you feel this is too high, use 15% or divide by 6.7.	$ 750	$ 9,000
3.	Your present installment obligations	$ 730	$ 8,760
4.	Your present safety margin—subtract line 3 from line 2.	$ 20	$ 240
5.	Your personal ratio—divide your installments obligation (line 3) by your take home pay (line 1).	19%	19%

It might be wise to use both the 15% and 20% figures to see the difference in your own situation.

and late charges on most debts, and they are barred from continuing any action against the debtors. If you default on Chapter 13 payments, the court will throw you into Chapter 7 proceedings.

Bank cards—does it make any difference which one?

There are over 19,000 financial institutions offering either MasterCard or Visa. You will have an incredible amount of choice when selecting a card. Cards will differ in:

annual fees ranging from $0 to $50
interest rates ranging from 8.5 to 21 percent
varying grace periods

In addition there are over 1,500 affinity programs. Affinity card relationships exist between many charities and nonprofit organizations, including professional organizations and alumni associations. Philanthropic and professional organizations benefit from these cards, receiving a portion of a cardholders' annual fee and/or transactions fees. Check with your favorite charity or professional group to see if an affinity card relationship

exists and request an application. In the environmental area, for example, affinity groups exist with both national and local organizations—the World Wildlife Fund, the Zoological Society of Florida, and even the Federation of Fly Fishers.

Co-branded credit cards with airlines offer you the opportunity to build up frequent flier miles when you

HOW TO SEE TROUBLE COMING

To check for real trouble signs, ask yourself:

1. Am I lengthening the time between payments?
2. Am I charging more and more instead of paying cash?
3. Are new bills piling up unpaid?
4. Am I robbing Peter to pay Paul?
5. Am I letting certain bills slide?
6. Am I over my safe ratio of 15 to 20 percent of take-home pay?

Worksheet X: Yours
PERSONAL DEBT RATIO

Your ratio is based on take-home pay. You have figured out the amount of debt that you owe for installment loans. Is this too much for you?

		MONTHLY	YEARLY
1.	Your total take-home pay	$	$
2.	Use 20% (maximum for most consumers). Divide income by 5. If you feel this is too high, use 15% or divide by 6.7.	$	$
3.	Your present installment obligations	$	$
4.	Your present safety margin—subtract line 3 from line 2.	$	$
5.	Your personal ratio—divide your installments obligation (line 3) by your take home pay (line 1).		

It might be wise to use both the 15% and 20% figures to see the difference in your own situation.

charge any of your purchases on that card. Check with the airline of your choice to determine if it has hooked up with a particular bank card. Other co-branded cards give you money back, free gasoline, or credit toward purchase of products. The choice is yours but you might as well capitalize on whichever card gives you the most advantages.

Wise ways with credit
Your credit cards can be the closest thing you will ever have to "free" money. If you understand their billing cycles and how their finance charges are calculated, you can take advantage of them.

The best way to use credit cards is to pay the full amount due every month. Usually a credit card allows a grace period of 25 to 30 days from the date you are billed until you are assessed a finance charge. If you make a purchase immediately after your bill date (which is imprinted on your bill), and if you pay in full when you pay, you can gain free credit for almost two months. For example: Suppose your billing date is July 1. If you buy something on July 2, the purchase will not appear on your bill until August, and you will then have until September 1 (or the stated due date) to pay for it. If you

pay the full amount of your new balance by September, no interest will be charged and you will gain free use of your July 2 purchase until the first of September.

Translating and interpreting finance charges
Finance charges will be added to a bill if the amount due is not paid in full. Finance charges may be calculated by a number of methods. The most commonly used is the *average daily balance method with newly billed purchases included.* This method does not allow the grace period for newly purchased items mentioned in the preceding paragraph. Under this method, it is important to note that the finance charge is based on the average amount you have charged during the month. As soon as your latest purchase goes into the computer, your average changes and your finance charge increases. The finance charge then continues to be calculated on your latest average daily balance until it again changes. Therefore, if this method is used by your creditor, it is better to pay as soon as you receive the bill, rather than waiting (as you might have done when paying in full) until the end of the month. In other words, if you decide to leave part of a bill unpaid for just one month, you will be charged interest. (See Exhibit 7.)

Exhibit 7
FINANCE CHARGE CALCULATION

FINANCE CHARGES AS CALCULATED USING AVERAGE DAILY BALANCE WITH NEWLY PUR-CHASED ITEMS INCLUDED. The finance charge *depends on the date the payment is received* as illustrated. In the first example the payment is made on the 15th of June and in the latter on the 24th. Note there is $1.13 difference by paying it 9 days later.

6/1	Previous Balance	$300.00 × 5	1500.00
6/5	Purchase of $10.00	$310.00 × 5	1550.00
6/10	Purchase of $65.00	$375.00 × 5	1875.00
6/15	Payment of $200.00	$175.00 × 6	1050.00
6/21	Purchase of $18.00	$193.00 × 3	579.00
6/24	Purchase of $7.00	$200.00 × 7	1400.00
		31 days	7954.00

7954.00 divided by 31 (number of days in billing cycle) equals 256.58 (average daily balance) times 1½ equals $3.85 (finance charge).

6/1	Previous Balance	$300.00 × 5	1500.00
6/5	Purchase of $10.00	$310.00 × 5	1550.00
6/10	Purchase of $65.00	$375.00 × 5	1875.00
6/15	Purchase of $18.00	$393.00 × 5	1965.00
6/21	Purchase of $7.00	$400.00 × 6	2400.00
6/24	Payment of $200.00	$200.00 × 5	1000.00
		31 days	10,290.00

10,290.00 divided by 31 equals 331.93   331.93 times 1½% equals $4.98 finance charge

Trouble and high finance charges rise together when you make only partial payments month after month. Here's why. Whatever amount you pay, the creditor takes his full finance charge out before deducting anything from the balance you owe. This means that if you pay only the minimum due, you reduce the actual amount you owe only by that amount *less* the finance charge.

Let's say you send in a minimum payment of $50, the amount called for on a hypothetical monthly statement. If the finance charge on the *total* balance you owe is $10, the creditor will take $10 to pay that finance charge and deduct only $40 from the total you owe. If the balance you owe is quite large, your required minimum payment may be mostly interest (or finance charge) month after month and the principal amount you owe will be reduced very, very slowly—much too slowly to be called sound money management.

Watch for sneaky tricks

Among issuers of credit cards, competition is fierce. Often they come up with offers that sound too good to be true. Heed the old adage: If it seems too good to be true, it probably is. Read the fine print with great care, for that is where the ploys are buried. Some examples:

- The no-fee card with ultra-low interest. The headline, or the lead paragraph in the letter, says "no fee" and promises a delightfully low rate of interest. The small print discloses that after a certain amount of time (usually six months to a year) the interest jumps higher and an annual fee may be imposed.

- The reduced rate. If the bank that issued your card suddenly announces it is reducing the interest rate, don't assume you will get the lower rate. You may first have to pay off your entire remaining balance at the old rate. You may save money by simply switching to another credit-card issuer —one that is competing by also offering the lower rate.
- The spending requirement. The card offering a very low rate of interest may demand that you charge a certain amount annually. Otherwise, it keeps your rate higher than for someone who is spending at the required level.
- The bait-and-switch tactic. You get an invitation to apply for a "pre-approved" gold card with no annual fee. But then, despite the "pre-approved" promise, you are turned down. The issuer may then send you the standard non-gold card instead, with a higher interest rate, lower spending limit, and an annual fee. You do not have to accept it, however. You can cut it up and send it back. But remember: You filled out and signed an application, so the account may show up on your credit history even if you never use it, leading some other creditor who is looking you over to think you are already overextended.
- The tier-rate system. Many credit-card issuers offer lower rates to preferred customers. If you are unhappy with your current card, or have been offered a better deal elsewhere, the issuer may waive your annual fee or offer you another card with a more attractive rate. It never hurts to ask for a better deal, for credit-card issuers do not want to lose your business. It costs more to land a new customer than to hang onto an old one.

How to apply for a low-interest card

Those who issue low-interest cards are working on a tight profit margin. They can't afford to take on customers who may default or declare bankruptcy. So they ask you to fill out an application that is longer than usual, and they look you over very carefully and approve fewer people. If you want to be sure you get approval for a low-interest card, here's how to increase your chances:

1. If you are behind on any of your bills, get caught up before you apply.
2. Avoid looking like a high risk. If you have more than four credit cards with large outstanding balances, pay off one or more of them by transferring the balances to one of your other cards —preferably one that offers lower interest rates.
3. Pay off your outstanding balances down to not more than 70 percent of your approved credit limit.
4. Reduce the total amount of credit that is available to you. Got any cards you are not now using? Cut them up, if they have no outstanding balances, and write the issuer saying you want to close the account. *Important*: Be sure to request that this information be reported promptly to the credit bureau, and then check your credit history to verify the cancellation.
5. Don't apply for too many low-interest credit cards all at the same time. When your application for a new credit card comes in, the issuing company will request your credit history. All requests show up on the credit bureau's computer, and too many inquiries over a period of a few months or a year can make you look like a poor risk.

HOW THE GOVERNMENT WILL CONTRIBUTE TO YOUR FINANCIAL FITNESS: SOCIAL SECURITY BENEFITS

○   ○   ○   ○

"How do I know what I'll get from Social Security?"

"My wife hasn't worked in 35 years—will she get Social Security?"

"How can I be sure they've kept accurate records on me?"

"Is it true that Social Security might not be able to pay everybody it is supposed to in the future?"

○   ○   ○

Before you can plan retirement or life insurance, you should know what benefits you will be entitled to under Social Security. Few people understand what Social Security is and what it will provide when they retire, or if they become disabled, and what—if anything—it will provide for their dependents when they die.

Just what is Social Security?

It is a program run by the U.S. government to provide continuing income to those whose earnings have ceased because of retirement, disability, or death. The program is practically universal, reaching nearly every U.S. citizen. It is a form of social insurance and it is contributory; you and your employer both pay for it while you are working.

Early in your working career, you build up protection until you are a fully insured worker entitled to all the benefits that Social Security provides. This is achieved by earning what Social Security calls "quarters of coverage." The number of quarters of coverage you need in order to draw benefits depends on your age, but once you have 40 quarters of coverage you are fully insured from then on. A quarter of coverage is three months, or a quarter of a year, so 40 quarters is ten years.

Exhibit 8
AGE AT WHICH YOU CAN RECEIVE FULL SOCIAL SECURITY BENEFITS

YEAR OF BIRTH	FULL RETIREMENT AGE
1937 or earlier	65
1938	65 and 2 months
1939	65 and 4 months
1940	65 and 6 months
1941	65 and 8 months
1942	65 and 10 months
1943–1954	66
1955	66 and 2 months
1956	66 and 4 months
1957	66 and 6 months
1958	66 and 8 months
1959	66 and 10 months
1960 and later	67

Ever changing

The important thing to understand about Social Security is that the amount of benefits available is constantly changing. So is legislation involving Social Security. You must, therefore, view the following figures as examples only and not as the final word. I will show you how to obtain the figures that apply to your own case.

The baby-boomer worry

The fast-approaching day when the baby-boom generation—those born between 1946 and 1964—starts collecting Social Security benefits is cause for big worry. The baby-boom population is 77 million. By 2030, most of them will have retired. At that point, only two workers will be paying into Social Security for every one who is retired, whereas in 1995 the ratio was 3.2 to 1. Statisticians figure that unless Washington either beefs up the financing of Social Security or cuts down its benefits, the system will start going into the red in the year 2015.

The rules change again in 2000

Starting in the year 2000, and because life expectancies have become longer than when the original rules were made, the age of eligibility for full retirement benefits will gradually rise from 65 to 67. If you were born in 1938 or later, this change includes you. (See Exhibit 8.)

What do you get if you are a fully insured worker?

When anyone who has contributed to Social Security dies or retires or is disabled, he or she or their dependents are entitled to receive:

- Retirement benefits (a monthly payment starting at any time after age 62); at 65, the spouse receives a payment of 50 percent of the retired worker's amount, even if the spouse was never employed.
- A monthly payment for a surviving spouse, if 60 or older; if the survivor is caring for a child or children under age 16, additional payment is made, subject to a family maximum.
- A monthly payment to unmarried children who are under 18. Children receive 75 percent of a deceased worker's benefit and 50 percent of a retired or disabled worker's, subject to a family maximum. In general, payments may not exceed 150 to 175 percent of a worker's personal benefit, no matter how large the family.
- A monthly payment to a fully disabled worker, regardless of age.

What do you get if you work beyond age 65?

Suppose you are feeling great, you like your work, your employers need you and want you—can you increase your Social Security benefits by continuing to work full-time after you reach 65? Yes. You can gain two ways. First, remember that higher lifetime earnings result in higher benefits. Adding a year of earnings can help your total picture.

Second, the longer you delay retirement, up to age 70, the greater your Social Security checks will be. The increases will be added automatically. The percentage of increase depends on when you were born. (See Exhibit 9.)

Exhibit 9
INCREASES FOR DELAYED RETIREMENT

YEAR OF BIRTH	YEARLY PERCENTAGE INCREASE
1916 or earlier	1%
1917–1924	3%
1925–1926	3.5%
1927–1928	4%
1929–1930	4.5%
1931–1932	5%
1933–1934	5.5%
1935–1936	6%
1937–1938	6.5%
1939–1940	7%
1941–1942	7.5%
1943 or later	8%

Important: Even if you are delaying your retirement, be sure to sign up for Medicare to start when you are 65.

What do you get if you are not fully insured?

What if you have less than 40 quarters of coverage, and thus are not fully insured? Then you are what Social Security calls "currently insured." This means that if you die your survivors are eligible for benefits if you have had at least six quarters of coverage in the three years before your death. "Survivors" are qualified dependents: husband or wife, children, and other dependents who qualify.

The "currently insured" status is important to young people who sometimes wonder just what they are getting for their payments into the Social Security system.

How can you tell what your benefits will be?

Your benefits are based on your earnings during all the years you have worked. This figure is on file at Social Security headquarters and is regularly updated. It's a good idea to find out, at least every three years, what your records show. The way to find out is to obtain a Request for Earnings and Benefit Estimate Statement from your nearest Social Security office or by writing to Social Security Administration, P.O. Box 57, Baltimore, Maryland 21230. (See Exhibit 10.)

Fill in your name, address, date of birth, Social Security number, and current earnings.

If you are over 60, the estimate can be obtained with a telephone call to the Social Security Administration.

Social Security will send you a statement of earnings and an estimate of benefits. (See Exhibit 11.) Checking your records is important. If an error occurs, and you wait more than three years, three months, and 15 days to report it, it may be too late for a correction.

The estimate of benefits will help you to determine how much you might receive upon retirement, how much you would receive if you were disabled, and how much your survivors would receive if you died. The estimate may be lower than what you will actually receive at 65. All your earnings covered under Social Security, up to the time you apply for benefits, will be considered in figuring the amount of your retirement benefit. If you have additional earnings covered by Social Security between now and the time you retire, your monthly payment probably will be higher than what we have estimated. With such figures at hand, you can then calculate how much income you will want in addition to Social Security in order to have a comfortable retirement, and how much life insurance you need to protect your dependents.

o   o   o

MR. MID'S BENEFITS

Mr. Mid sent for his statement of earnings and estimate of benefits from Social Security. It shows he will receive

Exhibit 10

REQUEST FOR EARNINGS AND BENEFIT ESTIMATE STATEMENT

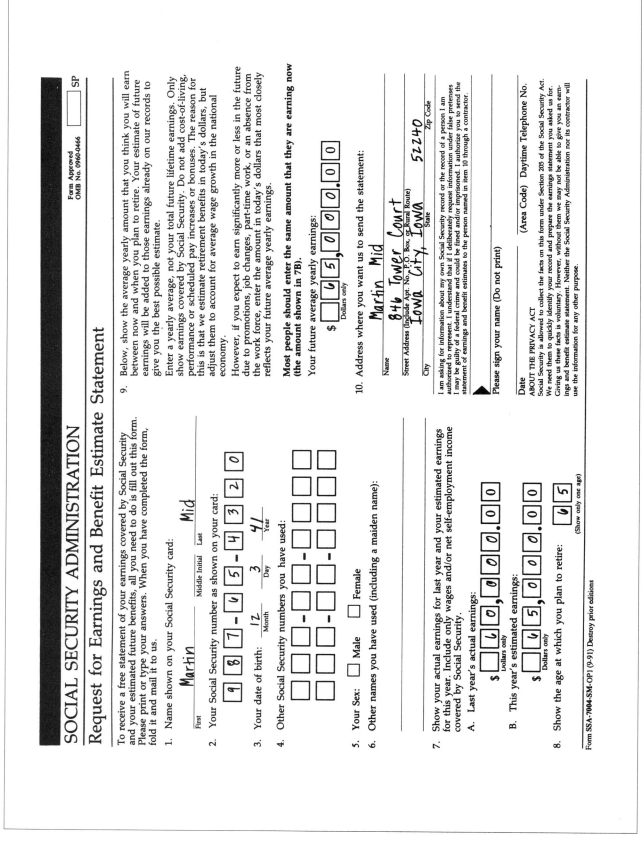

SOCIAL SECURITY ADMINISTRATION

Form Approved
OMB No. 0960-0466

SP

Request for Earnings and Benefit Estimate Statement

To receive a free statement of your earnings covered by Social Security and your estimated future benefits, all you need to do is fill out this form. Please print or type your answers. When you have completed the form, fold it and mail it to us.

1. Name shown on your Social Security card:

Martin   Mid
First   Middle Initial   Last

2. Your Social Security number as shown on your card:

9 8 7 - 6 5 - 4 3 2 0

3. Your date of birth:

12   3   41
Month   Day   Year

4. Other Social Security numbers you have used:

☐☐☐ - ☐☐ - ☐☐☐☐
☐☐☐ - ☐☐ - ☐☐☐☐

5. Your Sex: ☐ Male   ☐ Female

6. Other names you have used (including a maiden name):

_____

7. Show your actual earnings for last year and your estimated earnings for this year. Include only wages and/or net self-employment income covered by Social Security.

A. Last year's actual earnings:

$ 6 0 , 0 0 0 . 0 0
Dollars only

B. This year's estimated earnings:

$ 6 5 , 0 0 0 . 0 0
Dollars only

8. Show the age at which you plan to retire:

6 5
(Show only one age)

9. Below, show the average yearly amount that you think you will earn between now and when you plan to retire. Your estimate of future earnings will be added to those earnings already on our records to give you the best possible estimate.

Enter a yearly average, not your total future lifetime earnings. Only show earnings covered by Social Security. Do not add cost-of-living, performance or scheduled pay increases or bonuses. The reason for this is that we estimate retirement benefits in today's dollars, but adjust them to account for average wage growth in the national economy.

However, if you expect to earn significantly more or less in the future due to promotions, job changes, part-time work, or an absence from the work force, enter the amount in today's dollars that most closely reflects your future average yearly earnings.

Most people should enter the same amount that they are earning now (the amount shown in 7B).

Your future average yearly earnings:

$ 6 5 , 0 0 0 . 0 0
Dollars only

10. Address where you want us to send the statement:

Name   Martin Mid

Street Address (Include Apt. No., P.O. Box, or Rural Route)   846 Tower Court

City   Iowa City,   Iowa   52240
   State   Zip Code

I am asking for information about my own Social Security record or the record of a person I am authorized to represent. I understand that if I deliberately request information under false pretenses I may be guilty of a federal crime and could be fined and/or imprisoned. I authorize you to send the statement of earnings and benefit estimates to the person named in item 10 through a contractor.

Please sign your name (Do not print)

_____

Date _____ (Area Code) Daytime Telephone No. _____

ABOUT THE PRIVACY ACT

Social Security is allowed to collect the facts on this form under Section 205 of the Social Security Act. We need them to quickly identify your record and prepare the earnings statement you asked us for. Giving us these facts is voluntary. However, without them we may not be able to give you an earnings and benefit estimate statement. Neither the Social Security Administration nor its contractor will use the information for any other purpose.

Form SSA-7004-SM-OP1 (9-91) Destroy prior editions

Exhibit 11
FACTS ABOUT YOUR SOCIAL SECURITY

FACTS, CREDITS AND EARNINGS
February 15, 1995

THE FACTS YOU GAVE US

Your Name . . . . Martin Mid
Your Social Security Number 987-65-4320
Your Date of Birth . . . . Dec. 3, 1941
1995 Earnings $59,000
1996 Earnings $61,000
Your Estimated Future Average Yearly Earnings $65,000
The Age You Plan To Retire 65
Other Social Security Numbers You've Used . . . . None

We used the facts you gave us and the information in our records under your Social Security number to prepare this statement for you.

When we estimated your benefits, we included any 1995 and 1996 earnings and any future estimated earnings you told us about. If you did not estimate your future earnings, we did not project any future earnings for you.

YOUR SOCIAL SECURITY CREDITS

To qualify for Social Security benefits and Medicare, you need credit for a certain amount of work covered by Social Security. The number of credits you need will vary with the type of benefit. Under current law, you do not need more than 40 credits to qualify for any benefit or for Medicare.

Our review of your earnings, including any 1993 and 1994 earnings you told us about, shows that you now have at least 40 Social Security credits.

YOUR SOCIAL SECURITY EARNINGS

The chart on the next page shows the earnings on your Social Security record. It also estimates the amount of Social Security taxes you paid in each year to finance benefits under Social Security and Medicare. If you have government earnings that help you qualify for Medicare, those earnings also are included on the chart under the heading "Medicare—Your Taxed Earnings."

We show earnings only up to the maximum yearly amount covered by Social Security. These maximum amounts are shown on the chart. The chart may not include some or all of your earnings from last year because they may not have been added to your record yet.

YOUR EARNINGS RECORD

| YEARS | SOCIAL SECURITY | | | MEDICARE | |
	Maximum Yearly Earnings	Your Taxed Earnings	Estimated Taxes You Paid	Your Taxed Earnings*	Estimated Taxes You Paid
1937–50	$3,000	$ 0	$ 0		
1951–54	3,600	0	0		
1955	4,200	0	0		
1956	4,200	0	0		
1957	4,200	4,200	94		
1958	4,200	4,200	94		
1959	4,800	4,800	120		
1960	4,800	4,800	144		
1961	4,800	4,800	144		
1962	4,800	4,800	150		
1963	4,800	4,800	174		
1964	4,800	4,800	174		
1965	4,800	4,800	174		
1966	6,600	6,600	277	$ 6,600	$ 30
1967	6,600	6,600	290	6,600	30
1968	7,800	7,800	343	7,800	40
1969	7,800	7,800	374	7,800	40
1970	7,800	7,800	374	7,800	40
1971	7,800	7,800	405	7,800	40
1972	9,000	9,000	468	9,000	45
1973	10,800	10,800	864	10,800	108
1974	13,200	13,200	1,042	13,200	135
1975	14,100	14,100	1,113	14,100	140
1976	15,300	15,300	1,208	15,300	150
1977	16,500	16,500	1,303	16,500	160
1978	17,700	17,700	1,070	17,700	180
1979	22,900	22,900	1,403	22,900	220
1980	25,900	25,900	1,587	25,900	240
1981	29,700	29,700	1,975	29,700	272
1982	32,400	32,400	2,170	32,400	334
1983	35,700	35,700	2,391	35,700	374
1984	37,800	37,800	2,532	37,800	397
1985	39,600	39,600	2,591	39,600	514
1986	42,000	42,000	2,701	42,000	609
1987	43,800	43,800	2,765	43,800	635
1988	45,000	45,000	2,853	45,000	652
1989	48,000	48,000	2,976	48,000	696
1990	51,300	51,300	3,180	51,300	702
1991	53,400	53,400	3,335	53,400	730
1992	55,500	55,500	3,458	55,500	749
1993	57,700	57,700	3,636	57,700	778
1994	60,600	60,600	3,757	60,600	879
1995	61,200	61,200	3,943	61,200	922
1996	62,700	Not Yet Recorded			
1997	65,400	Not Yet Recorded			

*Earnings were taxed for Medicare beginning in 1966. From 1983 on, these earnings include Medicare-Qualified Government Earnings (see page 7). In 1991, the maximum yearly earnings taxed for Medicare are $125,000. For 1992, the amount is $130,200.

about $1,248 a month starting at age 65, if he retires then. His wife will get $500 a month starting when she is 62.

If Mrs. Mid decides to wait until she is 65 to start collecting on his account, however, and assuming that his account is larger than her own Social Security account, she will receive $624 a month. She would not receive any benefits until she reached 60 if Mr. Mid were to die now. She may then decide whether to start benefits at 60 or at any age until she is 65. If she elects to start

receiving benefits at 60, she will get about $887 a month. If she holds off until 65, her monthly payments will be $1,248.

○　　○　　○

A woman will not receive both a wife's benefit and her own old age or disability benefit. If her own benefits are larger than those she would receive as a wife's benefit, she will receive a benefit based on her own

Exhibit 11 *continued*

ESTIMATED BENEFITS

Retirement

You must have 40 Social Security credits to qualify for retirement benefits. This is the same number of credits you need to qualify for Medicare at age 65. Assuming that you meet all the requirements, here are estimates of your retirement benefits based on your past and any projected earnings. The estimates are in today's dollars, but adjusted to account for average wage growth in the national economy.

If you retire at 62, your monthly benefit in today's
dollars will be about . . . . $ 998

The earliest age at which you can receive an unreduced retirement benefit is 65 years of age. We call this your full retirement age. If you wait until that age to receive benefits, your monthly benefit in today's dollars
will be about . . . . $ 1,248

If you wait until you are 70 to receive benefits,
your monthly benefit in today's dollars
will be about . . . . $ 1,680

Survivors

If you have a family, you must have 22 Social Security credits for certain family members to receive benefits if you were to die this year. They may also qualify if you earn 6 credits in the 3 years before your death. The number of credits a person needs to qualify for survivors benefits increases each year until age 62, up to a maximum of 40 credits.

Here is an estimate of the benefits your family could receive if you had enough credits to be insured, they qualified for benefits, and you died this year:

Your child could receive a monthly benefit of about . . . . $ 936

If your child and your surviving spouse who is caring
for your child both qualify, they could each receive
a monthly benefit of about . . . . $ 936

When your surviving spouse reaches full retirement age,
he or she could receive a monthly benefit of about . . . . $ 1,248

If more family members qualify for benefits (other children, for example), the total amount that we could
pay your family each month is about . . . . $ 2,184

We may also be able to pay surviving spouse or
children a one-time death benefit of . . . . $ 255

Disability

Right now, you must have 22 Social Security credits to qualify for disability benefits. And, 20 of these credits had to be earned in the 10 year period immediately before you became disabled. If you are blind or received disability benefits in the past, you may need fewer credits. The number of credits a person needs to qualify for disability benefits increases each year until age 62, up to a maximum of 40 credits.

If you were disabled, had enough credits, and met the other requirements for disability benefits, here is an estimate of the benefits you could receive right now:

Your monthly benefit would be about . . . . $ 1,248

You and your eligible family members could receive
up to a monthly total of about . . . . $ 1,872

These estimates may be reduced if you receive workers' compensation or public disability benefits.

IF YOUR RECORDS DO NOT AGREE WITH OURS

If your earnings records do not agree with ours, please report this to us right away by calling the 800 number shown below. We can usually help you by phone. When you call, have this statement available along with any W-2 forms, payslips, tax returns or any other proof of your earnings.

IF YOU HAVE ANY QUESTIONS

If you have any other questions about this statement, please read the information on the reverse side. If you still have questions, please call 1-800-537-7005.

Social Security considers all calls confidential. We also want to ensure that you receive accurate and courteous service. That is why we may have a second Social Security representative listen to some calls.

---

record. If her own benefit is less than she would receive as a wife (50 percent of his primary insurance amount at 65) then she will receive the wife's benefit.

There is an advantage for a woman collecting on her own benefit. She will receive it whether her husband is receiving benefits or not. As a wife, however, she can receive only a wife's benefit when her husband starts to collect on his account.

○   ○   ○

THE YOUNGS' BENEFITS . . .

Suppose that either one of the Youngs becomes widowed or disabled. Since neither one has worked for 40 quarters, neither is fully insured. Social Security considers both "currently" insured for survivor benefits. And they are both considered fully insured for disability benefits because each has worked in jobs covered by Social Security for half the quarters since each was 21 years old.

A widowed parent taking care of a child under 18 is eligible for benefits, but Social Security applies an

Exhibit 12

SOCIAL SECURITY BENEFITS AS PERCENTAGE OF PRIMARY INSURANCE AMOUNT (PIA)

OLD-AGE BENEFIT

    Starting age 65 or over . . . .   PIA
    Starting age 62–64 . . . .   PIA reduced

DISABILITY BENEFITS . . . .   PIA

WIFE'S BENEFIT (wife of retired or disabled worker)

    Caring for child (under 16 or disabled) . . . .   50% of PIA
    Starting age 65 . . . .   50% of PIA
    Starting age 62–64 . . . .   50% of PIA reduced

HUSBAND'S BENEFIT (husband of retired or disabled woman worker)

    Starting age 65 . . . .   50% of PIA
    Starting age 62–64 . . . .   50% of PIA reduced

CHILD'S BENEFIT

    Child of retired or disabled worker . . . .   50% of PIA
    Child of deceased worker . . . .   75% of PIA

MOTHER'S OR FATHER'S BENEFIT (widow or widower caring for child under 16 or disabled) . . . .   75% of PIA

WIDOW'S BENEFIT (widow not caring for child)

    Starting age 65 . . . .   100% of PIA
    Starting age 60–64 . . . .   100% of PIA reduced

WIDOWER'S BENEFIT

    Starting age 65 . . . .   100% of PIA
    Starting age 60–64 . . . .   100% of PIA reduced

DISABLED WIDOW'S OR WIDOWER'S BENEFIT

    Starting age 50–60 . . . .   50% to 71½% of PIA

PARENT'S BENEFIT (dependent parent of deceased worker)

    One dependent parent . . . .   82½% of PIA
    Two dependent parents . . . .   75% of PIA (each)

---

earnings "test" to the benefits. If a person entitled to benefits makes more than a certain dollar amount in a year, Social Security reduces or eliminates its benefits. Because of Dolly's and James's earnings, any benefits for either of them—if either were widowed—would be eliminated, but their child would receive a benefit.

○   ○   ○

How much can you earn during retirement without giving up Social Security benefits?

If you are 65 or older but not yet 70, you may not have earned income totaling more than $13,500 a year or you will lose some of your Social Security benefits. If you are under 65, earned income may not be more than $8,640. Over 70, you lose no benefits because of employment.

Important: The limits on earnings will increase $1,000 a year from now until the year 2000, when the limit will hit $17,000. Then it will jump to $25,000 in 2001 and $30,000 in 2002.

If you are under 65, $1 in benefits will be deducted for each $2 you earn above the limit. If you are between 65 and 69, $1 will be deducted for $3 you earn above the limit. For example, suppose you are 66:

Benefit amount	$800 per month ($9,600 a year)
Earnings	$20,000 per year
Earnings limit	13,500
Difference	$6,500 divided by 3 = $2,167

You will get $9,600 less $2,167, or $7,433 in Social Security benefits. With your $20,000 in earnings, your gross income will be $27,433.

Now, suppose you limit your earnings to $10,700. You will get your full Social Security benefits of $9,600, plus your earnings of $10,700, for a gross of $20,300. But don't forget—you will face further reductions, because you must pay income taxes and Social Security tax on earned income. That means you may have to pay federal tax on up to one-half of your Social Security benefits.

If other family members receive benefits on your Social Security record, your earnings may affect their benefits. (The benefits of any family members who are working, however, are affected only by the earnings of those particular family members.)

Note: Special rules apply to your earnings during your first year of retirement. Check them out when you notify Social Security that you are officially retiring.

Here are some important points to remember about Social Security:

- Up to 50 percent of Social Security benefits can be taxed if your adjusted gross income plus tax-exempt interest plus one-half of your Social Security benefits exceeds certain base amounts. The base amounts are $25,000 for a single taxpayer and $32,000 for married taxpayers who file a joint tax return.

- Since 1993, single taxpayers with incomes greater than $34,000 and couples with incomes greater than $44,000 must pay tax on 85 percent of their Social Security benefits.

  Note: 85 percent is not the tax rate. It is the portion of Social Security benefits that is subject to federal income tax.

- Some states tax Social Security benefits. Others do not. Usually any state that has an income tax follows federal guidelines. Be sure to check on what your state does. It is worth checking out any state that you may be considering a move to.

- Until a claim is actually made, the exact amount of benefits can only be estimated. Computations will be reestimated when you file a claim.

- You cannot and will not receive any benefits unless you file for them. Social Security must be notified of your retirement, your disability, or your spouse's death.

- Such notification must be made within six months after the retirement, disability, or date of death. The law in almost all cases does not permit any retroactive payment of benefits for a period longer than six months.

- Social Security should be notified at least three months *before* you retire, if you want benefits to start promptly upon your retirement.

- A widow or widower should notify Social Security immediately upon the death of a spouse.

- Survivors of fully insured and currently insured workers are entitled to a lump-sum benefit of $225; this goes to the wife if she is entitled to benefits or to children if they are the recipients of benefits.

- The amount you are entitled to annually is increased automatically as wage levels rise; it is tied to the Cost of Living Index.

- You should check regularly on what is happening to Social Security rules and regulations and how they affect you.

Once you have established a good estimate of your Social Security benefits, you are ready to talk about life insurance needs and retirement and pension plans.

SAVING AND INVESTING FOR FINANCIAL FITNESS

○   ○   ○   ○

"Should we keep our savings in a passbook account?"

"Why is savings 'passive' and investing 'active'?"

"What's the reason for not buying Treasuries through the mail?"

"How can I decide among all the various types of investments—including mutual funds?"

"What's the most important key to investing?"

"What is 'phantom income'?"

○   ○   ○

The difference between saving and investing

There are important differences. Saving is accumulating money for a specific purpose or to use in an emergency. It is a way of preserving capital and guaranteeing steady income. It is also a way of maintaining liquidity. You can always get at your money if it is put away in savings.

Investing is different. You take a chance when you invest. You accept risk—on the premise that you will get returns higher than those from the dependable but conservative practice of ordinary saving.

Investing not only involves risk. It involves your time and effort. You must be willing to devote time to it, to

study, listen, compare, and make sometimes difficult choices. Investing is a much more active exercise than saving.

Saving is passive. Investing is active. If you are looking for your money to grow, it is time to begin an investment program. The important thing to remember is that investing takes time—and don't try to outguess the market. Over the long haul there will be slumps, but there will also be rallies.

Saving is itself one of the foundation stones for investing. For you must have a solid foundation upon which to build an investment program. Such a foundation consists of several fundamentals, including:

- savings for an emergency
- savings for one or more specific goals
- adequate life insurance
- IRAs
- a home of your own.

And you need one more fundamental: enough income to use for investing. Only when you have enough income to meet living and saving expenses and maintain a positive cash flow, or liquidity, should you consider yourself ready to take the risks that are involved in investing in stocks and bonds or any of the other possibilities of "the market."

Savings account

Money in a checking account is like cash in your pocket. It burns a hole. It will be spent.

Having at least one savings account is a must. Open one when you open your checking account or accounts. And start the habit of paying yourself immediately after payday by putting money into your reserve for emergency fund and fixed expenses.

1. *Passbook savings.* This is the old standby. Its chief advantage is that your money is available any time you want it, without you paying any penalty for taking it out. Its disadvantage is that it doesn't pay as much interest as other types of accounts, so the idea is to save in a passbook account. Not all passbook accounts are alike, so:

- Shop around to see where you can get the best deal on interest.
- Watch out for evaporation: Some banks impose a $5 service charge every month on accounts with less than a $300 balance (if you have $100 in a passbook account in such a bank and you forget it for a year, you will have $40 in the account).
- Ask how interest is credited: Is it compounded annually, semiannually, quarterly, or daily? The answer tells you where you will get the highest *effective yield*, or total interest paid on the account. (How do you figure out *compound interest*? To your balance, or principal amount, you add the interest earned for the period—year, half-year, month, or day—to get a new principal amount. Then calculate the interest on *that*, and add it, for still another new principal. Obviously, the more frequently the interest is compounded, the higher the effective yield. What you want, ideally, is interest compounded daily from the day of deposit to day of withdrawal.)
- Check also on *when* interest is credited. In some banks, even though compounding is daily, the money earned may not be credited to your account until the end of a three-month period. If you withdraw money before it is credited, you can lose the interest on it for the entire three-month period. Again, day-of-deposit to day-of-withdrawal compounding is what you want.

2. *Money market account.* While not as tightly regulated as they were a few years ago, these accounts, which generally pay higher interest than passbook savings, usually require a minimum deposit of $1,000. Key points to be aware of:

- You have instant access to the account and you incur no penalties.
- Banks may determine their own rates of interest, based on what they consider to be market conditions, so careful shopping around is called for.
- Banks may not *guarantee* a rate of interest for longer than one month. Most guarantee by the week; this keeps them competitive with the popular money market funds on Wall Street.
- The chief advantage is that you can have your money market account in the same bank as your checking account and transfer funds when you need them, thus earning interest until you need to use the cash.

Exhibit 13
COMPOUND INTEREST CHART

Investing small amounts of money over time can prove to be very profitable. The chart below shows the effect of $1,200 per year ($100 per month) invested at varying rates compounded *annually.*

END OF YEAR VALUES	6%	8%	10%
5th year	$7,170	$7,603	$8,059
10th year	16,766	18,774	21,037
20th year	46,791	59,307	75,602
30th year	100,562	146,815	217,131
40th year	196,857	335,737	584,222

3. *CDs or TDs.* Certificates of deposit or time deposits are also worth considering. With these, you are committed to keeping a certain amount of money on deposit for a minimum period. These fixed-term savings were deregulated on October 1, 1983. Every bank may now set its own minimum investment size and interest rate; and while there used to be specific time limits, you may now purchase a certificate for virtually any term you want—from three months to 10 years. You may also decide on the maturity date you want. Want a certificate to mature on your wedding anniversary or on a child's birthday? Just say so when you're buying it. You may select the term or the interest rate and the bank will design a certificate to match what you want.

Deregulated investments demand close scrutiny. Take the time to read the bank advertisements and ask hard questions. The choices are many, and so are the decisions you will have to make.

> *Tip*: With deregulation, the penalties that used to be imposed if you withdrew your money before the maturity date have been relaxed. They are far less severe.

"The market" and its risks

The typical investor faces a bewildering range of choices: stocks, bonds, mutual funds, real estate, tangible goods, precious metals, and a good many other alternatives.

Besides all the choices, there is no shortage of people to give you advice: brokers, analysts, accountants, lawyers, etc. Remember, it is your money, and you may want to participate in the decisions to buy or to hold certain investments. Not only should you understand your investments, but most importantly you should be comfortable with the way that your money is invested. You hear stories about people who have "made a killing in the market." You dream that one of those people will be you. But what you seldom hear is that for every one who has made a killing there is a loser—someone who took the risk that goes with investing and then took a loss. That's why it is vital that you establish the solid financial foundation you need.

The loser who was prepared to lose and took the risk is in one situation. Unhappy, yes, but not in trouble. There are few sadder moments than when you find you need the money you have invested for some other purpose, decide to sell, and discover that you must sell at a loss and get back less than you had before.

So you must understand that investing is risky, and you must figure out what your "risk temperature" is—no two people ever have exactly the same one. One person may feel comfortable investing in blue-chip stocks while another keeps his or her cool best in tax-sheltered limited partnerships, and a third goes in for municipal bonds. No one should ever be talked into any type of investment that makes him or her feel uncomfortable. Yet you cannot make money without taking some risks, and the faster you hope to make it—and the greater the amount you hope to make—the greater the risks you will have to take. What kinds of risks? Here are some to consider, but note that you, as an investor, have little control over them.

- *Macroeconomic risk.* Change in monetary policy. Outbreak of a war. Change in OPEC policy.
- *Market risk.* Shifts in capital flows and psychology, unrelated to economic news, that can cause advances or declines in the market (e.g., changes in interest rates).
- *Industry risk.* Changing circumstances within a particular industry: for example, the changes in the automotive industry brought about by OPEC and by fuel-efficient imports.
- *Business risk.* The competitor of the company whose stock you buy comes out with a better product than your company's.
- *Management risk.* Mergers, reorganizations, results of poor management judgment—even an unforeseen event (a plane crash, a fire).
- *Information risk.* Rumors or information that are misleading or false.
- *Natural disaster risk.* Floods, hurricanes, drought, tornadoes that could affect, for example, a livestock or crop investment.
- *Liquidity risk.* Insufficient demand for your investment when you decide to sell (or when you *must* sell to gain cash).

The liquidity risk is the one that affects most people. If you cannot risk liquidity—if you *must maintain liquidity*—put your savings where they will not only preserve the asset (i.e., the amount you have saved) but will give you a nice steady income or rate of return. Whether you can handle the liquidity risk should be your primary criterion as to whether or not you should get into investing.

Decide on investment objectives

How do you decide what your investment goals are? Ask yourselves these questions:

1. Are we looking for income and high yield: steady income that we can depend on, at a fairly high percentage of the investment?
2. Are we looking for current growth: Do we want to see our investment itself grow steadily—and

not be so concerned about its producing income—so it will be worth a lot more when we sell it?

3. Are we looking for *aggressive* growth—do we want to make some quick bucks, then sell and do it again?

4. Are we investing to gain tax advantages (e.g., maybe defer taxes or buy tax-free municipal bonds)?

The answer to questions such as these can help you set some investment objectives. You should plan your strategy before you buy specific investments. The issue isn't where the market is but what your needs are. Your goals will also be determined by your ages, your temperaments, your current and future financial needs.

Once you have set your objectives—and it is a good idea to write them down and file them with your investment papers—you must stick to them until the time comes when you know they should be changed. If your income is moving upward and you do not have children to feed, clothe, and educate, your needs probably run in the direction of investing for growth and for tax advantages. If your children are in the expensive teenage and college years, or you're retired, you'll be looking for income and high yield.

What type of investment?

Assuming that you have looked carefully at your budget and net worth and have decided you have enough income to maintain a positive cash flow and take care of expenses, let's look at the kinds of investing you'll want to consider.

Investments are of two types. In a *fixed-income investment*, you are lending your money to a corporation or a government agency (local, municipal, county, state, or federal) that issues bonds. You become, in effect, a creditor of the corporation or government. It pays you interest at a rate that is set, or fixed, when you buy the bond.

You make an *equity investment* when you buy stock in a company. You own part of that company, however small or large your investment may be, and you expect to take advantage of its growth and profits.

Fixed-income investments

1. *Government securities.* Since the U.S. government borrows $200 billion a year, new issues are readily available. These are safe investments simply because the government can print new dollars to repay old debts. There are three types of government securities:

- *Treasury bills.* Sold every week, these reach maturity within three, six, or 12 months. The minimum

investment is $10,000. You buy them at a discount. For example, if you buy a three-month Treasury bill worth $10,000, it is possible to purchase it for $9,850. Three months later it can be presented for full payment of $10,000, realizing $150 in interest.

- *Treasury notes.* These are sold every four weeks or so. They mature in anywhere from one to 10 years and usually require a minimum investment of $5,000. You pay the full value of the note you buy, and you get cash interest from the government twice a year during the term of the note.

- *Treasury bonds.* These are not sold on a regular schedule. You have to watch for them (check with your banker regularly if you are interested). Treasury bonds take anywhere from 10 to 30 years to mature, so they are definitely in the long-range category. Usually you can get them for $1,000 apiece. Like Treasury notes, they pay cash interest twice a year and you buy them at full face value.

Where do you buy Treasuries? You can purchase them directly at any Federal Reserve Bank. You can buy them through the mail, but this requires a certified check one week in advance. You can also buy them through a broker or a bank (either will add a sales charge).

> *Tip*: If you buy Treasuries through the mail, you won't know what interest rate you are getting until after you have made the purchase.

Hold on to Treasuries until they mature. You can always borrow against them or sell them in the secondary market, where you will get more or less what you paid for them, depending on whether the interest rates have fallen, risen, or stayed the same since you bought them.

> *Note*: Treasuries are not taxed at the state or local level. If you live in a state that imposes a tax on interest income, Treasuries can thus give you a certain tax advantage.

2. *Government savings bonds.* The government now pays a floating interest rate on savings bonds. The rate will increase if interest rates go up and, if held for five years, the bonds will pay a guaranteed minimum return. The interest is exempt from state and local taxes and no federal tax is due until the bonds mature or are cashed in. Series HH bonds can be purchased only in exchange for EE bonds, with interest also deferred until maturity. Savings bonds have excellent liquidity—you can cash

them in at any bank after holding them for six months —and they are extremely safe, but their yields are lower than other investments that are just as safe. Why buy them? One reason is if you can't afford any larger kind of government security. Another reason is to force yourselves to save, by buying them through a payroll deduction plan. *Note*: Like other Treasuries, savings bonds are not taxed at the state or local level.

3. *Corporate bonds.* When you buy a bond, whether it is a government bond or a corporate bond, you are lending your money to that particular government body or corporation for a specified length of time. At the end of that time, that is, the date of maturity, the issuer of the bond pays you back the full amount, or face value, of the bond. Meanwhile, you receive a fixed rate of interest, paid twice a year in most cases. The rate of interest is imprinted on the bond. A 9 percent rate means that a $1,000 bond will pay you $90 a year. This rate does not change once the bond is issued, whether or not bond prices fluctuate.

What is the risk in bonds? The creditworthiness of the corporation that issued the bond can deteriorate. And, as interest rates rise, the value of the bond drops. Bonds that were issued a number of years ago are likely to have lost their value because interest rates might be higher than they were when the bonds were issued. Such bonds are called *discount bonds*.

Here's an example of how they work:

Bond prices move up and down with changes in interest rates because yields on existing bonds must compete with those on new bonds that are being issued. Let's say that interest rates go up after you have purchased a $1,000 bond with a 9 percent rate. If interest rates rise to 10 percent, no one will pay $1,000 for your 9 percent bond. The price of the bond will drop to roughly $900 so that its yield to maturity will be 10 percent. The yield to maturity takes into account the coupon rate of 9 percent and any gain or loss in the price of the bond between the time when you buy it and the maturity date. When purchasing a bond after it has been issued, make sure you ask the broker what the yield to maturity is. Bond prices are also dependent on the length of time between purchase and maturity. The longer the term to maturity, the more volatile the price. The price of a 10 percent coupon bond with a 30-year maturity will generally fall about 8.7 percent if interest rates rise one percentage point. But a 10 percent bond due in three years will drop about 2.5 percent with a similar rise in rates. So, a change in interest rates affects the price of a bond with a longer time to mature than the price of one with shorter maturity.

The opposite of all this is that if interest rates go down, a bond increases in value and can be sold at a premium.

Here's how *current* yield can fluctuate:

	Interest Payment	Current Yield
If you buy at par—$1,000	$80.00	8%
If you buy at discount—$800	$80.00	10%
If you buy at premium—$1,200	$80.00	6⅔%

In a word, bonds adjust—they adjust to interest movements by changing price.

4. *Tax-exempt bonds.* States, communities and their agencies issue bonds that are usually called "municipals." Their yields are not taxed by the federal government. These are usually recommended only for people in high income brackets. In deciding between tax-free and taxable bonds, you have to figure the tax-equivalent yield—i.e., the yield a taxable bond would need to equal that of a tax-exempt issue. The answer depends on your federal and state income tax rates. If you are in the 28 percent tax bracket and live in Connecticut, a tax-exempt yield of 6 percent would be equivalent to a 9.46 percent taxable bond. Bonds with longer maturities will provide extra yield.

Tip: You avoid not only the federal tax but any state or local taxes when you buy a bond issued by the state you live in.

5. *Mortgage-backed securities.* These are pools of mortgage loans. Among the most popular are those backed by the Government National Mortgage Association or "Ginnie Mae." If a borrower on a mortgage in the pool fails to make a monthly payment of principal and interest, the agency will make good in the event the issuer of the security does not. Ginnie Maes pay interest and a small amount of principal each month. The actual yield of a mortgage-backed security depends on how rapidly its underlying loans—i.e., the mortgages held by the lending institutions participating in the pool —are paid off ahead of time. If interest rates drop, for instance, borrowers may either sell their homes or refinance them. As a result, you may receive a return of a large share of your principal, which you will have to invest at lower interest rates.

The yields on GNMAs are usually higher than on long-term Treasuries. GNMA certificates come in $25,000 lots. Many investors, however, find managed funds of mortgage-backed securities in which they can invest in lots of $1,000 or more.

6. *Zero-coupon bonds.* These bonds are sold at a deep discount from face value and pay interest at maturity. These are good for such long-term investment needs as retirement or a child's education. The longer the maturity, the higher the rate of interest.

You can purchase zero-coupon Treasuries, corporate or municipal bonds, but note that zeros pay no current interest. Unless you purchase tax-free or municipal zeros, you must pay income tax on the deferred or "phantom income." The value of a zero will fluctuate with interest rates, but there is no effect on the value of the bond if held to maturity. An advantage: You can purchase varying maturity dates to coincide with such particular needs as tuition payments.

Equity investments: the stock market

A stock market investment means that you become a part owner of a corporation. You buy a share in it. There are two obvious reasons for making such an investment.

- You believe the company will succeed and that the price of its stock will rise as a result, and eventually you can sell your share in it for more than you paid for it.
- You believe that while you own a share in it, the company will be so well run that it will make a profit and that the company will divide that profit among its shareholders, including you.

In the stock market, you will find no guarantees. A company may do well, or it may not. Stock prices change daily and if you are the nervous type who could be easily upset by a slight drop in the market price of a stock you own, you probably should not be in the market. You must also be willing to do your homework: You should never buy a stock that you have not studied thoroughly, so you know what kind of company issued it, who runs the company, what its goals are, what its record is. Such study is, of course, the specialty of the *securities analyst*, who works full-time at this.

Your best approach to the market is through a good stockbroker. Shop for one as you shopped for your banker: Find a person who will take the time and make the effort to understand you and your particular needs. If a stockbroker fails to ask about your entire financial situation—your savings program, your insurance coverage, your respective incomes, your net worth today—he or she is not worth *your* time or your commission payments. If you really know what you're doing, and can choose your own stocks or bonds without assistance, consider using a discount broker, whose commissions for executing a trade are anywhere from 40 to 70 percent less than those of a regular broker.

Stocks are bought and sold, or traded, on exchanges. The largest in the United States is the New York Stock Exchange. That's where the major stocks—shares in the blue-chip corporations—are traded. The American Stock Exchange (AMEX) generally lists stocks of smaller, less well-known companies. In addition there are regional exchanges located in other major cities. Many stocks are "unlisted" or sold "over-the-counter," or are listed by the National Association of Security Dealers (NASDAQ).

> *Tip*: To get an idea of the listings, open the business section of a good daily newspaper and you will find them. *The New York Times* or *The Wall Street Journal* will give you the most comprehensive listings.

To buy or sell stocks, you must go through a stockbroker or any bank. The broker or the bank charges a commission on each transaction—buying or selling. The commission rate will vary, depending on whether it is a full-service or a discount brokerage service.

The risk in the market? That depends. On the economy in general. On the stock you buy. You can lose your shirt. You can make a bundle.

> *Tips* (these are tips on what to do if you're going into investing in the stock market; "tips," or advice based on rumors, in the market are something else, and usually they are worthless):

- If you are looking for income, look for stocks that pay regular dividends.
- If you are looking for growth over a long period, buy stock in companies that show clear signs of growing. Probably they will not be paying out high dividends right now, but instead investing their profits in research and expansion to make the company grow.
- If you are building a portfolio of stocks for the long term, do *not* put all your eggs in one basket. Diversification is a must. Buy stocks of companies in several industries, and make different types of investments.

What about mutual funds?

If you are new to investing and can't decide where to begin, consider a mutual fund. The mutual fund gives you a way to spread out your risk and, in effect, buy diversification in a single purchase. With an investment of $1,000 in some mutual funds, you become part owner of a variety of stocks. The fund is managed by professionals who devote their full time to studying the market and making investment decisions.

If you and your company are putting money into a 401(k) (more about that later, in chapter 12) or profit-sharing plan, chances are the company asks you to select a mutual fund to invest in. Probably it offers several choices, ranging from fixed-income to stock funds. Most people, lacking sophistication on the subject, choose guaranteed-income contracts (GICs), which are nice and safe but will not give you long-term growth.

Some 5,000 mutual funds are alive and well today in America, up from about 500 back in 1979. The secret of their success is the simple fact that a mutual fund puts together the money of many participants and buys a large portfolio that is widely diversified. The risk is thus spread among many—ideal for a small investor.

When you buy mutual funds, you avoid the headache of doing your own research on stocks and bonds. Instead, you let the fund management do the analyses. But of course you have to make the decision on just which fund or funds to buy. You will find plenty to choose from. They vary according to their investment objectives. You can even find a "family of funds"—a group, all run by the same basic company and each with its own management, that aims at a variety of objectives.

The various types of mutual funds are:

- *Income or corporate bond fund.* Designed to return a high level of income, these funds are invested in bonds, preferred stocks, and high-yielding common stocks.
- *Growth fund.* If you are looking for long-range capital gains, keep in mind these funds that are invested in companies that are expected to grow faster than the rate of inflation. Emphasis is on preserving capital, but with an effort to produce dividends.
- *Aggressive growth fund.* The idea here is to go for big profits, usually by investing in small companies and in developing industries. These funds concentrate on more volatile issues and, as you might expect, the greater the push for high profits, the greater the risk.
- *Specialized fund.* In this category, you might find a fund that buys stocks of many companies in a single field, such as high tech. Usually, specialized funds concentrate on only one or two industries.
- *High-yield bond fund.* This type of fund purchases lower-rated bonds of corporations. While producing a rate of return that is usually better than that of higher-rate bonds, it runs greater risks.
- *Balanced fund.* The balance is between stocks and bonds, with the idea of providing both income and capital appreciation.

- *Tax-free or municipal bond fund.* A fund for those in high-income tax brackets who want tax-free income. It invests in municipal bonds. Some concentrate on the bonds issued by a single state, giving residents of that state the advantage of earning income that neither the state nor the federal government may tax.
- *International fund.* These funds invest in companies in foreign lands, mostly Europe and Asia, expecting to gain from economic growth around the world.
- *U.S. government income fund.* This type of fund buys such government securities as U.S. Treasuries, guaranteed mortgage-backed securities (GNMAs) backed by the federal government, and other notes.
- *Money market fund.* These large funds (many are gigantic) buy a wide variety of interest-yielding securities, including short-term certificates of deposit in large denominations, U.S. Treasury bills, and other short-term assets.

A fund receives interest and dividend income and realizes gains and losses on its investments, then distributes its profits to you in proportion to the number of shares in the fund that you own. Funds make distributions at various times—some monthly, others quarterly, semiannually or annually.

Selecting the fund category that suits you best requires balancing your tolerance for risk against the investment's expected return. Once you have decided on a mutual fund, you will be relieved of the need to study specific stocks and make decisions on them. The professional managers of the fund do that.

When you think about a mutual fund, you must have one or more of three basic goals in mind:

- Stability (your principal is protected).
- Growth (your principal increases through capital gains).
- Income (the fund produces consistent income for you).

You must decide among these goals, and pick funds oriented to the objectives you want. No single fund can give you all three.

Cost of mutual fund investing

Mutual funds are either "load" or "no-load." A load fund is bought through a broker, who charges a commission (the load is the commission, or sales charge). If you buy directly from a specific fund, there is no sales charge; it is a no-load.

Exhibit 14
MUTUAL FUND COST BASIS

CONFIRM DATE	TRADE DATE	TRANSACTION		DOLLAR AMOUNT	SHARE PRICE	SHARES THIS TRANSACTION	SHARE BALANCE
10/3	10/3	Purchase		1,000.00	19.97	50,058	50.058
01/06	12/23	INCOME REINVEST	.550	27.53	22.15	1.243	51.301
01/06	12/23	SHORT TERM C G	.430	21.52	22.15	0.972	52.273
01/06	12/23	CAP GAIN REINV	1.670	83.60	22.15	3.774	56.047
03/28	03/14	INCOME REINVEST	.300	16.81	24.16	0.696	56.743
04/15	04/15	PURCHASE		695.00	24.37	28.519	85.262
06/28	06/14	INCOME REINVEST	.300	25.58	25.17	1.016	86.278
09/27	09/13	INCOME REINVEST	.300	25.88	24.98	1.036	87.314
Cost basis 9/27				1,895.92			

A redemption fee may be charged when you sell shares in a mutual fund. Some redemption fees are imposed to discourage frequent trading. The fee may be set at very high levels for short holding periods. For instance, a fund may charge a 5 percent redemption fee on the sale of shares sold within one year of purchase, while shares sold in the second year incur a 4 percent fee, and so on down to 1 percent in the fifth year, then nothing thereafter. Others impose small redemption fees at all times.

Nearly all funds allow the interest and capital gains to be reinvested without a sales charge. However, a few funds impose "reloading" charges on the reinvestment of capital gains distributions. There is a growing trend among funds to have a "hidden" load charge. These funds—known as "12b-1" plans—may charge up to 1.25 percent per year. The money may be used only to advertise and promote the fund to prospective investors. In addition to loads, reloading, and hidden loads, all funds require their shareholders to share the operating expenses, transaction costs, and portfolio fees that a fund incurs each year. These fees usually range from .25 percent to 1 percent per year.

The success of your mutual fund depends, of course, on market conditions, but the idea of the fund is to spread the risk of owning securities. The return you get depends on the type of fund you decide to get into. An income fund will emphasize dividends, while a growth fund will give you smaller dividends but greater capital gains.

Taxing of mutual funds
Income distributions from mutual funds are taxed as ordinary income, whether you receive a check during the year or have the distributions reinvested. Each fund you own will send you a 1099-DIV. For each mutual fund you are in, keep accurate records to determine what you paid for the original shares and all the reinvested shares. This will help you calculate your profits when you sell the shares. You want to avoid double taxation on the reinvested distributions—investors need to add the amount of reinvested distributions to their original purchase price when determining a capital gain or loss. Many investors in mutual funds fail to keep accurate records as they reinvest. Thus they pay taxes twice on their reinvested distributions. For example: suppose you buy $1,000 of shares in a mutual fund and receive $200 of distributions, on which you pay taxes, and then sell the shares for $1,500. The taxable profit is based on the original cost of the shares —$1,000—plus the $200 of taxed distributions. Thus, the taxable gain would be $300 instead of $500.

When you sell shares in a mutual fund, it is a taxable event. If you redeem or sell all your shares, there is no problem about having to sort out how many shares have been sold. Many people will sell only part of their shares without specifying what shares they want sold. It is then assumed that the first in are the first sold (FIFO), or those owned the longest are sold first. You can, however, specify what shares you want sold. Your gain or loss is then based on what those particular shares cost when you bought them. You must keep careful records and advise the fund about exactly which shares you want sold.

Mutual funds give you a number of advantages:

1. *Small minimum investment.* A small amount can get you started, and subsequent purchases can be even smaller.
2. *Diversification.* Each share you buy in a mutual fund gives you an interest in a broad range of stocks, bonds, or any other kind of investment the fund specializes in. Diversification helps soften the blow that can come from wide price fluctuations when you own individual securities.
3. *Liquidity.* When you want to sell, the mutual fund will always buy back its shares—at a time, you hope, when you will realize a gain and not a loss.
4. *Automatic reinvestment.* You can ask most funds to reinvest automatically dividends earned, so your account keeps growing. Capital gains can be reinvested, too.
5. *Automatic withdrawal.* If you want regular cash income as your fund produces dividends, most will set up an automatic withdrawal plan for you. (This can be particularly valuable in your retirement years—far from now.)
6. *Exchange privilege.* Since many funds manage a "family" of different kinds of mutual funds, they can let you switch your investment from one type to another as your needs and objectives change or as you want to take advantage of changes in the market, known as "investment timing." But it is important to remember that when you switch, you are selling shares in one fund and buying shares in another. If there is a gain on the fund, you will have to pay taxes on that gain.

A mutual fund's total net assets (the total of all the stocks and bonds and other investments it has bought) are divided by the number of shares it has outstanding (i.e., all the shares that have been bought by people who have invested in the mutual fund). This gives the value of one share in the fund—called the *net asset value.* The net asset value rises and falls with the market prices of the fund's holdings. It is figured daily. The number of shares you buy when you invest depends on the amount you are investing divided by the net asset value on the day you make your purchase. For example, in a no-load fund, if you invest $1,000 on a day when the net asset value is $21.21, you will own 47.147 shares of that particular fund.

If you are the type of person who has real self-discipline, you might go for dollar-cost averaging—a conservative approach to investing in mutual funds. What you do is invest a fixed sum of money at regular intervals, regardless of market conditions. The idea is that you lower your average cost per share by buying more shares when the prices are low and fewer when the prices are high. Dollar-cost averaging is a long-term strategy. What you must do is ignore all fluctuations in the market and stick to your plan. That's where the self-discipline comes in. Maintain your dollar-cost averaging no matter what happens from day to day—not allowing the market or your emotions to change your strategy.

Investing in mutual funds is one of the easiest and most convenient ways to begin your investment program. Most funds can be opened with $1,000. Some have a lower minimum. Others have a higher one.

> *Important tip*: If you are planning to use dollar-cost averaging, make sure the minimum amount required by the fund after the initial investment is not higher than the amount you had planned to invest.

Before you invest in a mutual fund, look over your needs and objectives carefully—and study up on mutual funds. You will find annual surveys on the performance of mutual funds in many magazines. Compare their performance, noting especially how they do when the market is good and when it is bad.

Study before you buy

Before you make a commitment to buy any mutual fund, look it over carefully. Get the fund's prospectus. Study it. What are the fund's objectives? How has it performed over the years? What fees does it charge for sales or for maintaining your account? What procedures must you follow in buying or selling shares? In particular, look for:

- A *statement of investment objectives* that reveals exactly what kind of fund this is. If it is an aggressive growth fund, look for the words "maximum capital appreciation" as a goal. If it is a balanced fund, look for such words as "income," "capital growth," and "stability."
- A *per share table* that tells you how much each share of the fund has earned annually since its inception, or over 10 years or so. Earnings will include dividends as well as capital gain distributions. The table portrays the fund's performance—erratic or steady—in both an up market and a down market. Some tables include comparisons with the Standard & Poor's 500 or the Dow Jones. Don't count on the table as a guarantee of future performance, however, because changes in the market or changes in its own management can nullify the best promises.

- A *fee table* that lets you know whether you must pay a sales commission—known as a "load"—on purchases, or whether it is a "no-load" fund that does not charge up front when you buy in. Watch out for funds that charge you for "re-loading" when they reinvest a distribution for you. Some fees to look for:
  a. *12b-1 fee.* Some funds make this assessment as high as 1.25 percent per year. These charges are used to defray the cost of marketing and distributing funds.
  b. *Redemption fee.* This may be a small fixed charge, or it may be a percentage of your redemption price. Funds use it to cut down on recurrent buying and selling.
  c. *Contingent deferred sales charge (CDSC).* This is imposed to discourage you from holding shares for very short periods. It may be as high as 5 percent if you sell during your first year, then 4 percent the next year, down to no fee after 5 years. It is a sort of "back-end load."
  d. *Operating and management fee.* This covers the handling of your account. Expect it to average from 0.5 percent to 1.0 percent annually. You will probably find it defined as a percentage of the fund's average assets. Be sure to compare, against other funds you are considering, to see how earnings have been affected by fees not only in the past year but over earlier periods— say, from three to ten years.
- A statement of *investment policies and risks.* Look this over carefully. Imagine yourself dealing with the risks it describes. Check out what kinds of securities, in terms of quality and grade, the fund buys. See what risks its managers take—or avoid —in working to meet their objectives.
- A description of *distributions* that informs you on just when dividends or capital gains are distributed, and what choices you have about how you receive them. The fund should permit you to take both dividends and capital gains any way you want—either one in cash, either one reinvested.
- A policy on *how to buy and redeem shares* that establishes the minimum purchase you must make to open an account as well as the minimum for additional purchases. Check on whether telephone transfers may be made. Note whether you get the advantage of dollar-cost averaging.

Annuities

An annuity is an investment contract. It is purchased from an insurance company. The idea is to provide the annuitant (the person who buys the annuity) with payments at regular intervals over a fixed period of time, starting sometime in the future. The money in an annuity accumulates, compounding tax-deferred until the funds are withdrawn.

There are two types of annuities: fixed and variable. In a fixed annuity, the insurance company invests the funds in fixed-income investments, such as bonds and mortgages, and guarantees the principal and a minimum rate of return. The funds in a variable annuity are invested in stocks, bonds, and mutual funds. Neither the principal nor the minimum payout is guaranteed. Some companies allow you to split your investment between fixed and variable accounts.

When you want to start payouts, you have a number of choices. A straight life annuity will pay periodic benefits for your lifetime—but with no payments to any beneficiary. A periodic annuity will pay benefits for only a specified number of years. If you die before the payout is finished, a beneficiary will continue to receive payments for the time specified. A joint-and-survivor payout will provide you with a specified payout, and upon your death, a reduced amount will go to a beneficiary for the remainder of his or her lifetime. The amount of the payout will depend on the payout option you select.

You can buy annuities with a single premium or through periodic installments. Insurance companies have minimum dollar investments for each. They also impose a penalty on early withdrawals from an annuity. The penalty is usually 6 or 7 percent in the first year; it then decreases by 1 percent per year until there is no penalty.

Annuities are one of the few tax-deferred investments you can find today. Many people have taken a closer look at annuities since Black Monday (October 19, 1987).

High-risk investments

If you do not need current income and if you can take some high risks, consider investments in some of the more esoteric forms: precious metals (gold or silver), coins, diamonds and other precious gems, stamp collections, art objects. If you want to become really sophisticated, get together with your stockbroker and find out about puts and calls, buying and selling on options, commodities, futures contracts, oil and gas exploration, real estate. There are countless ways to make—and lose —money through investments. Just be sure you know your situation and your objectives before you put any money into the more aggressive and speculative investments.

Don't be afraid of the stock market. Take the long view.

Everybody has heard about someone who lost money in the stock market. And many people have heard just enough to scare them—just enough so they don't feel safe about putting their money into stocks or stock funds.

In planning your future financial security, remember that when you buy stocks, you own something. When you buy fixed-income investments—Treasuries, CDs, guaranteed-income contracts (GICs), and money-market accounts—you are lending money. Owning is better than lending.

You have to understand investing. It is for the long term. If you think you will make a killing overnight, or that you will have instant gains, you are likely to be disappointed. What you have to do is know your own objectives and your own time frame, and you must realize that over the long haul equity investments have steadily outperformed fixed-income investments.

Over the long term, the stock market has performed much better than other means of investing. Take the decade of the 1980s, for example. Standard & Poor's 500 index of common stocks revealed an average return of 17.5 percent. In the same period, Treasury bonds produced 12.6 percent, while Treasury bills came in at 8.9 percent. And all that time, inflation was steadily doing its dirty work.

Look at it this way: If you had invested one dollar in a Treasury bill on the last day of 1925, you would have had $12.87 by the last day of 1995.

If you had put one dollar in a long-term government bond at the same time, it would have increased to $34.04.

But if you had put your dollar in large companies at the same time, you would have had $1,113.92 by the end of 1995.

Which would you prefer?

Yet many people feel safe with fixed-income investments, and they forget that inflation is always eating away at the value of their holdings. Furthermore, the longer they hold them, the more inflation consumes.

Yes, you may say, but the stock market can decline suddenly, and it can stay down for a long time. Agreed. That is why you must think long-term when you buy stocks. The longer you hold them, the lower the risk.

Does all that tell you something?

Avoiding investment mistakes

Some basic tips:

1. Make sure you have a solid foundation. Is money put away somewhere for a rainy day? For a specific goal? Do you have enough life insurance? A positive cash flow? Do you already have the dream house?
2. Work out an investment plan. Decide on middle- and long-range investment objectives. Do you want to accumulate a down payment for a house, in a hurry? Are you looking for security over the long term? Are you going into the market on a long-term or short-term basis? Do you want (or expect) to "make a killing"? Are you *willing* to invest for the long term, and do you have the patience to do so?
3. Know where you stand financially. Review your situation regularly. Do a Net Worth Statement and a cash-flow analysis.
4. Understand your risk factor and your risk temperature. Don't invest in anything that keeps you awake at night. Know yourself—and how much risk you are willing to take.
5. Be informed. Read financial publications. Know what you are buying. Ask educated questions (they won't be educated questions unless you keep yourself informed) of a broker or an investment adviser. Take charge. Formulate your own plan—with advice.
6. Be ready to make changes. Remember—you are not married to any stock. If you have a loser, admit you made a mistake and get out. As your needs and objectives change, reevaluate your investments. *Never* get sentimental about a stock.
7. Don't expect miracles. There aren't any. It is easy to talk about gains. You will have losses, too. Remember—there is a trade-off between risk and return—if you want a high return, you have to take high risk.
8. No one type of investment works best all the time.
9. To avoid reversals, you must diversify. Do not put all your eggs in one basket.
10. Think *liquidity* at all times. Know what you will sell to get cash if you have to.

A ROOF OVER YOUR HEAD

○   ○   ○   ○

Owning a home is as American as Mom, apple pie, and the stars and stripes. To own your own home is the culmination of the American dream. It is a symbol of financial security, of having made it. It is also probably the best single investment available to the average American, because the house bought for $20,000 some 25 years ago is now worth (if it has been maintained well) $100,000 or more, depending on location. The only problem is that, for you and many other couples, inflation and high interest rates have made home ownership nearly impossible. Home ownership has declined over the last 10 years for people between the ages of 25 and 29. The decline is due to the high cost of purchasing that first home, which has a median price today of $115,000.

What are the advantages of home ownership? These three are basic:

1. It is your best chance to accumulate tangible capital. It is an investment you can walk around, improve, add to.
2. It is one of the few almost foolproof ways to shield an investment from inflation. (Real estate values are a barometer of economic changes.)
3. It gives you tax advantages. By allowing you to lower your income taxes through itemized deductions of the interest you pay on your mortgage and the taxes you pay on the property, your Uncle Sam provides an indirect subsidy for your house.

Today you must ask yourselves a lot of questions and do a lot of figuring before you can determine how much house you can afford. Start with this checklist, and make notes as you go, for you are sure to come up with more questions than these—questions that pertain to your own particular situation.

1. How large a down payment can you make? Obviously, the more you can put down, the lower your monthly payments will be.
2. How long a mortgage term should you sign for? Mortgages can be set up to span 20, 25, or 30 years; the shorter the period, the less you spend on interest but the higher your payments will be.
3. How large a monthly payment can you comfortably make? Your budget determines this. After you have figured out how much you need for non-housing expenses (including savings and an emergency fund), what is left is what you have to work with for housing. But remember: Insurance, utilities, property taxes, and maintenance are part of your monthly housing costs, too. This question also calls for plenty of thoughtful long-term planning. Look not only at what you are both making now but how much more you can reasonably expect if you get raises regularly . . . at what will happen to your joint income when you have a baby and one spouse leaves the work force either temporarily or permanently

. . . at what the cost of child care, if necessary, will do to your budget.

4. What does the location of the home you are buying do to your expenses? Will you be adding commuting costs? A major increase in the weekly mileage on one—or two—cars? Where are the stores? Services? Recreational facilities? Will you have to drive five miles to get a loaf of bread?

5. Just how much will utilities add to the monthly housing expense? What about heat? Heat was part of the deal in a rented apartment. Now you'll have to pay for it. Better check with the fuel company that has been supplying the house and see how much fuel was used last winter—or the last two or three winters, so you can average it out.

6. How much more will insurance cost? It is bound to be greater than what you have been paying to cover your apartment.

7. How much will the property taxes be? This one can be ticklish. Find out when the last reassessment occurred. If it's been a while, another could come around soon and hit you with an unexpected hike in taxes after you move in. Check with a resident who is knowledgeable about what the local policy is. Or call the town or city hall.

8. What local services do you get? Are they free? Do your local taxes pay for garbage collection, or will you get a monthly bill from the garbage collector?

9. Are there child-care facilities nearby?

10. How are the schools? This could be the most important question on your list. If you are planning to raise a family in this house, take the time and trouble to investigate the schools thoroughly. Stop in at the school superintendent's office, or at any school principal's office, and ask questions. What is the average ratio of pupils to teacher in the classroom? How much does the community spend each year per pupil—and where does it rank among cities and towns in your state? What percentage of the high school graduates move on to higher education? Some basic demographic statistics about the school system can tell you a lot about whether or not you really should be buying this home.

11. What about the closing costs? At the time of the closing you may have to pay some "points." This is a one-time expense. Each point equals 1 percent of your mortgage ($1,000 on a $100,000 mortgage). Most lenders charge two to three points. A mortgage with a higher interest rate might have less points than a mortgage with a lower interest rate. And don't forget about title and mortgage insurance, attorney's fees, title search, prepayment of taxes and insurance, credit report, and appraisal. You should figure closing costs of 2.5 to 3.5 percent of the amount of the mortgage.

12. Do you have sufficient reserves to pay the cost of moving and to buy those incidentals that you may not realize you need until you actually start to live in the house: fuel, insulation, lawn mower, garden hose, gardening tools, rake, snow shovel? How about landscaping? If you are buying a brand-new house, it is likely to come with a minimum of trees and shrubs. And a new house will probably lack screens, storm windows, and storm doors.

A lot to think about? You bet. But the amazing thing is—millions of Americans have survived the entire process.

How much for a down payment?

If you have asked yourselves all these questions and have come up with a firm "yes" on the ultimate one: "Can we afford a house?" you must now produce the down payment.

Let's say you have worked hard to put away $200 every month for five years. Assuming 8 percent interest on your money, compounded quarterly, you should have close to $15,000 salted away. This should give you enough for a down payment of $10,000, with the balance to be used for closing costs, moving, and all the incidentals I've mentioned. You have watched the pot grow—and now you can put it to work! The next question is: What type of housing? House and lot? Condominium? Cooperative apartment? Mobile home? Let's look at each.

House and lot

Any house you look at is going to be either new—or old. If you're looking at a new house, you are pretty much assured that everything will function properly. The builder should stand behind the work. Furnace and appliances will come with guarantees. You may have plenty to do in the area of landscaping and perhaps painting the interior, if it has been left undecorated.

If it is an older house, you will want to be sure it is in acceptable condition. It takes expertise to evaluate an older home; don't hesitate to get it. If you are not an expert yourself, pay a professional to make an inspection. Don't just ask a friend. This will give you a reliable check on plumbing, heating, paint condition, roof, electrical wiring, insulation—a million and one details that could make the difference between frustration and satisfaction for you as buyers. Nothing is worse than having to buy a new roof or a new septic field for a house just after you bought the house itself. If the inspection reveals that something is wrong, you can start to renegotiate the price with the seller, taking into account the cost you face in fixing the problem.

Condominium

The condo is rather new on the American home owning scene. It is usually a structure on the order of an apartment house, in which you are deeded the title to, or ownership of, your unit. It becomes your property. You also own a proportionate interest in the common facilities, such as hallways, grounds, elevators, and recreational areas (tennis courts, swimming pool, even a golf course in some condos). Each month, you pay common charges that cover taxes on the property (the tax portion of your common charge is deductible on your income tax return), maintenance, heat, and utilities. Warning: Common charges have a way of increasing, so make sure your budget is elastic enough to accept increases in them. As owners, you will join a condominium association in which each member has one vote when decisions about the condominium must be made (all members will have agreed to abide by the provisions of a condo agreement).

As a condo owner, you have the same advantages as the owner of a house and lot. Your equity builds up as time goes by (generally, condos have appreciated to match inflation, just like houses). The tax benefits that you can itemize on your income tax return are the same. Your responsibility for repairs and maintenance within your individual unit is also the same as in a house. And, generally speaking, you are entitled to sell your unit to anyone you choose.

> *Tips:* Watch the recreational facilities. Don't be fooled into buying into a condo where the swimming pool and tennis courts are "going to be built soon." And turn your back on any place that has a tiny swimming pool or a single tennis court for a hundred condo units.

Cooperatives

In a co-op apartment, a nonprofit corporation owns your unit. What you own is stock in the corporation. The amount of stock you own depends on the size and value of the apartment you take. There is one common mortgage on the building (unless the corporation has bought the building outright or already paid off the mortgage) and all the owners make monthly payments, varying in size according to the value of the individual units, to the corporation. These payments cover, in effect, taxes, interest payment, and maintenance. As a shareholder, you are entitled to list as deductions on your income tax return your share of the property taxes and the interest on the mortgage. When you want to "sell the apartment," you are really selling your shares in the corporation.

> *Note:* Some co-ops stipulate that any prospective owner must be approved by the other shareholders. The corporation may exercise the option of buying back the shares if the prospective owner isn't approved.

Some questions to ask before you buy into a co-op or purchase a condo:

- What are the rules and regulations? Do you want to agree to abide by them?
- Are those now living there pleased with the living conditions? Is the place noisy? Too hot? Too cold?
- Is it clean and well maintained, indoors and out? Trees and shrubs healthy? Lawn green and manicured?
- Are the recreational facilities adequate? Well maintained?
- How's the parking? Plenty of room?
- What about lighting? Parking areas well lighted? Paths and entryways clear and bright?
- Who pays for utilities? How are the costs apportioned?
- Are you permitted to rent your unit?
- What are the costs of settlement?
- Are there any lawsuits pending against the developer or officers of the association?
- Are most owners living on the premises—or have they rented out their units?

Mobile homes

This is probably the cheapest form of home ownership. It can be your first way—maybe for now your only way—to own low-cost housing.

Here's how it works. Either (1) you rent a small piece of property in an "open" park, then have your manufactured house installed on that property at your own expense, or (2) you buy a home from the management of a "closed" park. This is what many retired people do. In fact, many closed mobile-home parks are designed mainly for retired people.

In some parks, the mobile-home owners may buy their land instead of renting it. This has a certain advantage: If your mobile home is set up on your own land, some banks will offer you a regular real estate mortgage. Otherwise, they want you to finance the purchase of your mobile home like an auto loan, with a low down payment, short repayment period of three to five years at best, and high monthly payments. Recently, the U.S. government has begun insuring mobile-home loans through the Federal Housing Administration (FHA) and the Veterans Administration (VA).

A mobile home may well be a viable start for you. Before buying one, check with a number of lenders about the type of financing they offer. It's worth the effort to find the best possible deal.

Financing

You've analyzed the possibilities. You've got the down payment. You've reviewed your budget and tried to answer the nagging questions about the future. You've decided to do it. Now, how do you finance the purchase of the home you want?

Very few can come up with the full purchase price of a home. So they buy with the help of some kind of mortgage financing. Banks now look at debt-to-income ratios. Mortgage debt, which includes property taxes and homeowners insurance, should not exceed more than 28 percent of total household income. The bank will also look at total debt—mortgage debt plus such other monthly debt obligations as car payments and student loans. This ratio should not exceed 36 percent. These ratios usually apply to buyers who have 10 percent of the purchase price for the down payment. Some lenders will let you have financing with a down payment of as little as 5 percent. This means that if you have very little debt and a spotless credit history, you can buy a house sooner. Usually, because they figure you have a higher risk of defaulting on your mortgage, such lenders will say that your mortgage debt must not go over 25 percent, and your total debt not over 33 percent—rather than the 28 and 36 percent limitations mentioned above.

Just what is a "mortgage?" By definition, it is simply a pledge of property to a creditor as security for a loan. As the borrower, you are the mortgagor. You give the mortgage to the lender, or mortgagee, who takes the mortgage and holds it until you have paid the debt.

A mortgage has three elements: the amount the lender provides, the repayment period, and the rate of interest. Until very recently, once a mortgage loan was closed, none of these elements could be changed. You "got a mortgage" for a certain number of years at a certain rate of interest and that was it—period. But lately lenders, finding interest rates fluctuating, have come up with new types of financing. The result is that today you may choose between the old-fashioned conventional fixed-rate mortgage and a new type, the adjustable-rate mortgage (ARM). Let's look at each.

1. *The conventional fixed-rate mortgage.* With this type you pay a fixed monthly payment, at a fixed rate of interest, for the life of the loan—as long as 25 to 30 years. Many banks still offer the fixed-rate mortgage, but today the cost is likely to be initially higher—maybe 2.5 percent higher —than the cost of an adjustable-rate mortgage. If interest rates do go up over the long haul, you get the advantage and the bank, or lender, finds that it has loaned you money at a lower rate of return, or profit, than it might have gained by some other investment.

2. *The variable- or adjustable-rate mortgage.* With this type the initial cost is lower, because you start off at the lowest interest rate the bank, in order to meet competition from other lenders, dares offer today. But you agree to abide by regular review and escalation or deescalation as interest rates are adjusted up or down by the lender to meet the conditions of the money market. Under strict government guidelines, the rates may change every month. The adjustment, however, is usually scheduled every six months or once a year, with the rate permitted to increase no more than a maximum of two percent a year. The rate changes are tied to a number of interest-based indices published by the federal government, and usually there is a "cap," or ceiling, beyond which the rate may not be raised, as well as a downward floor. In theory, however, there is no limit on how high or how low the rate may go over the life of the loan.

While the ARM interest rate is usually lower at first than that on a fixed-rate mortgage, the risk you take is that it will eventually equal it or even exceed it. If, on the other hand, the adjustable rate holds steady or goes down, you may come out ahead.

Tip: Very often the initial interest rate is a bargain rate. Find out what you would be paying if you weren't getting the come-on bargain rate because if interest rates don't change, that's what you'll be paying.

Under an ARM, the amount you have to pay to the bank could change at every adjustment date. With most ARMs, you sign up for a fixed monthly payment that will stay the same through a given period before an adjustment is made. If you are hit with an upward adjustment that is more than your budget can stand, see if the bank will keep the payments the same and extend the life of the loan. What the bank does is determine, based on the current interest rate, how much of your payment to apply to the principal that you borrowed and how much to pay interest at the current rate. If the interest rate goes down, the bank puts more of your payment toward paying back the principal. If the interest rate rises, on the other hand, the bank applies more and more of your payment to interest charges and less and less to paying off the principal. Conceivably, this could increase your debt: If the interest charge becomes higher than the total payment you are sending in each month, you get into what is called "negative amortization," actually increasing rather than "paying down" your loan. Let's look at an example.

Suppose you obtain an adjustable-rate mortgage for $45,000 for 30 years at 7.5 percent annual interest. Your monthly payment will be $315. In the second year, however, the interest rate rises to 8.5 percent. Now your payment should be $346—but you elect (and the bank allows you) to keep the payment the same. Thus, when each monthly check comes in from you, the bank first takes its payment of interest, at 8.5 percent, then applies anything left over to reducing your principal. As long as the rate of interest stays at 8.5 percent (or goes even higher) you will be falling further and further behind in the amount that is being applied toward your principal. For instance, with a payment of $315 at 7.5 percent, let's assume that $281 of your initial payment is for interest and the balance reduces the principal. If you make the same payment at 8.5 percent, the amount going toward the interest will increase to $315, and thus nothing will go toward paying the principal. If, on the other hand, the interest rate should fall to 6.5 percent, which would call for a monthly payment of $284, and you continue to send in your fixed payment of $315, the bank will apply less of your payment to interest and more to reducing your principal balance—and you will be paying down your loan at a faster rate.

Tip: Some ARMs have no cap on the interest rate they may charge you. They can just go up and up. *Avoid them.*

The moral of all this is to try to find a bank that offers an ARM with infrequent adjustment and with a cap on increases in the interest rate or in monthly payments.

Some variations on the ARM that you should know about:

- *Graduated payment mortgage.* With this type of mortgage the monthly payments are relatively low in the first few years. Then they rise until they are higher than conventional monthly mortgage payments would be. The idea is that payments are scheduled to increase at fixed intervals and by fixed amounts. The problem is that the payments in the early years might not be covering the interest, so you are not building any equity in your home unless property values are increasing generally.

- *Renegotiable-rate mortgage.* With this type the interest rate comes up for renegotiation after a set period, usually one to five years, rather than when market factors, such as a change in the prime rate, force it to change. The new rate is determined, as is the adjustable rate, by the Federal Home Loan Bank Board.

- *Roll-over mortgage.* This is similar to the renegotiable-rate mortgage. The rate is set for from three to five years. Then it is totally renegotiated, or "rolled over." In effect, the roll-over involves a series of short-term loans, with the entire loan coming due at the end of each period and then being replaced by another short-term loan. This goes on for a total of 25 or 30 years, as in conventional mortgages.

- *Balloon mortgage.* For the first few years, this one is similar to the variable, or adjustable-rate, mortgage, and you are paying it off like the conventional loan of 30 years. But at the end of a specified time, usually three to five years, you get hit with a "balloon" payment of the entire balance, which you pay by obtaining a new loan at the interest rates that then prevail. This type of loan is often used in second mortgages. If on the second time around, when the balloon is due, you can borrow at lower interest rates than you were able to get the first time, you have the advantage. This is not a sure thing, however, and, in addition, you could then be in an economic situation that makes borrowing difficult.

- *The assumable mortgage.* Sometimes you can assume the existing mortgage of the person who is selling the house. But you must come up with the difference between the asking price and the balance that is due on the mortgage. Suppose you are buying a $110,000 home on which the owner still owes $50,000 on the mortgage. If the owner's rate of interest is low, this could be an advantage for you, but now you will have to come up with $60,000. You may already have part of that amount as your planned down payment. To provide the missing difference, you could try to

YOUR HOME AS AN INVESTMENT

A home can be a valuable source of tax savings, inflation protection, and capital growth.

In many cases, the cost of buying a home isn't any higher than renting. Fill in the following information to determine the difference between owning and renting.

OWNING (Annual Costs)

Home Expenses:		Income Tax Deductions:	
Real Estate Taxes	$ 1,200	Real Estate Taxes	$ 1,200
Mortgage Interest	$ 9,900	Mortgage Interest	$ 9,900
Mortgage Principal	$ 520	**Subtotal II**	$ 11,100
Homeowner's Insurance	$ 360	**Your Income Tax Bracket:**	
Repairs	$ 500	State	_____%
Utilities	$ 1,500	Federal	28 %
Subtotal I	$ 13,980	**Subtotal III**	28 %

- Multiply your income tax deductions (II) by your personal tax rate (III) to discover your total tax savings (IV).

$$\underset{\text{II}}{\$\ 11,100} \times \underset{\text{III}}{28} = \underset{\text{IV}}{\$\ 3,108}$$

- Subtract your total tax savings (IV) from your total home expenses (I) to find the cost of owning your home after taxes (this figure does not include the value of appreciation of your home).

$$\underset{\text{I}}{\$\ 13,980} - \underset{\text{IV}}{\$\ 3,108} = \underset{\text{V}}{\$\ 10,872}\ \textbf{Total Cost of Owning Your Home}$$

RENTING (Annual Costs)

Rent	$	8,100
Renter's Insurance	$	350
Utilities	$	643
	$	9,093 **Total Cost of Renting**
		VI

- Subtract Total Cost of Renting (VI) From Total Cost of owning (V).

$10,872 − 9,093 = 1,779 per year, or $148 per month.

obtain a second mortgage. Or you might try making a deal with the bank that holds the previous owner's low-interest mortgage. They might be willing to make a "composite" loan—a new loan at a lower rate than is now prevailing, in order for them to "retire" the previous owner's loan, which has recently been giving them no profit margin at all.

Tip: Banks do negotiate. Banks do make deals. Banks do bend their own rules, if they see that you have a secure future. They will bend over backward for a young doctor, or for someone who is going into a successful, closely held family business. When they know you are on a fast track, they anticipate future business—and they will negotiate. They will not, however, bend government

Worksheet XI: Yours
YOUR HOME AS AN INVESTMENT

A home can be a valuable source of tax savings, inflation protection, and capital growth.

In many cases, the cost of buying a home isn't any higher than renting. Fill in the following information to determine the difference between owning and renting.

OWNING (Annual Costs)

Home Expenses:		**Income Tax Deductions:**	
Real Estate Taxes	$_____	Real Estate Taxes	$_____
Mortgage Interest	$_____	Mortgage Interest	$_____
Mortgage Principal	$_____	**Subtotal II**	$_____
Homeowner's Insurance	$_____	**Your Income Tax Bracket:**	
Repairs	$_____	State	_____%
Utilities	$_____	Federal	_____%
Subtotal I	$_____	**Subtotal III**	_____%

• Multiply your income tax deductions (II) by your personal tax rate (III) to discover your total tax savings (IV).

$_____ × _____ = $_____
  II   III   IV

• Subtract your total tax savings (IV) from your total home expenses (I) to find the cost of owning your home after taxes (this figure does not include the value of appreciation of your home).

$_____ – $_____ = $_____ **Total Cost of Owning Your Home**
  I   IV   V

RENTING (Annual Costs)

Rent	$_____	
Renter's Insurance	$_____	
Utilities	$_____	
	$_____	**Total Cost of Renting**
	VI	

• Subtract Total Cost of Renting (VI) From Total Cost of owning (V).

---

rules. Don't expect them to. If you cannot get the loan you want and the amount you need, consider what is known as "creative financing." Many lending institutions will handle second mortgages. Often a seller, especially if he or she is anxious to close the deal, will finance part of the buyer's purchase price (a "take-back" mortgage). Many real estate developers offer special financing on new homes.

○   ○   ○

HOW MUCH OF A MORTGAGE CAN THE YOUNGS TAKE ON?

They have a monthly gross income of $6,479—28 percent is $1,814. This is the most they can spend per month on their mortgage payment, taxes, and insurance. But what would be their total debt-to-income ratio if they added their car to that mortgage figure—$1,814 plus

$275 (car loan, see their budget on page 34). It would be $2,089, which is less than 36 percent of their gross income. Thirty-six percent of their income is $2,332.

○   ○   ○

Remember: Buying your home will probably be the largest and most important investment you will ever make. It's worth taking the time and trouble to check every aspect of your purchase and make the very best deal you can on the house and on the mortgage terms. Remember, too, that even if the price is high and the bank's interest rates are high, your home can be a valuable source of tax savings, capital growth, and protection against inflation. And if it works out right, owning a home often costs no more, or very little more, than renting.

Tax deductions and other savings.

What are some of those tax savings you gain as homeowners? Here are ways you can take deductions from your income tax:

1. *Mortgage interest.* The interest you pay to a lender on a mortgage loan is tax-deductible, whether the mortgage is for a place that is for personal use (a place to live in), business use (a place to operate a business in), or income-producing use (a place you've bought as an investment, to rent to others). The interest you pay is deducted from your adjusted gross income. It may be claimed as an itemized deduction only on Schedule A, Form 1040.

   Your monthly mortgage payments cover interest on the principal amount you owe, plus repayment of some of the principal. In addition, some banks pay your real estate taxes and insurance for you and add that to the total, so you are paying one-twelfth of those costs each month. Most lending institutions provide you with a statement at the end of the year specifying how much you have paid during the year for each item.

   At the time of the closing on your mortgage, you may have to pay some "points." This is a one-time expense. Each point equals one percent of your mortgage ($450, for example, on a $45,000 mortgage). If points are considered to be prepaid interest, they are usually deductible on your income tax return. If they are considered a service fee, they are not deductible, so this is a question to ask when you are shopping for your mortgage. If the points are deductible, insist on paying for them with a separate check, so you have a record, rather than letting the bank automatically take them out of your loan.

2. *Real property taxes.* These are local taxes imposed on all property owners. They are deductible from your federal income tax. The money they bring in is, in most communities, the main revenue that pays for schools and roads and municipal services such as police and fire departments and refuse collection.

   Don't be surprised to find that taxes have a way of increasing as the value of property increases. Your city or town will reassess property every few years and increase taxes based on the new assessments. As mentioned earlier, this could happen soon after you move into your home, so before you buy find out what's going on in the locality where you are buying. Then at least you won't be surprised.

○   ○   ○

HOW THE YOUNGS WILL MAKE THEIR DECISION . . .

Dolly and Jim are doing a lot of paperwork before they start looking at houses. Every weekend they study the real estate section of the local newspaper. They are also keeping a watch on mortgage rates. Home prices have come down in the last couple of years, which is certainly to their advantage. They want to be good and sure they can afford a house, so they have figured out what it will cost them to buy a house for $125,000 and take on a $112,500 mortgage.

They have worked out the finances and here's how some of the figures come out: The average monthly total expenses of living in their apartment come to $758 ($9,093 per year). They figure the new house will cost $1,165 per month ($13,980 a year)—or $407 more per month than they are paying now (assuming a 30-year fixed mortgage of $112,500 at 8.5 percent). On a yearly basis, however, the average will be less, for on their income tax return they will be able to deduct from their gross income the interest they will pay to the bank as well as their real estate taxes. The total federal tax savings will be $3,108. Over the years the difference between owning and renting will narrow because their rent has increased every year.

In a year they will have saved over $13,000, which is enough for the down payment. Both sets of parents have said they will help with closing and moving costs.

○   ○   ○

FINANCIAL FITNESS FOR YOUR CHILDREN: EDUCATION FUNDING

○   ○   ○   ○

"How much will it cost me to educate my child in 15 years?"

"What is the 'kiddie tax'?"

"What type of investments should I consider for my child?"

○   ○   ○

One of the most common financial errors that young parents make is their failure to plan ahead for their children's education. You need to calculate future college expenses. The future costs will depend on the annual cost in today's dollars, inflation, and the ages of your children.

Tuition at a private college will probably cost you more than anything you will ever purchase except a home. College costs have skyrocketed since 1980. Tuition has been increasing by a minimum of 6 percent a year, almost doubling college costs every ten years.

So if you wait until your child is in high school to start a fund for education, it is bound to be too little and too late. Just take a look at what it can cost.

To find the factor by which inflation will increase college costs over the years, figure the number of years until your child starts college and then find the inflation factor. (See Exhibit 15.)

Scary, isn't it? It would be so easy to bury your head in the sand and hope the money for college will come out of thin air. Well, that's not going to happen. "But we'll get financial aid," say some people. But you'll find it hard to get enough. Federal student grants cannot keep up with the increasing costs of higher education. In addition, government funds for college grants and loans have been cut. The elimination of tax advantages for minors has also made it harder and more expensive to save for education.

Now that you have an idea of what it is going to cost to send your child to college, you'll need to figure out how much you have to invest—each year—and the yield on investment needed to meet the goal. To determine the factor by which a 10 percent rate of return, compounded annually, increases your investment, figure the number of years until your child starts college and find the return rate factor. (See

Exhibit 15
INFLATION FACTOR FOR FUTURE COLLEGE COSTS

YEARS TO START OF COLLEGE	FACTOR: RATE OF INFLATION (6%)	YEARS TO START OF COLLEGE	FACTOR: RATE OF INFLATION (6%)
1	1.06	10	1.80
2	1.12	11	1.91
3	1.19	12	2.02
4	1.26	13	2.14
5	1.34	14	2.27
6	1.42	15	2.41
7	1.51	16	2.55
8	1.60	17	2.70
9	1.70	18	2.87

Source: Fidelity Investments

Exhibit 16.) See Worksheet XII on page 97 to fill in your own numbers.

Now, divide the total cost of college by the rate of return factor to determine the amount you will need to invest each year.

The Tax Reform Act of 1986 eliminated certain tax advantages for minor children, creating what has become known as the "kiddie tax." Before tax reform, a child could earn $1,080 from interest or dividends tax-free. Any investment income (interest and dividend income) over that amount was taxed at the child's rate, most likely 15 percent. Now, for children under 14 the first $650 is tax-free and the second $650 is taxed at the child's rate, most likely 15 percent. If the investment income (what the IRS calls "unearned income") is more than $1,300, it is taxed at the parent's rate, regardless of the source of income. At a 9 percent return, more than $5,000 can be held in an account before any of the investment, or unearned, income will be taxed. Investment income for children over 14 is still taxed at the child's rate.

If you have children under 14 you should think in terms of tax-deferred investments or fast growing stocks. If taxation on investment returns can be deferred, it is likely that the funds will grow at higher after-tax rates. U.S. Government Series EE Bonds are an example of a tax-deferred savings vehicle. If you hold the bonds for more than five years, the interest is tax-deferred until you redeem them. The trick here is to make sure that the bonds you purchase will mature after your child reaches age 14.

Another tax-deferred investment is zero coupon bonds. These bonds have been stripped of their interest coupons. The bonds can be corporate bonds, Treasury bonds, or municipal bonds. You receive no income while you hold the bonds. The full amount is paid when the bond matures. The problem is that you must pay taxes yearly on the income earned, even though you don't receive the income directly. So invest in municipal zero coupon bonds because municipal bond interest is not taxable. But, remember to work it out so the bonds will mature when the first tuition bill is due.

Fast-growing stocks or mutual funds are another investment for the child under age 14. Here, you are buying into investments that have great growth potential over the years but currently do not pay much in dividends (see chapter 8). When your child reaches 14, these investments can be sold and the proceeds put in safe high-yielding investments. Another tax-deferred investment to consider: single-premium whole-life insurance policy. In this one, you invest in a whole-life insurance policy, letting the earnings accumulate. While they are accumulating, you pay no federal or state tax on the earnings. When your child turns 14, you can withdraw the accumulated earnings and invest the money in your child's name. Or if you would rather not turn the funds over to your child, pay the tuition bills from the policy's tax-free earnings.

Besides the type of saving or investment, you must think about how you want the accounts set up. Parents or grandparents can set up custodial accounts under the Uniform Gift to Minors Act (UGMA). The custodian is responsible for managing the funds until the child reaches majority—usually at age 18. Remember that if the child is under 14, the account can earn up to $1,300 in interest

Exhibit 16
INVESTMENT RETURN RATE FACTOR FOR FUTURE COLLEGE COSTS

YEARS TO START OF COLLEGE	FACTOR: RATE OF RETURN (10%)	YEARS TO START OF COLLEGE	FACTOR: RATE OF RETURN (10%)
1	1.00	10	15.94
2	2.10	11	18.53
3	3.31	12	21.38
4	4.64	13	24.52
5	6.10	14	27.98
6	7.71	15	31.77
7	9.49	16	35.95
8	11.43	17	40.55
9	13.58	18	45.60

Source: Fidelity Investments

tax-free. This type of account has one major drawback: Once the child reaches age 18, the child can do whatever she or he wants with the money—go to college, buy a flashy sports car, or take a trip around the world.

But you can consider setting up a trust under Section 2503(c) of the 1986 Tax Code. The trustee, usually a parent, has complete control over the income and principal until the child reaches age 21. The trust pays income taxes at its own rate, thereby avoiding the age 14 "kiddie tax" rule. This means that the first $5,000 of income in the trust is taxed at the 15 percent rate. Amounts over $5,000 are taxed at the 28 percent rate.

Some universities are coming up with their own ideas for helping parents foot the education bills. Some arrange for a parent to buy future tuitions in one lump sum at a discounted cost—"pay now, attend later," or "tuition future" plans. The discounted cost is based on when the student will enter and what the college believes it can earn on your money between now and then. The interest is supposed to make up the difference between the current tuition and what will be charged in the future. One problem is that if your child decides not to go to that college, you might be refunded only your original investment, with the college keeping all the earnings. If the school cannot earn sufficient return on the investment to meet future costs, the school will have to come up with the shortfall. Because of spiraling education costs and the changes in interest rates, uncertainty about these plans is growing. And to allow for a quicker response to changes in the financial markets, many contracts are set quarterly rather than annually.

Many banks have savings plans that are designed for college savings. Here's a type of prepayment plan that can be used at any school. The bank sells certificates of deposit based on the average tuition rates at various groups of schools and guarantees that investment income will keep up with rising college costs. Because college costs have been rising faster than inflation, an up-front premium of several thousand dollars is required.

There will probably be several changes in the tax laws between now and the time your children attend college. And new ways to invest are sure to come along for parents who are wise enough to be saving for college costs. Keep an eye on what is happening in the world of saving for education. And when your child reaches high-school age, learn all there is to know about financial aid.

The lowest cost of funding is an immediate lump sum transfer of money to your children. The younger they are, the less you have to put away, as the funds will have a longer period in which to grow. But most young couples do not have money to set aside in one lump sum. The next best thing is to save on a monthly basis. (See Worksheet XII.)

Putting money in an account in your child's name may seem like a good idea when the kids are young. The modest tax break accorded to a child's investment can save you only a few hundred dollars a year. But later on, when college is near, you may be applying for student aid. Most financial aid people require a child to contribute as much as 35 percent of any assets held in the name of the student while parents are expected to use only 5 to 10 percent of their assets for annual college costs.

What will college cost? To estimate how much college will cost, and how much is needed to invest to meet the target, complete the following worksheet.

	YOUR CHILD	JANE SMITH
1. Enter your child's age	_____	6
2. Years to college; time to invest (18 minus child's age)	_____	12
3. Annual college costs* a. Enter your own estimate or b. $7,000, public school c. $16,000, private school	_____	$7,000
4. College Inflation Factors: According to the College Board, college costs are increasing 6% per year. Refer to Exhibit 15 for the inflation factor based on your time horizon.	_____	2.02
5. Future annual cost of college Step 3 × Step 4	_____	$14,140
6. Future total cost of college Step 5 × number of years of college	_____	$56,560

*According to the College Board, these are approximate annual costs of public and private colleges for the 1993–94 school year.

How much should I invest?

	YOUR CHILD	JANE SMITH
7. Assumed rate of return (10%)** Take the number of years your child has until college, refer to Exhibit 16, and enter applicable return rate factor	_____	21.38
8. Annual target amount to invest Divide Step 6 by Step 7	_____	$2,645
9. Monthly amount to invest Divide Step 8 by 12	_____	$220

**Assumed 10% pre-tax rate of return. This is the average rate of return of the S & P 500 for the 20 years ended 6/30/90.
Source: Fidelity Investments

It is time for college and you have not saved

Where are the funds for your child's education going to come from if you did not save?

Financial aid, in the form of scholarships, grants, and loans is available to those who need it. It is more readily available if you know how, when, and where to apply. Find out all you can about financial aid—start with your child's guidance counselor, the school library, and the public library. Don't wait until your child's senior year or you could miss out on financial aid that might be available.

If you do not qualify for need-based grants and loans, you can borrow money from other sources, providing you pass a credit check.

Federal loans

Stafford loans are offered by the Department of Education. First-year students can receive up to $2,625 annually; second-year students $3,500; third- and fourth-year students $5,500. The rate equals the 91-day Treasury bill plus 3.1 percentage points, adjusted annually with an 8.25 percent cap. Repayment begins six months after the student leaves school, with the government covering the interest in the interim. The unsubsidized version of the Stafford loan is available to all families, whether they meet the government's qualifications for aid. The terms are similar except borrowers must begin paying interest immediately.

Plus loans and *Supplemental Loans for Students* (SLS)—This government-sponsored program lends the parents or student the full cost of education, less any other financial aid. The variable rate adjusts each July and is based on the 52-week Treasury bill rate plus 3.1 percent. There is an insurance premium of up to 3 percent of the loan principal. This covers the cost of loan defaults. Repayment of interest begins 60 days after the loan is taken. You can take up to 10 years to repay. Deferral is possible only under special circumstances.

Private-sector college loans

Hundreds of educational organizations offer them. They act as direct lenders or as servicers that collect your payments. These loans cover all or most of college expenses, less any financial aid that your child receives. The rates are generally higher than those on federal loans. Get information from your child's guidance counselor or the public library.

Select/Plus loans are offered by the Student Loan Marketing Association (Sallie Mae) and the program is similar to the Plus loan program except that you can defer repayment of both principal and interest until your child leaves school.

Excel loans are offered by the New England Education Loan Marketing Association (Nellie Mae), a nonprofit organization of colleges, and you can borrow up to the full cost of education, less financial aid. You can choose between a variable interest rate that adjusts monthly (prime rate plus two points) or an annual rate that adjusts once a year (prime rate plus three to four points). There is a 4 percent insurance premium. Principal repayment can be deferred for four years.

These loans are considered personal loans and are intended for families who do not qualify for federal aid. The interest is therefore not tax deductible.

Tapping your 401(k) retirement account

You can use the balance in your company retirement account. Rates are generally low, typically prime plus one percent, and you are essentially paying the interest to yourself. Generally, you can borrow as much as one-half of your vested interest or $50,000, whichever is less. The money must be paid back in five years or immediately if you change jobs or are fired. Interest is not tax-deductible.

Using the equity in your home

You might want to consider borrowing against the equity in your home. A home equity loan is a line of credit secured by a mortgage on your property. You borrow as you need the funds just by writing a check. The interest rate is variable and is usually based on the prime rate plus a margin. The margin and repayment schedule vary from state to state and from bank to bank. Most lending institutions have a maximum annual percentage rate. You make interest-only payments, with the principal payment due some time in the future. This can cause a problem if you have to come up with one payment at maturity. The advantage of the equity loan is that the interest on $100,000 is tax-deductible.

If you plan to use the equity in your home, shop around comparing rates, payback schedules, and fees. They can vary greatly from bank to bank.

○   ○   ○

IF THE MIDS HAD USED AN EQUITY LOAN

The value of the Mids' house is $150,000. If they had wanted to use the equity in their house to finance their child's education, they could have borrowed 75 percent of the value of their house less their first mortgage of $26,145.

Current market value	$150,000
times 75 percent	$112,500
less mortgage	$26,145
equals amount they can borrow	$86,355

They would have been charged an annual percentage rate of 1.5 percent over prime rate but not exceeding 15 percent. With this loan, they would pay interest only, with principal due in full in 20 years.

○   ○   ○

HOW MUCH INSURANCE DO YOU NEED TO BE FINANCIALLY FIT?

o   o   o   o

"How much life insurance coverage do we actually need?"

"The company is buying me Blue Cross—isn't that enough health insurance?"

"Does my homeowner's policy cover my son's stereo equipment at college?"

"How can I cut down on that expensive auto insurance?"

o   o   o

Almost everybody has life insurance of one sort or another, yet few people seem to understand it completely or use it to its best advantage. Insurance companies add to the confusion by bombarding us with words and concepts that simply leave us baffled. The "experts" seem to be either super-salespeople who tell us only what they want us to hear, or dodos who have not managed to succeed in other lines of work.

The prime purpose of life insurance is to protect the income part of the budget. It exists to replace the income that stops if the breadwinner dies. But life insurance can also be used for a secondary purpose: to accumulate savings.

The key word in thinking about life insurance is *now*. Now is not ten years ago, and it is not ten years from today. Yet countless people carry life insurance that was right for them ten years ago, or will be right for them ten years from now, but is dead wrong for them now. The fact is that your life insurance needs to be changed as your life changes, and at any given moment you may be overinsured or underinsured. It is important to recognize this and cope with it.

Fortunately, this does not mean that you have to revise your life insurance coverage every year. But if you go more than five years without a thorough review of your needs and coverage, you may be either wasting money on insurance or not buying enough.

The basic types of life insurance

It seems as if each and every insurance company has its own variations on the different types of policies, so it is impossible to describe them all. But here are the basic types:

1. *Term insurance.* This is just what its name implies: You buy life insurance for a specific term, or period of time—usually one to five years. The cost is low; in fact, term is the cheapest form of insurance you can buy. It provides nothing but protection. In other words, it pays off only if you die. At the end of the term, you have nothing—but you have had the protection during the term.

If you renew for another term, the cost is higher because you are now older and the likelihood of death is greater as you get older. Usually by the age of 45 or 50, you will find the premium cost for term insurance rising rapidly, much faster than in earlier years. Still, by this age you should either not be buying term or buying less of it.

Term insurance is ideal for a young couple. It provides greater amounts of protection for less money than whole or straight life insurance.

> *Important*: If you are buying term, be sure you get a policy that can be renewed without your having to pass another physical examination. Also be sure it contains a clause that permits you to convert it into a whole policy without a physical exam and has a guaranteed rate. Renewability and convertibility will become important if your health changes. If you become uninsurable or become a high risk, the rate will be prohibitive.

2. *Whole or straight life insurance.* This gives you more than just protection. It includes savings. The amount of the premium is determined by your age and state of health at the time when you buy the policy; it does not increase as long as the policy is in force. Therefore, the younger you are when you buy a whole or straight policy, the less it costs you.

During the first few years, the insurance company credits only a small amount to savings. Then, as time goes on, the savings build up. This amount remains yours even if you cancel the policy. Or you can borrow from the insurance company the amount that is in savings, paying interest on it at a rate you will find stated in your policy. If you "borrow against the policy," you continue to pay the premium, thus keeping the policy in force. However, if you die, the insurance company reduces the amount it pays your beneficiary by the amount you borrowed. For example, if you have a $25,000 policy but have borrowed $8,000 on it, the company will pay only $17,000.

This "policy loan" provision is a valuable right. It enables you to draw upon the "cash value" that has built up in your policy in order to meet financial needs.

3. *Universal life.* This is a variation of a whole life insurance policy with a tax-deferred investment program. You may vary your annual death benefit and annual premium. Some years you might put more money toward the policy, thus building up cash values faster. Other years, you might put in less.

4. *Variable life insurance.* A portion of the premium pays for insurance protections and the other portion is invested according to your wishes. Thus, the money could be invested in stocks, bonds, mutual funds, or zero coupon bonds. The insurance company manages the funds that your investments are in, so you must choose from the investments that the company offers. You may switch from one type of investment to another. This type of policy is for those who know about investments and feel comfortable with them.

5. *Single premium life.* The premium is made in a single lump sum, usually with a $5,000 minimum. The cash value buildup is tax-deferred. The policyholder can borrow from the policy at any time. However, many companies impose a back-end load, that is, a charge if you make withdrawals during a certain time.

Which to buy—term or whole life?

Many people today question which is better. They wonder if the savings aspect of whole life is worth it. Since it takes a number of years to build up a sizable cash value, the savings are eroded by inflation. So you must ask yourself whether there are other ways to build up savings more quickly and with a greater return, that is, interest or dividends paid on the amount saved. A key point to remember about whole life insurance is that the policy with the lowest premium might not be the best choice. Premiums are just one factor in building cash value. The other factors are investment results, interest-rate guarantees, fees and charges for mortality risk, commissions, and favorable borrowing rules.

If you expect to keep a term policy for some years, then look at the total premiums for that period of time. Don't just look at the first year's cost, since term prices rise as you get older. Compare the cost per $1,000 of death benefits. Premiums will depend on age, sex, or health status and amount of coverage.

Ask yourself: How much coverage do I really need now? How much can I afford? Am I being sold on a whole or straight life insurance policy when I need greater protection and could buy it for the same amount of money by taking a term policy? In other words, you must understand what your individual needs are at each point in your life.

○   ○   ○

THE YOUNGS NEED PROTECTION. . . .

Jim and Dolly Young have discussed the fact that, since they have one child and expect to carry a large mortgage within the next year, protection is their first need. They hope to have more children, too. Each of their incomes is a much-needed, integral part of their total finances. If Dolly were to die, Jim would need to replace not only her lost income; he would probably also need to hire a live-in housekeeper, especially if he continued to travel for his company.

○   ○   ○

THE MIDS HAVE USED CASH VALUES. . . .

The Mids used some of the cash value to help pay college expenses. Now, with no child in college, their financial responsibilities have decreased but their need for life insurance has not. They know that inflation affects long-term purchasing power.

○   ○   ○

THE ELDERS NEED LITTLE INSURANCE. . . .

But it is hard to convince their generation. Many people of this age continue to pay premiums on policies they no longer really need. (See chapter 12 on retirement for a discussion of their options.)

○   ○   ○

How to decide how much you need

The important thing when buying life insurance is to determine how much you need, and buy no more than that. How do you determine the amount? Worksheets are the only way. You must also refer back to the worksheets on Budget, Asset Evaluation, and Social Security and Pension Benefits.

With insurance on your mind, look at your budget sheets. What income will be available for the family if you die?

- Spouse's income, if he or she works or can return to work.
- Social Security payments, if the spouse is eligible for them.
- Income from dividends and interest from investments (see your Asset Evaluation Worksheet).
- Benefits from a pension plan.
- Proceeds from insurance already in force or included in coverage at your place of employment.

Your insurance proceeds, invested at a reasonable rate of interest, should generate the income your beneficiaries need to fill the gap between their other financial resources and their financial need.

Now look at the expense side of your budget. Which expenses will decrease for the rest of the family if you die? Probably food, clothing, transportation, and life

insurance premiums. Usually a family needs at least 75 percent of previous take-home pay in order to cover expenses and maintain its lifestyle. Imagine how tough it would be to plan insurance needs accurately if you did not have a good picture of what it costs you to live! Also an adjustment has to be made to account for inflation's effect on purchasing power.

In addition to replacing income, it is a good idea to figure out the cash requirements that insurance should cover in the event of the death of the breadwinner. Some you have already listed in the liabilities column on your Net Worth Statement. Be sure to include:

- Mortgage, installment loans, current bills, and other debts.
- Education expenses. If your children are near college age, you will have to calculate more closely than if they are younger. If the children are younger, it would be hoped that if an insurance policy had to pay off, the amount earmarked for college could be invested at a rate of return that would keep up with the ever-increasing costs of college.
- Final expenses. These include administration of the estate, probate costs, attorney and accountant's fees, appraisal fees, taxes, final unreimbursed medical expenses, and funeral expenses. Rule of thumb: Allow 2 to 5 percent of the total estate, plus up to $5,000 funeral expenses, to cover these.

With so many variables, you can see how the amount of insurance you need can change as life changes. So reevaluate your needs at least every five years to account also for changes in inflation and taxes. And remember: Financial Fitness doesn't mean being overinsured. Careful planning can give you the amount of coverage you need—not the amount an agent wants to sell you. Your Net Worth Statement, Budget, and Asset Evaluation worksheets have helped you to learn which assets will produce income, which liabilities should be paid off with insurance, and what it will cost you to maintain your lifestyle.

How to handle the proceeds?

When an insured person dies, the insurance company may pay out the policy in any of several ways, known as *settlement options*. The choice may be specified in the insurance policy. However, this is an unfair method because it is impossible to know in advance, when the policy is created, what will best serve the family's needs later on. The intervening years can change too many things. So a decision on the choice of settlement options should not be made when the policy is bought.

By the same token, the decision does not have to be made immediately after the death of the insured person. The insurance company can hold the proceeds of the policy until the beneficiary makes the decision. If you are making the decision, do not be rushed into it. And do not let anyone else make it for you. Here are the options:

1. *Lump sum.* This means you get a check immediately for the full amount of the policy (less any amount that may have been borrowed out). If you have alternate investments, and if you are knowledgeable about investing (or have good advice and are willing to learn), this is a good option. When interest rates are high, the lump sum settlement offers many advantages, for you should be able to get a better return on investment than the insurance company provides.

2. *Interest only.* This means the insurance company holds the principal amount but pays you the interest it is earning. This is a good holding position while you decide what to do with the proceeds.

3. *Fixed installments.* At stated intervals, you receive a check for a fixed amount until the money is all used up. The company also pays interest on the remaining balance it is holding.

4. *Fixed period.* The company agrees to pay you the proceeds, plus accrued interest, over a certain period of time. The size of each check depends on the amount of time that the proceeds are spread over.

Important tips:

- If you choose the fixed installment or fixed period option, be sure you have the right to change your mind and withdraw the entire sum at any later date.
- If you choose an annuity, check out what is available from your insurance company versus other annuity contracts. Get the highest monthly income possible for each $1,000 you invest.
- Paying off the mortgage may *not* be the best thing to do, even if you have enough proceeds from the insurance policy to do so. The money you will use to pay it off might be invested at higher rates of interest. If the mortgage has been established for a long time, monthly payments are probably small, with little left to pay, and the rate of interest is probably low. So take a good close look at the mortgage situation and use the money the best way.

What about life insurance for women?

Traditionally, life insurance has been sold to cover the male breadwinner. But with changing roles come changing attitudes. Many women should be covered.

KEY POINTS ABOUT LIFE INSURANCE

In summary, remember these key points about life insurance:

1. Buy whole life, or cash value, insurance if you want the premium to stay the same and if you want to build up savings.
2. Buy term insurance if you want maximum protection. Be sure the policy is renewable and convertible.
3. Shop around. Costs and policy terms vary.
4. If possible, take advantage of group insurance. It costs less than an individual policy. Check at your place of work.
5. Remember that your life insurance program is not carved in granite. Review your needs regularly—at least once every five years—recalculating your income and expenses and deciding whether you need more or less coverage. Always match your coverage to your needs.
6. Do your homework. Know what you want before you start pricing individual policies.
7. Be aware of the long-term effect of inflation. Insurance you buy based on today's dollar will be worth less and less tomorrow in purchasing power.

The single woman with no dependents has little need for life insurance. Probably she gets basic coverage as a fringe benefit with her job. This would cover final expenses if she died. More important is disability coverage, to maintain her lifestyle if she cannot work.

The wife and mother who has a job probably needs some life insurance, especially in a family that is dependent on two incomes to maintain its lifestyle. If her children are still young, insurance should be provided to replace her income and cover the added burden of child care. Again, a group policy where she works probably would cover immediate cash requirements, but would not replace income.

The single mother who works and is the sole support of her children must have life insurance. Whether widowed or divorced, if she maintains a career and a household she needs coverage until the children are no longer dependent on her.

Few people ever think of a homemaker as providing services to her family that would otherwise cost dollars and cents. Yet that is what she does: cooking, cleaning and child care must all be maintained to keep the family going, and these services will have to be paid for if she is not there. In addition, the expenses of a major illness and of a funeral should be considered—but seldom are.

To anticipate the insurance needed, both immediate and future needs should be considered. Immediate needs include the funeral and settling of the estate. Future needs include housekeeping and child care for a number of years. This will take some calculation. Figure the monthly cost in dollars, multiply by 12 months and then by the number of years before the children will be on their own.

Business partners need insurance

Many a widow finds herself left with a small business. Family and business life may have been intertwined, and probably the business is the largest asset that she and her husband possessed, or that the remaining partner or partners possess.

Life insurance is the key to protecting the business asset, insuring its stability and continuation if a partner or major shareholder dies. It can provide the funds for the surviving members of the business to purchase the share owned by the partner who died, thus saving his widow the possible nightmare of trying to take up where her husband left off, and saving the partners from the possible embarrassment of not having enough money to buy her out.

The amount of insurance coverage should be equal to the partner's or shareholder's interest in the business, and should be formalized in a buy-sell agreement among the partners.

In the case of a business owned by a single individual, life insurance can provide a widow with money to live on while the business is liquidated, again saving her the complications of taking over a business she may not understand, or want to be in, but which provides her livelihood.

o   o   o

WHAT IF MARTY MID DIED NOW. . . .

How would Mary Mid be left? She would get no monthly Social Security payments yet, for she is not old enough and has no dependent children still under her care. At age 60, a widow is entitled to receive reduced benefits if she prefers. But Mary would continue to work until she reached age 65, and then begin to collect her benefits. She estimates she would incur no more than 80 percent of the couple's present living expenses.

If Mary took Marty's $125,000 life insurance benefits in a lump sum, rolling it over into savings and investments, she could use the interest income to help with living expenses.

Under his pension plan, she would get 50 percent of his accrued benefit, since he has been with the company for more than 20 years. (The company plan pays no death benefits to those under 55 who have less than 20 years of service; the widows of those over 55 receive 50 percent of the accrued benefits.)

Here is a formula to work out exactly what share of his pension Mary can expect after Marty's 24 years with the company:

$5,468 (Marty's average monthly earnings) x 1.5% [the company formula] x 26 (Marty's years with the company) = $2,132. $2,132 x 75 percent [the share Marty is entitled to at age 55] = $1,599. $1,599 divided by 2 (Mary is entitled to one-half) = $800.

So Mary would get $800 monthly from Marty's pension plan if she became a widow now.

Based on these figures, the Mids need no additional life insurance. The income available to Mary would be greater than her needs.

o   o   o

Disability insurance

What happens if you are disabled by an accident or an illness? The odds of being disabled for an extended period before you reach 65 are greater than the odds of dying before then.* If you are disabled, chances are high that your income will drop and your medical bills will climb simultaneously. Not only would that be no fun, it would be disastrous. So whether you are male or female, if you are the breadwinner you must have disability insurance that ensures a monthly income. Use Worksheet XIV to calculate what eligibility insurance you need.

Social Security provides disability insurance for those who become severely disabled before they reach 65, but it is limited.** It covers those who have a physical or mental condition so severe it prevents them from working and which is expected to last, or has lasted, for at least 12 months, or which is expected to result in death. You have to wait five months after your disability begins before Social Security starts to pay. The amount it pays is the same as the amount you would start to get upon your retirement at age 65. To be eligible, you must be fully insured under the Social Security regulations.

---

* Only a small percentage of American workers are covered by disability insurance.

** It is important to know that seven out of ten disability claims under Social Security are rejected.

Worksheet XIII: Example One—Mr. Mid
HOW MUCH LIFE INSURANCE?

A. ANNUAL FAMILY LIVING COSTS *(80%)* $ 48,000

B. SOURCES OF INCOME AVAILABLE

- Spouse's Income $ 34,500
- Social Security Benefits 0
- Income from Income-Producing Assets (from Budget form) $ 1,550
- Income from Proceeds of Existing Life Insurance Policies (use an assumed rate of interest)
  6%—multiply amount of insurance by .06
  8%—multiply amount of insurance by .08
  10%—multiply amount of insurance by .10
  ~~$125,000~~ × .08 = $7,500
- Other Sources of Income $ 9,600 *(pension)*

  TOTAL SOURCES OF INCOME $ 53,150

C. ADDITIONAL ANNUAL INCOME NEEDED (Subtract B from A) *($ 5,150)*

D. NUMBER OF YEARS NEEDED 12

E. AMOUNT OF MONEY TO MAKE UP SHORTAGE

- Multiply Additional Income Needed (line C) times the number of years needed

  _____ × _____   _____

- Inflation Adjustment above total times inflation times number of years

  _____ × _____ × _____   _____

F. ADDITIONAL CASH REQUIREMENTS

  Final Expenses $ 7,500
  Education for Children _____
  Liabilities (including Mortgage) $ 37,005 $ 44,505

G. INSURANCE NEEDS (E PLUS F) 0

Disability insurance as a fringe benefit

Many employers provide some sort of disability insurance, using either of these two types of plan:

1. *Short-term.* This provides modest benefits for a short period. It usually pays weekly, based on your earnings, but with a maximum that is as low as $150 a week. The waiting period before it starts to pay is from seven to 21 days. Some plans pay out for as few as 13 weeks, while others may continue to pay up to 52 weeks.

2. *Long-term.* This is designed to take care of more serious disabilities. Most plans provide a certain percentage of earnings, usually 50 or 60 percent of your base salary, with the maximum monthly payment varying from $1,500 to $2,000 or above. The waiting period

Worksheet XIV: Example One—Mr. Mid
HOW MUCH DISABILITY INSURANCE?

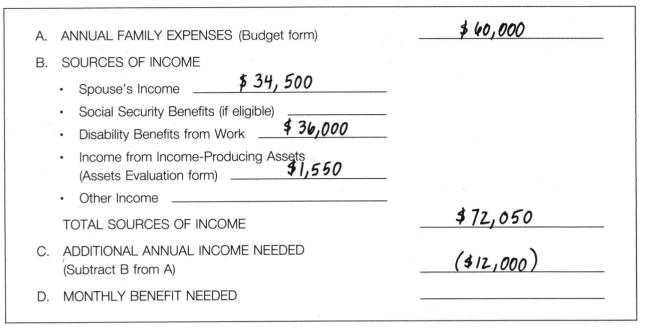

A. ANNUAL FAMILY EXPENSES (Budget form) _____ $ 60,000 _____

B. SOURCES OF INCOME

- Spouse's Income _____ $ 34,500 _____

- Social Security Benefits (if eligible) _____

- Disability Benefits from Work _____ $ 36,000 _____

- Income from Income-Producing Assets
  (Assets Evaluation form) _____ $1,550 _____

- Other Income _____

TOTAL SOURCES OF INCOME _____ $ 72,050 _____

C. ADDITIONAL ANNUAL INCOME NEEDED _____ ($12,000) _____
    (Subtract B from A)

D. MONTHLY BENEFIT NEEDED _____

---

may be anywhere from three to six months. The payments may continue any number of years (five, ten or twenty) or until you reach 65. If all this sounds like a wide variety of benefits and conditions, it's because there are almost as many different disability policies as there are employers, so you have to check out what your company is offering and hope it is one of the better long-range plans.

In case you are wondering why everything seems to stop at age 65, it's because that is when Social Security and Medicare take over. Since these two government programs are so universal, and since most people have traditionally retired at 65, the insurance companies just don't bother to work out actuarial tables or develop premium rates for employee group insurance after 65. However, any number of insurance companies do offer individual policies. Many advertise that they pay a certain flat amount daily, "from the first day of hospitalization," unrelated to any medical bills or hospital costs. Such policies are carried by many people who are over 65. They are, in effect, simple disability policies.

○   ○   ○

MARTY MID'S DISABILITY PLAN . . .

It covers 60 percent of his salary, up to a maximum of $3,000 a month. If he has to call upon it, it starts payments after a six-month waiting period and pays until age 65. Since his base salary is $65,600 or $5,467 per month, he could receive up to $3,280 per month (60 percent of his

$5,467). This comes in above the $3,000 maximum his group policy is willing to pay. (See above.) Social Security benefits were not added in because most claims are denied.

○   ○   ○

Coordination of benefits

There is one more wrinkle. In many disability policies you will find a "coordination of benefits" provision. This prescribes how other disability income benefits payable to the disabled person will affect the benefits of the group plan. If Worker's Compensation, Social Security, or any other policies are paying, the group policy may not pay as much as it otherwise would on a long-term plan.

Your group disability policy terminates, of course, if you leave your job for any reason, and when you reach 65.

Importance of individual policy

Since Social Security and group plans do not usually pay as much as you really need if you are disabled, individual policies are important. Your disability policy premium will be based on your age, condition of health, and income. Since policies can vary widely, be sure you know what you are buying.

Features that affect your coverage include:

- Maximum benefit period. The length of time during which the company will pay. Usually expressed

---

in weeks, months, or years. Some policies run for a lifetime.

Perils insured against: either accident only or accident and illness. Be sure you get coverage for both. Some companies loudly advertise their bargain rates but cover only accidents, something you don't realize until you read the policy carefully.

- Elimination period. This is the time that must elapse before the company starts to pay. It is usually 30, 60, 90, or 120 days after your disability begins.
- Definition of disability. The conditions under which you will be considered disabled for the purpose of collecting benefits.

In buying any disability policy, make sure:

1. The insurance company cannot cancel, raise the premium, or alter benefits during the life of the policy.
2. The policy is guaranteed renewable.
3. The period covered makes sense. It may be as short as one year, or continue until you reach age 65, or cover your lifetime. The longer the coverage, the higher the premium.
4. You know when benefits start. The longer the elimination period before payments start, the lower the premium.
5. A future income option should be added to the policy. This will allow you to purchase additional coverage as your income increases, without any evidence of medical insurability.

How to know how much disability insurance you can afford—and need

Again, go back to your worksheets, especially Budget and Asset Evaluation. Review what it costs you to live and what sources of income you would have if you were disabled. Look over your current expenses, and take into account the fact that expenses will more than likely rise if you are disabled. If you run into special medical provisions and care, they will go up like a rocket. Also consider the effect of inflation on your purchasing power.

o   o   o

WHAT IF JIM OR DOLLY YOUNG DIED, OR WERE DISABLED? . . .

The Youngs' living expenses are close to $47,000. If one of them were to become disabled or die, where would

the other find the money he or she needs? Would each need the same amount?

If either were disabled, expenses would probably increase, due to medical costs. If either died, expenses would decrease only slightly. Some expenses would certainly be eliminated. But the Youngs have a child who would have continuing needs—food, clothing, child care, and education. Jim and Dolly have listened as their friends complain—happily—that the expenses of raising kids go up every year. So far, the Youngs figure, if either had to go on without the other, he or she would incur about 85 percent of present expenses.

Since the earnings of each of the Youngs exceed the "test" applied by Social Security, benefits would be available only for their child. So it is important for them to consider not only replacing lost income but having money for final expenses, for educating their child, and to clear up the debt they now carry. Each now plans to buy an insurance policy and to make the policies large enough to cover the mortgage that they expect to be carrying in less than a year. This means buying two term policies for at least $200,000 each.

Finally, Jim and Dolly know that as their salaries and financial responsibilities increase, and especially when they have another child, they should review their insurance coverage carefully and increase it.

o   o   o

Health insurance

In recent years, medical costs have skyrocketed. Few people really know how much medical coverage they have or are entitled to, or how to file claims. They are staggered by the bills that come with a major illness.

It is essential to understand the various types of coverage, especially if you are covered by a group plan at your place of work. You should then pick out what is best for you and your family. Cost may be a major consideration, but you should get the best available for the amount you can afford to pay.

The purpose of health insurance is to protect you from high medical costs, including hospital bills, physicians' fees, and drugs. The types of coverage include:

1. *Basic hospitalization.* This is provided by private insurance companies and the various Blue Cross policies nationwide. The policy usually pays all or part of a person's hospital bills, including semiprivate room, food, X rays, laboratory tests, operating room fees, and drugs. Usually the coverage is limited to a specific number of days during any one period, with a waiting period between confinements. The better the coverage, the greater the cost.

2. *Basic surgical and medical expense.* Again, private companies provide these policies, while the nationwide

Worksheet XIII: Example Two—Mr. Young
HOW MUCH LIFE INSURANCE?

A. ANNUAL FAMILY LIVING COSTS *(85%)* $ 39,950

B. SOURCES OF INCOME AVAILABLE

- Spouse's Income $ 32,000

- Social Security Benefits $ 7,200

- Income from Income-Producing
  Assets (from Budget form) 0

- Income from Proceeds of Existing Life Insurance Policies (use an assumed rate of interest)
      6%—multiply amount of insurance by .06
      8%—multiply amount of insurance by .08
      10%—multiply amount of insurance by .10
      $40,000 × .08 = $3,200

- Other Sources of Income 0

  TOTAL SOURCES OF INCOME $ 39,200

C. ADDITIONAL ANNUAL INCOME NEEDED
    (Subtract B from A) $ 750

D. NUMBER OF YEARS NEEDED   20

E. AMOUNT OF MONEY TO MAKE UP SHORTAGE

- Multiply Additional Income Needed (line C) times the
  number of years needed
      750 × 20 $ 15,000

- Inflation Adjustment above total times inflation times
  number of years
      $15,000 × 4% × 20 $ 12,000

F. ADDITIONAL CASH REQUIREMENTS

    Final Expenses $ 7,500

    Education for Children $ 40,000

    Liabilities (including Mortgage) $ 116,600 $ 164,100

G. INSURANCE NEEDS (E PLUS F) $ 191,100

Blue Shield (usually associated with Blue Cross) is best known. Fees for doctors, whether surgeons or other physicians, are paid separately from hospital fees. Usually the insurance company sets a "schedule" of certain fees which it is willing to pay for certain operations. If your surgeon charges more than that fee, you must pay the difference. Obviously, again, the better the insurance coverage, the higher the cost.

Note: Often, basic hospitalization is combined with basic medical-surgical coverage, as in the Blue Cross/Blue Shield plans. Everyone should have at least this basic coverage.

Worksheet XIV: Example Two—Mr. Young
HOW MUCH DISABILITY INSURANCE?

		with Social Security	without Social Security
A.	ANNUAL FAMILY EXPENSES (Budget form)	$47,000	$47,000
B.	SOURCES OF INCOME		
	• Spouse's Income	$33,000	$32,000
	• Social Security Benefits (if eligible)	$7,200	0
	• Disability Benefits from Work	0	
	• Income from Income-Producing Assets (Assets Evaluation form)	0	
	• Other Income	0	
	TOTAL SOURCES OF INCOME	$39,200	$32,000
C.	ADDITIONAL ANNUAL INCOME NEEDED (Subtract B from A)	$7,800	$15,000
D.	MONTHLY BENEFIT NEEDED	$650	$1,250

3. *Major medical.* This type of policy starts where basic hospitalization and basic medical/surgical insurance leave off. It covers the big expenses that are above the maximums of those policies. Usually a major medical policy covers extensive hospitalization, surgery, other doctors' fees, private-duty nursing, home medical care, diagnostic work, therapies, medical devices, and rehabilitation. Major medical policies contain a deductible feature, so the patient pays a certain amount—usually from $100 to $1,000—before the insurance company pays anything. (Often, the deductible is annual: With each new year, you pay the first $100 or so of claims yourself before the insurance company pays anything.) Once you have gone beyond the deductible amount, most major medical polices pay 80 to 85 percent of each claim you file. You must pay the balance yourself. At a still higher level, however, the insurance company takes over and pays 100 percent of all legitimate claims (this is called a "stop-loss limit"). Some policies put no limit on the maximum amount of claims they will pay. Others are limited to $250,000 or $500,000. Most policies have a lifetime maximum.

Example: Suppose you have a major medical plan with an annual deductible of $100 and a stop-loss limit of $2,000. If you have a $1,800 claim, you will have to pay $440 out of your own pocket:

Total claim	$1,800
Less deductible	- 100
	$1,700

Insurance co. pays	
80 percent	- 1,360
You pay 20 percent	$340
Plus deductible	+ 100
Total you pay	$440

Coinsurance is the amount of the bill you pay above the deductible, with the insurance company picking up the rest, up to the policy limits.

Once your out-of-pocket expenses (i.e., the deductible and coinsurance amounts) reach $2,000, the insurance company will pay 100 percent. Thus, if your benefit period is one year, you will be responsible for $2,000 each year.

How can you cut down on the cost of a major medical policy?

1. Increase the deductible.
2. Ask for a higher stop-loss limit.

Either step will mean that you increase the risk that you are willing to take. You have to decide how much risk you can shoulder. Many people would rather pay a higher premium and not have to worry that out-of-pocket expenses will send them to the bank to borrow money if a major illness occurs.

4. *Medicare.* This covers everyone age 65 or older who pays Social Security taxes or is eligible for Social Security or Railroad Retirement benefits. It is also available to those under 65 who are disabled or who have chronic kidney disease.

Worksheet XIII: Yours
HOW MUCH LIFE INSURANCE?

A. ANNUAL FAMILY LIVING COSTS   _____

B. SOURCES OF INCOME AVAILABLE

  • Spouse's Income   _____

  • Social Security Benefits   _____

  • Income from Income-Producing
    Assets (from Budget form)   _____

  • Income from Proceeds of Existing Life Insurance Pol-
    icies (use an assumed rate of interest)
      6%—multiply amount of insurance by .06
      8%—multiply amount of insurance by .08
      10%—multiply amount of insurance by .10
      _____ × .08 = _____

  • Other Sources of Income   _____

    TOTAL SOURCES OF INCOME   _____

C. ADDITIONAL ANNUAL INCOME NEEDED
   (Subtract B from A)   _____

D. NUMBER OF YEARS NEEDED   _____

E. AMOUNT OF MONEY TO MAKE UP SHORTAGE

  • Multiply Additional Income Needed (line C) times the
    number of years needed
    _____ × _____   _____

  • Inflation Adjustment above total times inflation times
    number of years
    _____ × _____ × _____   _____

F. ADDITIONAL CASH REQUIREMENTS

  Final Expenses   _____

  Education for Children   _____

  Liabilities (including Mortgage)   _____   _____

G. INSURANCE NEEDS (E PLUS F)   _____

Medicare is divided into two parts. Part A is free of charge. It pays for hospital stays, and care in a skilled nursing home as part of after-hospital care. Part B covers physicians' fees and out-patient services at a hospital, as well as certain medical services and supplies. It costs a small monthly fee, and pays for 80 percent of "reasonable" medical costs (which often means that it pays considerably less than the actual cost). Part B does not pay for eyeglasses, dentistry, drugs, private nursing, custodial nursing home care, treatment in a foreign country, or routine physical examinations.

Clearly, out-of-pocket medical expenses can be high for senior citizens. It is imperative that they carry some supplemental policy in addition to Medicare, in order

Worksheet XIV: Yours
HOW MUCH DISABILITY INSURANCE?

A. ANNUAL FAMILY EXPENSES (Budget form)   _____

B. SOURCES OF INCOME

- Spouse's Income _____

- Social Security Benefits (if eligible) _____

- Disability Benefits from Work _____

- Income from Income-Producing Assets
  (Assets Evaluation form) _____

- Other Income _____

TOTAL SOURCES OF INCOME   _____

C. ADDITIONAL ANNUAL INCOME NEEDED
   (Subtract B from A)   _____

D. MONTHLY BENEFIT NEEDED   _____

to pay for items not covered by Medicare and for expenses that go beyond the Medicare program.

Warning: A retirement nest egg can be wiped out by medical costs not covered by Medicare. Anyone over 65 must carefully consider buying additional coverage.

5. *"Medigap" insurance.* This additional coverage is called "medigap" insurance because its purpose is to fill the gap between your medical bills and the amount that Medicare is willing to pay—usually less than the amount you have been billed by the doctor, hospital, or laboratory. Gaps occur because Medicare includes a deductible clause, just as your automobile insurance does, to help you pay a lower premium and because your doctor is charging more than Medicare thinks the particular treatment should cost. The largest gap comes in the area of "excess" physician's fees, as Medicare likes to call it. Medicare sets up what it considers "allowable charges" for every conceivable treatment. The problem is that there is no standard rate. Medicare's allowable charges, it has been found, can vary not only in various parts of the country but also in various neighborhoods of the same city.

Altogether, 10 different standard "medigap" plans have been created, labeled A through J. They are sold as "medigap supplements." Each state decides which of the plans may be sold to its residents, so you may not find all 10 plans available where you live. But wherever they are sold, all A plans are alike in the coverage they provide. So are all Bs, all Cs, and so on right down the line. That includes the look of the policy, what words it uses, and what those words mean. The only differences are the cost of the coverage among insurers and the efficiency with which they resolve claims.

6. *Health maintenance organizations.* While they offer prepayment plans that provide medical protection, HMOs do not provide health insurance as such.

HMOs are organized as nonprofit cooperatives. For a fixed price per month they provide medical care for their members, based on the premise that it is cheaper to prevent illness than to cure it. Since the premiums of members constitute their only source of income, HMOs must hold down costs, and preventive medicine is one way to do so.

The groups own and operate hospitals and clinics and hire doctors, nurses, and medical technicians. They pay annual salaries to their professional staffs, so the doctors do not charge patient by patient in the normal way.

If you belong to an HMO, your premium covers nearly all medical expenses and you are entitled to care in one place 24 hours a day, seven days a week. One disadvantage, though, is that usually you cannot choose your own doctor; you must use a doctor who belongs to the HMO.

Before making a decision about HMOs, find out how near the service is to you, and talk with some of its members.

The number of HMOs is increasing because most corporations are offering HMOs as an alternative to traditional medical plans.

7. *Long-term nursing home coverage.* Years of savings can be wiped out by a long-term stay in a nursing home or by lengthy custodial care at home. Worried by that well-known fact, many elderly people are buying insurance to pay for long-term care. But look out! Such a policy almost never pays all the cost of living in a nursing home or having someone come in and take care of you. The premium on these policies is based on three things: your age when you buy the policy, the elimination period (i.e., how soon after you enter a nursing home does the policy begin to pay?), and the benefits you receive.

Usually, a long-term policy pays a set dollar amount per day for care. But be realistic: A $50-a-day benefit will cover only a small portion of the daily cost of a

---

TIPS ON MEDIGAP

- If you buy one good "medigap" policy, you will have all you will ever need. You don't need more than one. So, once you have bought your policy, don't fall for impressive direct-mail offerings or for smiling personalities from the good old days on TV.
- Be sure that the policy you buy is *guaranteed renewable*—not conditionally renewable. Guaranteed renewable means that you can continue the policy, no questions asked, as long as you live and pay for it.
- The biggest out-of-pocket expense you are likely to run into is doctors' excess fees, so make sure the policy you buy covers them. Whenever Medicare says it will not pay the doctor's bill in full (except for your deductible) your "medigap" policy should pay a large percentage of the difference.
- Don't be misled by newspaper or magazine articles about certain policies. A policy may sound terrific in a national magazine but may be unattainable in the state in which you live. Or the company's basic policy might very well be available where you live, while the comprehensive policy that you read about and want is not available. Your state's insurance department can tell you exactly what is available in your state.
- Never buy insurance for a specific disease such as cancer, stroke, or heart disease. Any good "medigap" policy will cover *all* possibilities.

---

nursing home. Note also that the benefits period can vary from one year to a life-time, but that most policies have a three-year maximum.

Some things to look for in health insurance

- Combination plans. Many companies, as well as Blue Cross/Blue Shield, offer plans that combine basic hospitalization and medical and surgical benefits with a major medical plan. This package deal often has lower deductibles.
- Items not covered. Check on such items as cosmetic surgery, eyeglasses and routine examinations for glasses, regular physicals, and psychiatric care (if covered, the latter is usually under a special limitation).
- Guaranteed renewable and noncancelable policies. Some companies reserve the right to cancel at any time. This could be disastrous if, when they cancel, you are uninsurable or have an illness that existed before they canceled. A noncancelable policy cannot be canceled during the period of time it is stated to run. Nor can premiums be increased during this period. Usually when the stated period has ended, and it may be as short as one year, the policy has to be renewed if the policyholder chooses. However, the company may increase the premium.
- Shop around and consider the alternatives. Everyone should have major medical insurance. A major illness or accident can bring on economic chaos. If you are eligible for group medical insurance, take advantage of it. If not, compare the cost of Blue Cross/Blue Shield with other plans. Note the various features of each. Consider taking a larger deductible in order to pay a smaller premium. See if an HMO is near you. Often an HMO offers group coverage to an individual who is not otherwise eligible to be in a group medical plan.

Property, casualty, and home owner's insurance

If you had a severe fire in your home, or a hurricane or flood roared through your town, or thieves took your television and stereo and silver and priceless antiques, could you make repairs and buy replacements out of your financial assets? Few of us could. That's why property and casualty insurance is imperative.

Most of us understand the basic idea of the coverage: If a fire or theft, flood or wind damage occurs, we will be reimbursed for the loss. But few of us really understand what will be covered by the insurance company and what we must take care of ourselves.

Home owner's policies, as they are called, usually cover:

TIPS ON LONG-TERM CARE

- Be certain the policy is *guaranteed renewable* without question as long as you live and pay the premiums.
- The policy should cover four kinds of care:

    1. *Skilled care.* This means quality nursing home care under the direction or supervision of a physician, performed daily by a registered nurse or other skilled medical worker.

    2. *Intermediate care.* This also requires the skills of a medical worker, and is also performed under your doctor's orders, but less frequently—usually two or three times a week.

    3. *Custodial care.* This does not call for the skills of a medical worker. It takes care of the needs of daily living: eating, dressing, bathing, walking. This is the kind of nursing home care that is most commonly provided.

    4. *Home Care.* This covers a broad range of services, from skilled care by nurses, social workers, and therapists to shopping and housework performed by professional home-makers.

- Make sure the policy does not require you to be in the hospital before you enter a nursing home. Note that most people go directly from their own homes into a nursing facility. Does the policy include home care?
- Is Alzheimer's disease covered?
- Can you purchase an inflation rider? This option will increase your benefits to meet inflation's demands.

1. Fire insurance on the house.
2. Extended coverage for damage to the house by such things as wind, hail, falling objects, smoke, and motor vehicles.
3. Allowance for additional living expenses if the home owner has to live in a motel or rented house while repairs are made.
4. Allowance for personal property lost because of fire, theft, or mysterious disappearance. This covers items such as clothing, books, cameras, stereos, and household furnishings.
5. Liability. This covers claims based on any injuries suffered by others and caused by your property. Classic example: The mailman is bitten by your dog or slips on the ice on your sidewalk. The coverage includes payments for medical expenses.

- The policy always specifies an address and provides protection at that address. However, most policies also cover losses while possessions are in storage or at the cleaner's or when you are traveling.
- Items stolen from your children while at camp or away at school may be covered. Look closely at what the policy says about college dorms; most policies do not stretch all the way to a dormitory or, even less likely, to an apartment near a college campus. If your student son or daughter is living off campus in a rented apartment, better get insurance on the stereo, the camera, the walk-around headset, the guitar, the computer.
- Most policies limit the amount they will pay to the actual cash value of the property stolen or destroyed. The insurance company takes the age of the article into account and depreciates for each year you have owned it. (This is another area where your records come in handy, for if the suit lost in the dry cleaner's fire was new only six months ago you will have a way to prove it.) Since actual cash value may be substantially lower than what it will cost you to replace an item, especially considering the way property has appreciated in recent years, this insurance policy can be costly to you. However, you can get a replacement endorsement added to your policy by paying a higher premium. If a major loss occurs, you will consider the money well spent.
- The typical standard home owner's policy limits the amount the company will pay for a loss of personal property. Usually the limit is 50 percent of the total amount that the building is insured for. The loss is also limited to that caused by a fire, windstorm, or other specific peril listed in the policy. If you have a valuable collection of art, jewelry, silver, antique furniture, or other similar objects, you will be wise to ask for a "personal property floater schedule." It broadens the policy's coverage, but it can be expensive. By having appraisals made, the company gives a cash value to each item you list on the schedule. If you add this coverage, remember to reevaluate these items at least every couple of years, as the value of collectibles rises with inflation. (The trend can go the other way, too, of course: Remember what happened to the price of silver between 1979 and 1981? It shot up dramatically, then fell right back.) Also update the schedule to delete any items you no longer possess. Usually this type of coverage has a deductible amount, to help keep down the premium cost.

Important: Your record-keeping, including inventory of items, receipts for purchases, and photographs, is vital if you are carrying a personal property floater on your home owner's policy.

- Home owners are not the only ones who need coverage. If you are renting, you need both personal property and liability coverage just as much as if you were the owner. A person who falls and is injured can sue the tenant as well as the landlord.

What about the amount of insurance you should carry on your home? This mainly depends on the replacement value of the house and its contents. With inflation and the resulting appreciation of homes over recent years, you cannot just let your home owner's policy sit year after year without updating it. In fact, most of the insurance companies and their agents add an increment yearly for that upward spiral and simply bill you for the increase. The question, really, is whether that automatic increase is enough. Have you brought collectibles into the house? Do you need appraisals of certain valuables so you can take out a personal property floater? Since the floater is relatively expensive, do you want to insure only those items that would be really difficult to replace, such as heirlooms? Are you keeping smaller items in a safe deposit box and handling the risk that way? All these are questions that you should consider—and act upon.

Speaking of suing: an umbrella policy

You should be aware that while liability insurance covers you against a claim by a person bitten by your dog or injured on your icy sidewalk, it does *not* cover you in a situation where a repairman, cleaning woman, gardener, or painter is injured while working in your home. They should be covered by Worker's Compensation. Never just assume that a repairman or housepainter or other contractor has his or her own insurance, though. Ask to see proof.

How much liability insurance should you carry? Usually the range is between $25,000 and $300,000. With the number of liability claims and the size of the settlements in our society today, it is not a bad idea to increase your coverage to as high as $1 million if you have a fairly substantial income and assets. People who are suing are usually advised by their lawyers to try for as much as they can and to dig the well where the water is.

Automobile insurance

This is required by law in most states, and if you drive one inch without it you are courting financial disaster.

There are four things to understand about auto insurance:

1. *Liability coverage.* This protects you, the owner of the car, from claims that may result from the injury or death of another person, as well as from damage to property. The other person may be a pedestrian or a passenger or driver of another vehicle. The situation itself may be of any kind; the newspapers regularly report crazy happenings involving vehicles that no one could have anticipated. The property may be another vehicle or any kind of stationary object.

The liability part of the policy is written in figures that look like this: $100,000/$300,000–$25,000. What does it mean? The first two figures mean that the insurance company will pay up to $100,000 for bodily injuries to any one person and up to $300,000 for injuries to two or more persons in any one accident. The $25,000 means they will pay that maximum for property damage.

o   o   o

SUPPOSE MARTY MID IS CARRYING $100,000/$300,000–$25,000. . . .

In an accident he hits a Rolls-Royce containing four people; their injuries add up to medical claims of $400,000. If he cannot defend his situation and loses a lawsuit, he will be personally responsible for $100,000 of medical claims and for the difference between $25,000 and the replacement cost of the Rolls-Royce. Far fetched? No! Read your newspaper.

o   o   o

2. *Collision.* This pays for damage to your car caused by a collision with another vehicle, or with any other object, whether it is stationary or moving. To cut down the premium cost it carries a deductible, usually $100 or more, so you pay for minor repairs yourself. Usually the company pays for the cost of repairs above the deductible amount or pays the actual cash value of the car, less the deductibility, if you total the car. When buying a policy, you can usually choose how much of a deductible you want to risk. The higher the deductible, the lower your premium, of course.

3. *Comprehensive.* Many things, in addition to other vehicles, can damage your car. This part of the insurance covers loss due to fire, theft, wind, hail, and falling objects. Again, a deductibility clause may reduce your premium.

4. *Medical payments.* All passengers injured while in your car are covered by this section. It also covers the members of your family while they are riding in any other vehicle.

When you are buying auto insurance, or reviewing what you have, be aware of these important points:

- Like all other insurance, policies need to be reviewed and updated regularly. Nothing stays the same.
- Premium rates vary according to where you live, and according to the amount of risk you are willing to handle yourself by taking higher deductibility. Rates in big cities are higher than in small towns and rural areas presumably because the heavier the traffic, the more likely an accident.
- Unless you simply cannot afford it, your liability coverage should be the maximum possible. If you have substantial assets, you should have substantial liability coverage.
- As your car gets older, its value depreciates. Watch its cash value. If you keep a car several years, there comes a point when you may consider dropping collision coverage altogether because the annual premiums approach the replacement value of the car.
- Shop around. Auto insurance is high-priced stuff, but there are many insurance companies competing for your business. Your best approach is to work with an independent agent to get the best coverage for the lowest premium.

Summary

Whether you are considering or reviewing life, health, disability, property and casualty, or automobile insurance, ask yourself these basic questions:

What if? What if this, what if that? What risks do I take? What things could possibly happen?

Which of these risks must I assume myself, and which can I pay an insurance company to take over? That, in turn, will determine what kinds of policies and coverage you need.

How much will it cost? Shop around. Get several quotes, or bids, from various agents and companies. Make your decision based on coverage, service, and cost.

From time to time ask yourself this question: Am I carrying enough insurance, or too much, for my situation right now? Reevaluating and updating your policies every so often is most important.

KEEPING FIT AFTER 65: RETIREMENT

○ ○ ○ ○

"When can I qualify for retirement benefits?"

"When do I have a right to get the money in my pension account?"

"Do I have to pay taxes if I take it all out?"

"Can I move my money to another employer's plan if I change jobs?"

"Will my health decline?"

○ ○ ○

The problems facing the person who is retiring are psychological, medical, social, and economic. Many of the economic problems result from failure to plan for the time when work will no longer structure your day or define who you are and how you feel about yourself. Up to this point your job has given you a sense of belonging, as well as being a way of providing for your family. It has given you a sense of worth and accomplishment.

Now, for many a retiree, there comes a sense of emptiness and loss of identity. In numerous cases —though fewer and fewer each year—the wife has not had an outside job and the sudden continual presence of her husband makes her feel her domain is being invaded. The very fact that he is on hand for lunch every day, a meal she may not have had to cope with for 35 or 40 years, may mean completely altering her schedule. A period of adjustment, that may well involve an identity crisis at age 65 or so, is very likely inescapable.

More serious problems may stem from worry about money matters. Income during retirement generally comes from Social Security, pensions, and individual savings and investments, areas that may be hard hit by inflation. As Florida representative Claude Pepper, chairman of the Select Committee on Aging of the U.S. House of Representatives, said in a hearing on September 17, 1980:

> The current retirement income system has not kept its promise to the workers who faithfully paid into the Social Security [system], placed their faith in private pension plans, and tried to frugally invest in savings accounts during their working lives. Inflation has ravaged their retirement savings or made it impossible to save, while their pension expectations have vanished into an incomprehensible maze of requirements or often disappeared because of the requirements that a worker participate in a plan for ten years before he becomes entitled to pension benefits . . . We must come to grips with the failure of pension plans and savings plans to play their intended role in contributing to retirement income security.

This is the broken promise of retirement. It has made retirees dependent on others. It has shattered their dreams and created despair and want.

Few people stop to think that inflation is selective. It does not hit everyone in the same corner of the pocketbook, nor with equal severity. Its effects vary depending on where you live and on what products you buy and in what proportions. Those living in rent-stabilized apartments in large cities with good public transportation systems do not feel the impact of oil prices, for instance, in the same way as people living in rural or suburban areas who are dependent on cars and on oil for heating their own homes.

The elderly are probably the hardest hit. Their incomes usually stay essentially the same, no matter what inflation does. As inflation has zoomed skyward, it has left them with less and less to spend on nonnecessities. As incomes barely cover food, shelter, medical care, and transportation, inflation has reduced the standard of living of many retired people.

Today's business climate

It is more important than ever to prepare for retirement and to accept responsibility for planning your retirement yourself. That means saving. Nothing in Your Financial Fitness Program can be more important or, in the long run, more valuable to you.

The fact is that companies are giving up the paternal role in which they present you with a plan and all you have to do is stick around and keep working until the day when it all pays off for you. The traditional pension is no more. Employee contributions become more and more integral to the pension plan every day.

What happened? The 1980s happened. Mergers, acquisitions, corporate restructuring, tighter and tighter profit margins—one management factor after another entered the picture. Early retirement offers became and continue to be commonplace as companies try to stay competitive by downsizing—trimming, usually from the top, where paychecks are fattest.

Economic changes and corporate restructuring are forcing millions of Americans to reevaluate their careers, their company loyalty (it wasn't the thing to do a couple of decades ago, but today you *must* think of yourself ahead of the company), and their futures. They must—*you* must—think seriously today about retirement, no matter how far off in the future it seems to be. You must understand it and plan for it.

In your working lifetime, you will see an explosion of early retirements. Younger workers will be moving from company to company, holding a succession of jobs, switching not only jobs but careers and career skills several times. The "company man" or "company woman" who has been with the same outfit for 25 or 30 years will be a rarity.

All of which means that you are unlikely to build up the kind of pension benefits that your parents or grandparents enjoyed by staying with the same employers for most of a working lifetime. Inevitably, you will have to make retirement planning part of your financial fitness program.

What will your income and needs be after you retire?

Retirement planning has always been important, but today it is essential. You can't begin early enough to plan for your own retirement fitness and security.

First, you will have to figure out what your sources of income will be. There will be Social Security, retirement payments from a pension, and IRA and 401(k) payouts. Remember—when you're figuring retirement income, you must start with the amounts that you will receive . . . but you'll have to look at them in terms of today's dollar.

Next, figure what your needs will be after retirement.

Fares to and from work, business lunches, work clothes—all these expenses will be cut out. The kids' education will be paid for; chances are the mortgage will be, too. That leaves three key areas to think about:

- Emergency fund. Even if you haven't needed one all these years, it's a good idea to set up a fund for special emergencies.
- Lifestyle. It is time to rethink your priorities. Will the two of you still need two cars? Will travel become a larger budget item than before? Will you be entertaining more or less often? Some budget items will shrink, others stretch as your retirement lifestyle evolves.
- Budget. If you have kept a regular budget in force, you have a good fix on where the money goes now. Look over the various categories and see what they may cost in the future, assuming there is no change in lifestyle. Usually a retired couple can live on 75 to 85 percent of their pre-retirement gross income. This means you will have about the same net income as before retirement. The reason? Deductions from your gross income will decrease. You will no longer be paying into Social Security, unless you continue to work on a part-time basis: taxes will be less because Social Security benefits are not taxable for most recipients, and also because those over 65 may take an extra exemption on their federal income tax returns. Thus if a married couple are both over 65, they will have $6,100 in personal exemptions plus the standard deductions amount of $6,900 allowed by

the government for married couples. As a result, income up to $13,000 will not be taxed.

While certain expenses will be reduced or become nonexistent, others, such as medical care, will increase. And, of course, we cannot forget about inflation.

The difference between your estimated sources of income and estimated expenses will be your "retirement gap"—the additional income you will need for retirement. Look back to the Mids' goal on p. 6. The amount they need to save is their "retirement gap." The higher the level of income you want in retirement, the more you will have to depend on your own investments.

Is your pension plan fit?

A pension plan is a form of deferred wages. Under some plans, the employer puts in all the money; these are called "noncontributory" plans. In others, the employee puts in some earnings; these are called "contributory" plans.

Of all the workers in the country's private sector (that is, not in government jobs), only slightly more than half are covered by pension plans provided by their employers, whether contributory or noncontributory. There is a bewildering array of basic plans, though, with countless diverse provisions. For our purposes, it is almost impossible to come up with a sample pension plan. So, if your employer offers a pension plan, make a strong effort to become thoroughly familiar with it. Get to know it forwards and backwards, just as you get to know the necessary exercises for your physical fitness program.

There are two basic types of pension plans:

1. *Defined benefit plan.* This type specifies in advance the benefits the retired worker will receive. They may be *either* of the following:

   a. *Unit benefit, or percentage rate, plan.* If you have this plan, your benefits are based on your earnings over a specified period of service with the company. The unit may be a specific dollar amount, or it may be a percentage of your earnings. What you get annually is the sum of the benefits credited for each year you were employed. For example, ABC Company pays 1.1 percent of the average *monthly* earnings (counting the highest 60 months out of the last 120) for all years of service for a retiree with average base earnings of $25,000, or $2,083 per month, who has worked for 30 years. The benefit is $687.00 a month.

   b. *Flat rate plan.* Here a fixed dollar amount is paid for each year of service. If you receive, for example, $20.25 per month for each year of service, and if you have 30 years of service, you will get $607.50 a month. Often the flat rate plan's rate varies according to job classifications, so those who had better-paying jobs get higher pensions.

Over the four years from 1990 through 1994, the number of such traditional pension plans fell by 40 percent. Company after company has been discontinuing them in order to reduce costs. Usually, they replace them with "defined contribution plans."

2. *Defined contribution plan.* This type is also called an *individual account plan.* The amount of the contributions is fixed. However, the benefits are based on the amount accumulated in an individual's account at the time of retirement. The plan may specify either of the following:

   a. *The 401(k) plan.* The best known and most common type is the 401(k) plan. Between 1990 and 1994, these plans grew by 12 percent nationwide. First introduced in 1978 and named after a section of the Internal Revenue Service code that created it, the 401(k) plan is a voluntary retirement savings plan to which you make contributions from your gross income *before* taxes (one of its great advantages). Your employer is permitted under law to make matching contributions (another great advantage) that typically range from 25 to 100 percent of your contribution—up to a certain limit.

   A typical plan may say, "The company will match $0.50 for each $1.00 of the first 6 percent of your pay." Your contribution is limited to either a percent of pay or a dollar amount. Sup-

Exhibit 17
401(k) PLAN ACCOUNT GROWTH

Projected account at the end of:	Current salary	
	$35,000	$50,000
10 years	56,748	$81,070
20 years	214,953	307,076
25 years	370,677	529,538

Source: Hewitt Associates

Assumptions: 5% salary increases, employeee contributions of 6%, employer contribution of 3%, interest rate of 8% (credited quarterly on employee contributions and at end of year on employer's contributions).

pose, for example, you are making $50,000 a year and contribute 6 percent. Your account will be credited with $4,500—$3,000 from your payroll deductions, and $1,500 put in by your company. Now suppose you increase your contribution to 10 percent—$5,000. The company's contribution will still be $1,500, so your total for the year is $6,500.

The tax deferment is valuable. You pay no taxes until you start withdrawing money from the plan, usually when you retire. You get other advantages, too. Your plan may allow you to make contributions from your after-tax dollars, in addition to the before-tax payroll deduction. Some limitations apply: The maximum amount you may contribute in 1997 is $9,500; the total amount that may be contributed in any one year by you and your employer together is $30,000 or 25 percent of your gross salary minus your 401(k) contributions—whichever is less.

b. *Money purchase plan.* Here, a predetermined formula sets the amount of the contribution. This is a fixed dollar amount each year.

c. *Profit sharing plan.* In this case, the employer's contribution to the plan may vary from year to year as profits of the firm vary.

Where is the best place to put the money? Your employer will offer various investment alternatives, from money-market accounts to fixed-income investments to stock funds. Often company stock is offered. As you consider possibilities, note that the number of mutual funds out there keeps growing, adding to the choices you face.

One of the biggest problems in the whole pension world is that those who put money aside in defined contribution plans do not invest it as well as the professionals who manage defined benefit plans. About half of all the 401(k) assets in America are sitting quietly in low-interest guaranteed investment contracts. The fact is, most people play it too safe with their retirement earnings. The growth of your retirement funds can be seriously impeded, especially in the early years of long-term investing, if you are too conservative.

Think about vesting

You should be aware of a number of points when you are contemplating a job and considering the company's pension plan, or when your company offers any change in its existing plans:

- "Vesting" varies. Vesting means that the money credited to your name in the company's pension accounting is legally yours, without question or qualification. Usually you become fully vested only after you have worked a certain number of years or reached a certain age. Two typical vesting situations:

a. *Full vesting:* no vested right to benefit until five years of employment are completed, at which point you become 100 percent vested.

b. *Partial vesting:* under a new seven-year schedule, 20 percent after completion of the first three years, 20 percent for each of the next four years until 100 percent is reached.

- You are always entitled to all the money you have put in. If your plan is contributory, you may walk away with your share of the contribution before you have any vesting whatever.
- Once you are vested, you may not be forced to forfeit your pension benefits. That money is yours—with very few exceptions. However, many workers do not receive pensions upon retirement because they have not fulfilled the requirements for duration of service. In most firms, the longer you work, the larger your pension. (In our previous example under the flat rate plan, if you have 30 years of service your pension is $607.50 a month; a worker the same age who has been with the company for only 20 years will get $405 per month.)
- Changing jobs can raise problems about vesting. If you move to another job after you are fully vested, the value of your pension will be frozen at the moment when you leave.

You must consider a number of questions:

1. May you take a lump-sum distribution and "roll it over" into another form of retirement account?
2. Will you have to pay a tax if you take the lump sum?
3. May you move the money to another employer's pension plan, and will the second employer accept it?
4. May you leave the money with your first employer, and how much will you receive monthly?

○   ○   ○

HOW MR. MID IS VESTED . . .

Mr. Mid started work at his present company at age 25, before the passage of the 1986 Tax Reform Act. Consequently, at age 38 he was 50 percent vested, for his age plus seven years of service equaled 45. At age 43 he was 100 percent vested, having gained another 50 percent at 10 percent a year for the five years from age 38 to 43.

○　　○　　○

Receiving pension benefits

Whether you are retiring or moving to another job and claiming your vested interest in your former company's pension plan, you have to make the critical decision on how to take the money. Depending on your company's particular plan, you may have a couple of options:

1. *Lump-sum distribution.* If you can take the money in a lump sum, you will have to decide whether to "roll it over" into an individual retirement account (IRA) without having to pay taxes on it or not roll it over and pay taxes on the full amount. However, there are certain rules governing lump-sum distributions.

a. If you decide to take the money now rather than roll it over into an IRA, the distribution will be taxed as ordinary income. If you are over 59½, you will be able to use a five-year forward averaging provision. For those born before 1936 a ten-year forward averaging is also available. You can use forward averaging only once. In figuring the tax, you are considered a single person with no exemptions, whether or not you are married. The tax is figured separately, without taking other income into consideration. If you are under 59½, you will be subject to a penalty as well as to paying ordinary income tax on the distribution.

b. For those who do not need the funds immediately, a roll-over is the best bet. Just remember, you must put the funds in a roll-over account within 60 days from the date when you get the full distribution. The distribution must come from a qualified retirement or profit-sharing plan, i.e., the plan must be one that the IRS has approved. The funds that grow in a roll-over IRA are tax-deferred, which makes a roll-over very attractive for those who don't need the funds immediately.

The big advantage of a lump-sum distribution is that you keep control of the money and you decide what kind of investments you want to make. A roll-over IRA can be invested in savings and money market accounts, certificates of deposit, stocks and bonds, mutual funds or an annuity contract.

2. *Annuity.* For those who cannot or do not want to take a lump-sum distribution, an annuity will be provided. The Retirement Equity Act of 1984 requires that retirement benefits be paid in the form of a "qualified joint-and-survivor annuity."

The annuity automatically pays an employee and his spouse (if they have been married for at least one year) a certain amount. If one dies, the survivor is paid a percentage of the amount that both were getting.

The amount paid each month depends not only on how much the employee or the company, or both, have put into the plan but on the age at which payments are to begin, for it is based on mortality tables. If you start receiving payments at age 65, for instance, they will be smaller amounts than if you wait until age 70 to start. If your spouse is much younger than you, and thus can be expected to live much longer, the monthly payments will be less.

There is another angle that is important to understand: The amount of your monthly check will be higher if you purchase a straight life contract and give up any survivor benefits; this means that if you die, the remaining money that has not been used in payments will revert to the insurance company. You may decide you want a straight annuity paid on your life only. If so, the law requires the written consent of a spouse, usually the wife, if the employee wants to waive the joint-and-survivor provision. This waiver must be signed by both the employee and spouse and notarized. Under some contracts a refund is paid to a beneficiary. If, for instance, an individual dies before receiving total monthly payments that equal or exceed the single premium paid to the insurance company, it will refund the difference to the annuitant's beneficiary.

Under certain conditions it makes good sense to choose a straight annuity paid on your life only. It means that you receive a larger monthly check than if survivor benefits are in the plan. Suppose, for instance, you and your spouse figure out that with income from Social Security, investments, and proceeds from life insurance policies, she might not need a "survivor" annuity if she were widowed. The income from these other sources would enable her to live quite comfortably. Meantime, while you are alive, you can both profit from the larger pension check. In a word, figure things out. Plan.

What is the advantage of an annuity over a lump sum? You never have to worry about money management, for a start. You are guaranteed a fixed monthly income and you know you will never outlive your capital. Your monthly income will be based upon several things: the amount contributed by your employer and, if the pension plan was contributory, by you; the type of contract, whether single life or joint survivor benefit; and the age at which you begin to receive payments.

But there is a disadvantage to an annuity. Your monthly check remains the same, no matter what inflation does. You have no protection. Inflation can erode the value of your annuity, as many a retired person has learned bitterly in recent years. And there is no changing your mind. Once you have signed the contract and the annuity is paid for, that is it. It has no cash value.

Plan several years ahead

These alternatives, and the seriousness of the consequences of each, make it vitally important that you think your pension plans through with great care well in advance of your retirement. Six months before retirement is too late.

As you are working on your plans, many questions will occur to you. Here are the answers to a few of them.

1. What if you take early retirement? If your pension plan stipulates 65 as retirement age, you are likely to lose one-half if you retire at 60 and about two-thirds if you retire at 55.

2. What if you decide to stay on at work after you reach 65? In calculating pension benefits, most plans do not count the years after 65; that is, most employers stop contributing after age 65 even if the employee continues to work.

3. What happens to your plan if you take a leave of absence or are laid off temporarily? Check this carefully with your company. For pension purposes, the employer will usually honor all service before and after the break. However, some require a waiting period—usually one year—before you can get back into the plan.

4. Are your pension benefits affected by your Social Security benefits? Do not be surprised if your employer reduces your pension benefit by a percentage of the amount you are getting from Social Security. This can range from 25 percent to as high as 50 percent if you have 30 or 35 years of service. It can be a real shocker.

5. What if you die before you retire? First, your survivors receive a full refund of the money you have contributed to the plan. The law now requires that a pension plan give each participant the option of providing a survivor annuity from the time a married participant becomes eligible for early retirement until he or she retires. In other words, if you die at a time when you are eligible for early retirement, your spouse will receive benefits just as he or she would have if you had already retired and were covered by a joint survivor annuity. The amount of the death benefit may be determined by the amount of pay you were earning at the date of death, or it may be based on the amount of money that has accrued to you in the pension plan.

6. What if you become disabled? Many plans provide for you to become fully vested, regardless of usual vesting rules, if you are permanently dis-

abled. If you are temporarily disabled and unable to work for a while, most plans will hold the benefits that have accrued to you to date. If you have reached early retirement age, you may become entitled to an immediate annuity based on the amount that has accrued in your account up to that date. Some plans provide that a disabled employee may receive early retirement benefits at a younger age, and with fewer years of service, than an able-bodied employee would be entitled to.

7. How do you know the status of your plan? Legal requirements call for you to be given a summary report on the money in your plan once a year. It is important to be sure that you understand this statement thoroughly. If you have any questions, talk to someone in authority at your place of work who will explain it. Do not just accept the interpretations or guesswork of your fellow workers.

Since it is your retirement, and you want it to be as comfortable as possible, nothing is more important than checking regularly on your pension situation and knowing well in advance just what your benefits will be.

○   ○   ○

HOW DOES MARTY MID PREDICT HIS PENSION BENEFITS? . . .

This depends on his years of service with the company. First he works out the average final yearly earnings for his highest-paid 60 months (five years) in the ten consecutive years before he retires. Since he is eight years away from retirement, the assumption must be made that his income will be at its highest level.

For our purposes, let's take his present salary of $65,600 a year as his average. That means $5,468 a month. When he retires, he will have been with the company for 35 years. The company formula says he is entitled to 1.5 percent of his average monthly earnings, minus $1\frac{1}{3}$ percent of his Social Security benefits multiplied by his 35 years of service. So it works out as:

1.5% of $5,468 x 35 years =	$2,870
less 1.22% of $1,248 x 35 =	- 534
	$2,336

If Marty retires earlier, he will lose a certain percentage of his benefits. The company formula gives him 94 percent at age 62, 90 percent at 60, and 75 percent at 55.

We arrived at the $2,336 figure for Marty's pension by assuming he would take his pension in the form of a straight life annuity, which would pay out only as long as he lived.

If he decided to take it as a joint and survivor annuity, things would be different. In this case, the survivor could be either Marty or Mary, and either survivor would continue to receive 50 percent of the payment that came when both were alive. Since the money would now have to stretch further (insurance people, called actuaries, figure all this out from mortality tables), they would get $2,032 while he is alive and the survivor would get $1,016.

They could also take the annuity as a "ten-year certain." This means that the insurance company guarantees to pay a certain amount for 10 years whether or not Marty lives that long. Thus if he died after only five years, Mary would continue to receive the same amount for another five years. If he lived beyond the ten years, they would also continue to receive the payments. If he died, however, after the ten-year period ended, Mary would get no payments.

Assuming that Marty and Mary decide they want to take the 50 percent joint and survivor annuity, his projected retirement income will be:

his Social Security at age 65	$1,248
her Social Security at age 62	500
50% joint and survivor annuity (87% of $2,336)	2,032
total income	$3,780

This comes to only 45 percent of Marty's and Mary's present monthly income. That is why they are saving in 401(k) plans.

◯   ◯   ◯

MR. MID'S 401(k) PLAN

Mr. Mid is currently contributing 7 percent of his salary of $65,600 to a 401(k) plan. This comes to $4,592 per year. As a result, his income for tax purposes is $61,008 ($65,600 minus $4,592). The company contributes 50 cents for every dollar he puts in, or $2,296 yearly. There are certain limitations. In 1997, the maximum amount an employee may contribute is pre-tax $9,500. Another limitation is the total yearly amount both you and your employer may contribute: $30,000 or 25 percent of your salary after your 401(k) contributions—whichever is less.

The maximum amount that Mr. Mid and his employer may make to his 401(k) is $14,025 ($65,600 minus $9,500 equals $56,100 and 25 percent of that is $14,025).

◯   ◯   ◯

HOW MUCH COULD JIM YOUNG'S 401(k) BE WORTH IN THE FUTURE? . . .

Jim has been contributing a small amount to his 401(k) plan but recently saw figures that made him realize it could be a gold mine when he retires. His current salary is $45,000. Assuming that he has 5 percent salary increases, makes contributions of 6 percent (with the company adding an additional 3 percent), and the money earns 8 percent interest, he could have $73,667 in 10 years, $481,193 in 25 years and $797,892 in 30 years. By the time he is 65, his 401(k) could be worth over a million dollars! Since he will probably work for several companies, contributions to 401(k) plans are important.

◯   ◯   ◯

IRA: individual retirement account

Before 1982, only workers who had no pension or profit-sharing plans at their places of work were eligible to establish IRAs. From 1982 through 1986, anyone who had earned income could contribute to an IRA and deduct the amount from his or her federal income taxes. In effect, you could reduce your taxable income. However, starting in 1987, the rules regarding IRAs were changed. The maximum contribution of $2,000 per worker, or $2,250 per one-income couple, remained the same. The rules regarding the tax deductibility of the contribution were changed. If neither you nor your spouse are covered by a qualified pension plan, you may deduct the full amount—regardless of income. If your adjusted gross income is $40,000 or less ($25,000 if single), you may still deduct the full amount even if you are covered by a qualified plan.

For those with adjusted gross incomes between $25,000 and $35,000 on a single return or between $40,000 and $50,000 on a joint return, the maximum $2,000 deduction will drop—in steps. There will be a loss of $200 of the IRA deduction for each $1,000 of additional income. For example, if the adjusted gross income on a joint return is $42,500, a deduction of $1,500 may be taken; the deduction drops to $1,000 if the adjusted gross income is $45,000 and to $500 if the adjusted gross is $47,500. The deduction is completely phased out for the individual taxpayer with an adjusted gross over $35,000 and for joint filers with over $50,000.

Currently, couples with a stay-at-home spouse are limited to a maximum contribution of $2,250. The couple may divide the contribution between their two accounts as they choose, but no more than $2,000 may be contributed to the account of either one. *An important change*: Beginning with the 1997 tax year, a couple with one wage-earner can contribute $4,000 a year; that is as much as $2,000 per person. Couples can make 1997 contributions right after January 1, 1997. The contribution will be divided between two accounts, but no more than $2,000 may be contributed to the account of either one.

Control of the funds in either account is in the hands of the spouse in whose name the account is held. Should a divorce occur, a partner who gets alimony and has no earned income may use the alimony to continue the IRA contributions, up to $2,000 annually.

However, those who may not take the deduction may nevertheless continue to make nondeductible contributions up to $2,000. Earnings on the accounts will not be taxed until the funds are withdrawn. For those who are unable to deduct contributions, there will be no income tax on the contribution when withdrawn at retirement. Taxes will be due, however, on the earnings.

How about getting your money out of retirement accounts?

You are allowed to start taking money from your retirement accounts under the terms of your particular plan document. Usual conditions are:

1. You leave your present employment.
2. Any time after you reach age 59½.
3. If you become disabled.
4. If you are undergoing a financial hardship.

Money may be withdrawn from an IRA at any time after 59½ without penalty. Before that, withdrawals incur a penalty, except in the case of disability or death of the account holder. If you are leaving your job, take the lump sum amount and roll it into an IRA, which will continue to grow on a tax-deferred basis.

Minimum distributions

Nobody says you *have* to take the money out at age 59½. But you must begin to withdraw the money by the time you are 70½ or face some stiff penalties. You may also continue to make deposits until you are 70½, but no later.

Once you reach 70½, the rule is hard and fast: You have to start cashing in. The deadline for starting? April 1 of the calendar year after the calendar year in which you turn 70½. But there is a catch: If you wait that long—until the year after the year in which you become 70½—you will have to take your first distribution by April 1 and then take a second distribution by December 31. This, of course, could substantially increase your taxable income, because each distribution counts as income in the same single year.

To avoid that catch, take your first distribution in year one (i.e., the calendar year during which you turn 70½). Don't wait until April 1 of year two, even though the law allows you to wait that long. Each year after that, you will be required to take a distribution by December 31.

How much should you take? As little as possible, so your money can last as long as possible. The required minimum distribution is based on the amount you have in the account, and on whether you take the distributions based on your own single life expectancy or on a joint life expectancy with another person. The I.R.S. provides life expectancy tables based on single life expectancy and on a joint life and last survivor expectancy. (See Appendix.)

There are two withdrawal methods.

1) *Recalculation method.* Say you are a male who reaches 70½ this year and is using a single life expectancy, which at age 70½ is 16 years. You decide to take your first withdrawal from an IRA by the end of the year. If your account balance on December 31 is $75,000, and your life expectancy is 16 years, divide $75,000 by 16. You must withdraw $4,687.50. $75,000 minus $4,687.50 will leave you $70,312.50. Next year, the balance will increase by the interest earned by the fund, but it will be reduced by the distribution you took last year. If you assume an 8 percent return on your funds, your account balance at the end of the second year will be $75,937.50. And now that you are a year older, your life expectancy will be 15.3 years, so you divide $75,937.50 by 15.3 for a minimum withdrawal of $4,963.24. You must use the life expectancy tables every year.

2) *Term-certain method.* Here's another method for withdrawing IRA funds. It lets you *lock in* your payout period, based on your life expectancy. Using the same figures as in the previous example, your first withdrawal would be $75,000 divided by 16, for a minimum withdrawal of $4,687.50. At the beginning of the second year, the balance will be $70,312.50—i.e., $75,000 minus $4,687.50—but at the end of that year the balance (assuming an 8 percent return) will be $75,937.50. You divide that by 15, for a minimum distribution of $5,062.50. The following year, divide the year-end balance by 14, and so on.

Withdrawals based on two lives: joint life expectancy

Suppose you want to withdraw your money from your IRA as slowly as possible. Minimum distributions are allowed on the joint life expectancies of two or more people—you and your spouse, or you and your children. If you have named a beneficiary who is not a legal spouse, she or he will be treated as no more than 10 years younger than you are, while you are alive. Say you are 71 and your child is 45. For the purpose of figuring the minimum distribution that it insists on, the government considers your child to be 61 years old.

What is the difference? In the recalculation method, the money is drawn down at a slower rate while you are alive. In the early years, true, you withdraw smaller amounts. But the biggest difference comes when you die. If you have named a beneficiary, under the recalculation method, the minimum distribution is recalculated using the life expectancy of your beneficiary. This increases the amount of the withdrawals, incurs more taxes, and drains the estate more quickly. At the death of a beneficiary, all of the remaining money goes to *his or her* estate the year after death and becomes subject to income and estate taxes.

With the term-certain method, however, the payouts to a beneficiary continue at the same pace as before. Upon the death of the beneficiary, the remaining money is paid to the estate over the remaining period, thus prolonging the tax-deferred growth. If you want to protect a beneficiary's right to do this, you must arrange it in advance. Write to *each* bank or other custodian where you have an IRA account, specifying the original joint life expectancy, acknowledging that you will use the MDIB rule while you are living, and saying that the original life expectancy will apply if you die before your beneficiary. This "timely selection" must be made before your required minimum distribution date of April 1, following the year you turned 70½.

You can make everything easier if, before you retire or die, you consolidate your IRAs in a single custodian —either one mutual fund company (through which you may invest in any number of distinct funds) or with one stockbroker. However, this can be a problem if you have many beneficiaries. If, for example, you have three children as beneficiaries, it might be easier to set up three equal accounts.

Excess distributions have some rules of their own. Any annual withdrawals that are larger than $155,000, and any qualified employee-sponsored lump-sum distributions greater than $775,000, are subject to a 15 percent excise tax. *(This tax will be waived in 1997, 1998, and 1999 if you pull out the money as retirement income. The old rule will apply if you die and the money goes to a beneficiary.)* If you find youself in this category, you might want to take distributions before 70½ rather than risk falling into this excise-tax trap—as do so many people who wait until they are 70½ because they want to keep the money tax-deferred as long as possible. Note, however, that in the year you are rolling over a distribution from a qualified plan, it is exempt from the excise tax.

How is the money paid out to you? Again, you have choices.

1. You may take the entire sum in one lump payment.

2. You may decide to receive it in regular installments over a fixed period of time. This period may not be greater than your life expectancy or the averaged combined life expectancy of you and your spouse.
3. You may choose an annuity that will make regular payments for as long as you or your spouse live.

Important:
What about taxes on the money you put in the IRA? When you start to make withdrawals, the money you take out is taxed as ordinary income. That means, of course, that if you take it all out in one lump sum, you will be taxed in that year for the entire amount.

- What if you withdraw the money before you reach 59½? It will be taxed as ordinary income. A penalty of 10 percent will also be charged on the amount you withdraw. For example, if you take out $2,000 before you are 59½, you will pay tax on that amount and also a $200 penalty.
- What happens to the money when you die? A surviving spouse who inherits an IRA account upon the death of his or her spouse may make a tax-free roll-over to an IRA.
- Must you always keep the money in the same IRA account? No. You may move it to another account, in another bank, if you wish, either by direct transfer or by "roll-over." In a direct transfer, you never gain possession of the money during the transfer. It is moved directly from one trustee to another. For example, you may ask your bank to transfer the funds directly to a mutual fund. In a roll-over, on the other hand, you actually get a check or cash out of the bank. You must then deposit it in another IRA account within 60 days or pay tax on it as ordinary income and pay the 10 percent penalty.

Note: After any roll-over, you must wait at least 12 months before you may take another; direct transfers are not limited to any waiting period.

- What about taxes on nondeductible contributions? If you have made contributions to an IRA that were nondeductible (i.e., you made them with after-tax money, after you had already put in the maximum before-tax contribution allowed) the portion of any distribution you take that comes from that money is now tax-free—because you have already paid tax on it. How does the IRS decide what that portion is? Here's an example:

Let's say you withdraw $2,000 from your IRA, after making deductible contributions of $6,000 and nondeductible contributions of $10,000 over some eight years. At the end of this year, the balance in your IRA account is $22,000, including earnings over the eight years. Add the IRA balance at the end of the year and the withdrawal you made, and divide that figure (i.e., $24,000) into the total amount of nondeductible contributions (i.e., $10,000). This will give you 41.7 percent of your withdrawal tax-free, with the remaining 58.3 percent (i.e., $1,166) taxable.

Don't forget to keep good records. File away copies of Form 8606, which lists your nondeductible contributions every tax year. Put them with your tax returns for such years. And also keep all forms sent to you by banks or other institutions that hold your IRA savings and that show your contributions to IRAs and your distributions from them.

- Do you have to put the maximum into the IRA each year? No. You may put as much as you want to or feel you can afford. You can make a single deposit of your entire amount for the year or put it in dribs and drabs. Amounts may vary from deposit to deposit and from year to year, and if necessary you may skip one or more years. An IRA may be opened and first deposit made as late as the due date of your income tax return, usually April 15 of the year following.

IN A WORD: *PLAN*. THIS IS NOT SOMETHING YOU LEAVE UNTIL THE LAST MOMENT

Some key points to keep in mind:

- Unless you elect the term-certain method before April 1 of the year after which you turn 70½, you will be stuck with the recalculation method.
- Be sure to write to all custodians, specifying which method of distribution you want.
- Once you make the choice, it is irrevocable.
- Before you start minimum distributions, you may well find it valuable to consult an attorney who specializes in pension law.
- In any year in which you do not take your required minimum distribution, an excise tax of 50 percent of the excess in your IRA will be imposed.

- Does it make any difference when you make your contributions? It sure does. If you deposit money in an IRA early in the year, in January, say, that money and the interest it immediately starts to earn are tax deferred—protected from any tax for that year. And your money has that much more time to grow. If you put the money into a regular savings account or money market fund, to wait until you move it into an IRA before the April 15 deadline the following year, the interest it earns will be taxable.

○   ○   ○

IF THE YOUNGS START AN IRA . . .

Suppose Mr. and Mrs. Young start an IRA with $1,000 a year but wait until the end of the year to make the contribution. They have friends who put the same amount in at the beginning of the year. Each account earns 10 percent. At age 65, the Youngs will have about $442,592 in their account. Their friends will have about $486,852—or $44,260 more than the Youngs.

○   ○   ○

Does an IRA really make a difference?

Yes. If you put in the maximum of $2,000 a year for 10 years and it earns 10 percent, you will have about $35,062 in the account at the end of 10 years. If you put the same amount, at the same interest, in an account where you pay taxes on it, you will have about $23,000 in 10 years (assuming you are in the 25 percent tax bracket).

Does it make any difference where you invest the funds?

Yes. Plenty of banks, insurance companies, brokerage firms, and mutual funds are clamoring for your money. IRA funds can go into almost any type of account. So you need to look at all aspects of your situation and make a decision. How long do you plan to make contributions? What type of risk are you willing to take? If you are now in your 50s you may want to select an investment with a guaranteed yield. If you are much younger you may be willing to take a risk, knowing that if there are losses you will have time to make up the difference. How much are you willing to contribute each year? Some IRAs allow you to make small or frequent contributions. Others do not. Following are descriptions of some of the ways you can set up an IRA. Before deciding on any one, you should get specific information from the institution you are considering.

1. *Banks.* Most offer a variety of options patterned on the conventional certificate of deposit. Options involve the kind of interest, the amount of interest, and the length of time of the certificate. Some offer variable

4. *Mutual funds.* In this case you buy shares in a pool of money that is invested in securities chosen by professional money managers. In some mutual funds, your IRA is in a money market fund, where the investment is in short-term securities and the rate of return varies daily. In others, the investment is in stocks and bonds, some in blue chip companies, others in more risky emerging companies. As your investment objectives change, you may move your IRA from one mutual fund to another. In order to do this, many people choose a company that operates several funds. Most funds require a minimum deposit, some as low as $100. Usually a yearly maintenance fee of $2 to $10 is charged.

5. *Investment brokers.* These offer the widest range of IRAs. You can build your own portfolio, using a "self-directed" plan. You make the decisions on investing in stocks, bonds, mutual funds, unit investment trusts, or limited real estate partnerships. Each time you buy or sell, you pay commissions. There are also administrative fees. Most brokers expect you to invest the entire $2,000 at one time and it is really best to accumulate $10,000 to $15,000 before you start to self-direct.

> *Remember:* Investing in securities carries the risk of loss as well as gain, but it is the most flexible IRA route you can choose.

To summarize: It is never too soon to start an IRA. The commitment is long-term, but well worth it, especially in view of current widespread concern over the future of Social Security, pension plans, and inflation.

o   o   o

IF THE MIDS CONTINUE THEIR IRAs . . .

Since their adjusted gross income is above $50,000, they will not be able to deduct their $4,000 in IRA contributions. They want to save for retirement. Let's say they each put in $2,000 for eight years. They will each have contributed an additional $16,000. Marty's account will contain nearly $46,300 and Mary's $41,000 assuming an 8 percent rate. This fulfills nearly 30 percent of the Mids' goal of accumulating $300,000 in eight years. (See chapter 2 on goals.)

o   o   o

For the self-employed: Keogh plan

Any self-employed person should consider starting a Keogh plan as a nest egg for retirement. In all respects, Keogh has the same rules and regulations as an IRA, with one important exception: You may contribute as much as $30,000, or 20 percent of income (whichever is less) each year.

or floating interest; others do not, so you should compare interest rates offered by different institutions. In most, you can open the account with as little as $100.

2. *Credit unions.* Most credit unions design their IRAs to fit the size and nature of the union. The rate of interest is set by the board of directors. Your initial deposit may be quite low, and deposits may be deducted directly from your paycheck if your employer is willing to extend such a benefit. This means real convenience for you.

3. *Insurance companies.* An IRA set up with an insurance company is an annuity. A minimum rate of interest will be fixed through the years, possibly high in the early years, then lower as time goes on. You may have to pay an annual fee and sales costs, with a sizable penalty if you withdraw the money prematurely (probably even higher if you withdraw in the early years of the policy).

The IRA and the Keogh plan are bonuses given by the government. They may be the most important keys to maintaining your lifestyle during retirement. They can help to mend the broken promise of retirement, but only if you make the effort to learn about them, analyze your own needs, ask questions, understand the options, and be aware of changes in Social Security and pensions law.

o   o   o

THE ELDERS' BROKEN PROMISE

The broken promise of retirement. It *was* a promise to the Elders. Society promised them that if they saved and invested, they would be able to retire in comfort and with a standard of living they were accustomed to.

The Mids have had no such promise. They have seen what has happened to their parents and know that during the working years still ahead they must plan to help themselves—something that their parents never felt they had to do. In addition to Social Security and a pension plan, they must have another plan.

o   o   o

THE MID'S PLAN FOR RETIREMENT

The Mids have decided to develop a specific retirement plan. They are aware that with an inflation rate of 5 percent, they will need $1.79 in 2003 to buy what a dollar will purchase today.

Marty plans to increase the amount he is contributing to his 401(k) from 7 percent to 10 percent of his salary.

Will the Mids reach their goal of accumulating $300,000 by the time Marty retires?

The company will deduct $252 from his paycheck every two weeks. With his employer continuing to put in 50 cents for every dollar Marty puts in, the 401(k) will be worth $197,000 in 2003.

The Mids will each continue with their IRAs, contributing $2,000 each year. The amount they will have available at retirement will be:

Mary's IRA	$41,000 (assuming 8% return)
Marty's IRA	46,300 (assuming 8% return)
Marty's 401(k)	197,000
Mary's 403(b)	72,500
	$356,800

They will exceed their $300,000 goal. But the plan is based on Marty's working until he is 65. He is concerned that he might be offered an early retirement package. The company has been offering enhancements to pensions in order to make early retirement attractive to employees. The deal is this: five years are added to both the age and the length of service. So Marty, who is now 57 and has worked for his company for 27 years, would be considered 62 with 32 years of service. His monthly pension would be about 13 percent less than he now gets as salary. He would also get a severance check. But still—he figures things might be tight until he can collect Social Security at age 62. He might look for part-time work that uses his accounting and computer skills.

The Mids have talked about inflation and tried to grapple with it. They figure it is here to stay and must be part of their financial planning. From their letters and phone chats with the Elders, they have seen how it can hit retired people, especially since many of their expenses, such as food, transportation, medical costs, and utilities, are not inflation proof. They have sensed the anger and frustration of the Elders as their expenses rise and their retirement income stays the same.

Because they want to know how vulnerable they will be, the Mids are figuring out their own inflation index. Here's how they do it: Taking their total budget figure, they subtract the one-time home improvement expense. This gives them $55,448 annually. They then consider all current expenditures in the budget to see which are not inflationary, such as mortgage payments, loan repayments, or IRA contributions that do not change with time. The total affected by inflation comes to $36,699. They divide $36,699 by $45,208 to get an inflation index of 8 percent.

This formula, which is more accurate than government figures, means that they must keep their income and savings growing by at least 8 percent to keep abreast of inflation.

Since they have eight years to go before retirement, and knowing that right now they need little income from investments, they will be careful to make investments that are expected to increase in value and that can be converted into income-producing assets when they retire. All this gives them a hedge against inflation, which they know is likely to cut down on the purchasing power of their projected retirement income.

To accomplish this they will work closely with a professional investment adviser, and they will keep a close watch on their investments. They know the problems the Elders have run into and they intend to avoid the trap of noninvolvement.

○   ○   ○

Retirement planning requires discipline. It is not simple, for it involves projection of income and expenses. As you near retirement age, you must take into account interest rates, inflation, changes in the economy and in retirement benefits. The sooner you do it, the more likely you will enjoy those golden retirement years.

Now that you have looked at Social Security and pension plans, the question is: Will you have enough to live on when you retire? Will you need additional income?

The next step is to look at your assets and see if they can produce more income for you. You may have more alternatives than you think you have.

Warning: Law on 401(k) withholding

A law that went into effect January 1, 1993, may be important to you if you retire or change jobs and want to take a lump-sum distribution from your 401(k) or other qualified plan. Your employer is required to withhold 20 percent of the funds in your account and send it to the Internal Revenue Service. If within 60 days you deposit your remaining 80 percent in an IRA or other tax-deferred account *and add to it—from some other source—an amount equal to the 20 percent withheld*, you can then get the IRS to refund the 20 percent it took. How? By claiming additional allowances on Form W-4, so that you reduce your estimated tax payments, or by waiting until you get a refund on your tax return the following year. Either way, the government gets to use 20 percent of your money, without paying you interest, in the interim.

To avoid this procedure, do not take the lump-sum payment. Have your employer transfer the money directly to another trustee account—either at your new place of employment or with a bank or mutual fund or wherever you wish to put it. Talk with your accountant. Make your decisions *before* you leave the company.

The reason for this ruling is that the government wants you to roll over funds, especially if you are younger and changing jobs. It wants to discourage you from spending the money that is being put away for your retirement.

EVALUATING YOUR ASSETS TO MAKE THEM FIT

○　　○　　○　　○

"How can we get more income from our income-producing assets?"

"Is it costing us too much to maintain our largest non-income-producing asset—our home?"

"Is each of our investments doing the best it can—for us?"

"Those collectibles we have that produce no income: Should we sell some and invest the money?"

○　　○　　○

These are the kinds of questions that come up when you start evaluating whether your assets meet the Financial Fitness test. Now that you have analyzed your lifestyle and worked out your priorities, you should begin to consider your assets.

When, or how often, should you evaluate assets? The answer is, every couple of years at least, and more often if you have any major changes in lifestyle, family situation (such as children who have left the nest), or in the assets themselves.

A good reason for not evaluating your assets until now is the fact that assets usually cost you something—unless you inherit them—and it's important to work out your budget first.

Income is the key word when you talk about assets. Some *assets* produce income. Some do not. Always the hope is that assets that are not producing income right now will keep quietly growing until the day you sell or liquidate them. One hopes they are *appreciating*.

Different needs at various stages of your life dictate what you want assets to do for you. There are times when income from wages or salary is adequate—and times when it is not. When your children are in college or when you are in retirement, income from salary or from a pension may not be enough. Income from assets will then be extremely valuable.

View assets three ways

When you look at assets, you need three viewpoints: one of your assets, one of your insurance plans, one of your retirement program. If assets are large, insurance plans and retirement programs can be smaller. If assets are small, insurance and retirement programs should be larger. No two cases are alike, so you have to size up all the angles.

If you are like most young couples or young singles, the chances are you have no income-producing assets. The two of you are working, producing two salaries, and spending as much as you can on non-income-producing assets such as furniture, house, or collectibles. So this is the time to buy insurance, while young rates apply, and let cash surrender values start to build up—they will be future assets.

When a young couple makes the commitment to buy their first home, their net worth picture changes dramatically. From this point on, they add to personal possessions with furniture and other household possessions, often without keeping a tight rein on credit. Yet this is the very time when planning should be made for assets that will pay for college expenses in 15 or 20 years. (See chapter 2 on goals and chapter 6 on credit.)

With income increasing as the family grows in age, size, and number, insurance and its cash values should be looked at every few years. Investments should be watched more closely and bought for growth when the children are young, then realigned to produce more income as the college years approach.

Few people can pay college expenses out of salary. But if you have built up income-producing assets over the years, they can help meet this gigantic expenditure. And, before you start borrowing at high interest rates to pay for college, you may be pleasantly surprised by what you have built up over those 15 or 20 years.

When the kids move out

The empty-nest period brings another change. The years between the end of the children's education and retirement is the time to invest again for growth and appreciation and to make plans for the retirement years. If Mom returns to the work force, two incomes can now help build up the assets, especially with expenses dropping as the children move out on their own. (Surprise! Even the electricity bill drops a little when children no longer run hair dryers and stereos are not turned on 24 hours a day.) At this point, salaries should once again pay living expenses and leave some extra to build up assets.

The idea now will be to invest for capital appreciation that can be converted into actual income during the retirement years. Credit obligations should be avoided or kept to a minimum.

Now your Net Worth Statement will tell you what your assets are, and your Budget sheets will tell the cost of maintaining them.

There is never any real harm in selling off certain assets. You earned the money to buy them in the first place. You are not stuck with them forever. Must you stay in the same house, for instance, even if it has empty rooms? Now that your children are earning their own way, do you really need the same high insurance coverage you bought when they were in grade school? You have a number of options at this point, many of which we looked at in chapter 12 on retirement. Look at the Elders as an example.

Use the **Assets Evaluation Worksheet** to size up your income-producing and non-income-producing assets.

Income-producing assets

Pick up current assets (checking and savings accounts, securities, and so on) from your Net Worth Statement. (See pages 31–32.) Note that except for broker's fees or commissions, these cost you nothing to own or maintain. Fill in annual income from the "sources of income" section of your Budget sheet; yields should come from your Record-keeping sheets.

Non-income-producing assets

Fill in your real estate, personal property, and other long-term assets here. Don't forget such items as fine art and coin and stamp collections. In this area you do have annual costs of ownership: taxes, utilities, insurance, and maintenance on the house; insurance premiums on personal property such as a car or boat. The costs of owning these assets come from your fixed expenses budget.

Net sale value is the amount you would get if you sold a particular asset; the market value of your house, for example, minus such costs of selling as real estate commission, legal fees, and so on. There may also be a fee when you sell collectibles.

Analyzing assets in retirement

Your Assets Evaluation Worksheets can really prove their worth when you contemplate retirement. They sum up your acquisitions over the past 35 or 40 years—and raise many questions. They help you to look closely at each and every asset and think objectively about it. Should your assets, whether income-producing or non-income-producing, be exchanged for something that would produce additional income or benefit you in some other way?

People of retirement age do not easily change their way of thinking about money matters. After 30 or 40 years of investing in "safe" institutions such as passbook savings, they are not about to go into money market funds. Resisting change is easy. "I've been doing it this way for 35 years" . . . "I don't like it" . . . "It won't work—I know" . . . "It's too late to make changes now" . . . "It's not practical."

Just the opposite is true: It is highly practical to take hard-earned dollars out of a low-income-producing account and let them earn more for you. In fact, it is imperative.

The means for creating a better lifestyle—for you, not for your heirs—is probably right under your nose. Look at your assets. What alternatives do they offer? Can you get those that are already producing income to produce *more*? Do you keep too much cash in a checking account that pays no interest? Move it into a savings account, then transfer money to checking only when you really need to.

Have you got too much in a low-interest-yielding savings account? Buy a certificate of deposit or move it into a money market fund that will produce more income. Find the highest interest rates that are paid without tying up the money for extremely long periods (you should keep it reasonably available in case you need it).

Look at the stocks and bonds you bought some years back. Are they low-income investments? Do you have low-interest bonds sitting around? Countless people do. Often a safe deposit box reveals mature Series E bonds that have been forgotten. Some people think they shouldn't sell a stock because "we bought it so cheaply years ago and if we sell we have to pay taxes on it." Having to pay taxes should not be a deterrent to selling.

Getting more income from assets

Let's look at some ways that you can make assets produce more income.

We'll start with stocks. Say you have stocks that originally cost $10,000. You sell them now for $25,000. The gain is $15,000. You will have to pay a tax on the gain.

Suppose these stocks have been yielding 5 percent annually. The income would be $1,250. By selling the stocks you could have $21,570 available to reinvest, assuming you are paying tax at the 23 percent rate. If you put it into investments paying 8 percent, your income would be $1,725 or $476 more than you were getting before.

You may also have a loss that can give you an advantage. Many people in the 1950s and 1960s bought long-term corporate bonds which yield 5 percent. With higher interest rates such bonds may be worth less. You may even own a stock that is actually worth less on the open market than when you bought it. You can thus take a loss by selling such stocks and bonds.

Suppose you bought a corporate bond for $10,000 and it is now worth only $7,500 on the market. That is a loss of $2,500. You can apply that loss to your $15,000 gain from the sale of stocks, reducing your total gain to $12,500. Paying taxes should not be a deterrent to selling stocks and bonds.

What about assets that are not producing income? What are your choices with them? Is there a way to invest for more income? How can you turn an asset that costs a lot to own into an asset that produces income? Check out the following and please don't close your eyes and say, "No, I won't sell that," until you've read it.

1. *Your home.* The house is probably your largest investment, yet it also carries heavy expenses—fuel, taxes, insurance, upkeep. Are they getting you down? Have you had it with the crabgrass? Have you let the new roof you need go by the board because it is too expensive? Do you and your mate rattle around inside the house? When you get right down to it, is too much of your money tied up in this non-income-producing asset?

Look around in your area at the alternatives that might be suitable. Depending on where you live you might:

- Sell the house and invest in another, smaller house. You would have some money left over to invest in other ways. Or, if the new cost were about the same as the old, you would still gain because upkeep on the new, smaller house would be less.
- Sell and try a mobile home if you live in an area where they are suitable and popular.
- Sell and invest the money; use the income to pay rent.

Suppose you sell the house for $80,000 and buy a small condominium for $50,000. If you invest the remaining $30,000 at 8 percent, it will produce $2,400 in additional yearly income. You might start saving on expenses if the condo costs less to maintain. Or you might invest the entire $80,000 at 8 percent, producing an income of $6,400 a year, which can pay rent of $533 per month. If you rent for less, more income can be produced.

A caution on selling your house. Remember that there will be selling expenses: real estate commission, closing fees, moving expenses (which are high), such miscellaneous expenses as carpeting or drapes in the new place, and unforeseen expenses. Don't let any of these surprise you.

Another warning: If you are thinking about a major geographic move, give the place a trial at its worst time of the year. If you think Florida or the sunbelt Southwest is the place to spend your retirement, basking in hot February sunshine while those back home shiver and shake in the cold, go down there in July and see how you make out in 110 degrees. Some like it fine. Some find out too late that they should have stayed where they were.

There's another aspect to the retirement move, too. You'll want to have airfare to visit children and grandchildren. You might think right now that they will come to you, but it is doubtful that they will come frequently enough to satisfy your longing to see them, and the expense might be more than they can handle at this stage in their lives.

2. *Recreational property.* The cottage at the lake or shore, the ski hut in New England or northern Michigan—are you using it as much as you once did? With the children off in other areas, pursuing other interests, is it a justifiable expense? Chances are it is difficult to rent (and if you do rent it, you must manage its maintenance by remote control, which is no fun) and you are paying insurance and property taxes and getting little out of it.

If that sounds like *your* "second home," it is time to sell it and reinvest the proceeds to produce income.

3. *Cash value life insurance.* Do you really need the insurance? Is it paid up, or are you still writing checks for premiums? Every policy has a table of guaranteed values. For instance, for a $10,000 policy purchased at age 35, the following are some of the options available at age 65:

a. Cancel the policy. Say you have a $10,000 policy in force. The cash surrender value is $5,504, so if you surrender it now your wife would lose $4,496 if she were widowed. But if you surrender it you will save $230 annually on the premium. You will invest the $5,504 at 10 percent, producing $504 a year, and with the premium saving of $230 that will give you $734 per year you do not have now.

b. Borrow on the policy. Say you borrow the full amount of cash value: $5,504. This would leave $4,496 of insurance in force. However, you must still pay the $230 premium, and you will have to pay interest to borrow the $5,504, probably $275 a year. So between paying the premium and paying the interest, your income from the investment would be reduced to $229—surely an expensive way to keep $4,496 of insurance in force.

c. Take out a reduced paid-up policy. The $10,000 might provide about $7,860 in paid-up insurance. You would still have insurance, but it would be a smaller policy. Your only saving is the $230 annual premium.

d. Use cash value to buy a term policy. The table of guaranteed values will tell you the length of the term in years, months, and days. For instance, $10,000 of cash value at age 65 might buy 16 years and 147 days of term coverage. If you should live longer than that, the policy would be finished and you would be on your own with no coverage.

e. Purchase an annuity. Your policy probably also tells how large an annuity you may buy for each $1,000 of cash value. If an annuity is what you want, shop around for the best deal. You do not have to buy it from your present insurance company; nothing prohibits you from cashing in the policy and taking the money elsewhere if you can get more per $1,000.

4. *Collectibles.* Fine art, silver and gold, books, musical instruments, antique autos, rare coins and stamps,

Exhibit 18
DIPPING INTO YOUR NEST EGG

STARTING WITH A LUMP SUM OF . . .	. . . YOU CAN WITHDRAW THIS MUCH EACH MONTH FOR THE STATED NUMBER OF YEARS, REDUCING THE NEST EGG TO ZERO					. . . OR YOU CAN WITHDRAW THIS MUCH EACH MONTH AND ALWAYS HAVE THE ORIGINAL NEST EGG INTACT.
	10 YRS.	15 YRS.	20 YRS.	25 YRS.	30 YRS.	
$ 10,000	$ 116	$ 89	$68	$ 70	$ 66	$ 59
15,000	174	134	116	106	99	88
20,000	232	179	155	141	133	118
25,000	290	224	193	176	166	142
30,000	348	269	232	212	199	179
40,000	464	359	310	282	266	237
50,000	580	448	386	352	332	285
60,000	696	538	464	424	398	360
80,000	928	718	620	564	532	467
100,000	1,160	896	772	704	668	585

Worksheet XV: Mr. & Mrs. Elder
ASSETS EVALUATION

INCOME-PRODUCING ASSETS CURRENT ASSETS	NET SALE VALUE	ANNUAL INCOME (From Budget)	% YIELD (Income ÷ Market Value)	ANNUAL COST OF OWNERSHIP (From Budget)
Checking Accounts	$500	0	0	
Savings Accounts				
Credit Union Accounts				
Money Market Funds	$5,000	$150	3%	
Certificates of Deposit	$36,000	$1,800	5%	
Treasury Bills				
Treasury Notes				
Securities				
Stocks	$29,790	$1,544	5.1%	
Bonds				
Mutual Funds				
Total	$71,290	$3,494	5%	
NON-INCOME-PRODUCING				
Personal Residence	$40,000			$2,776
Recreational Property				
Cash Value Life Insurance				
Business Interests				
Home Furnishings	$10,000			
Automobiles	$5,000			$800
Jewelry	$10,000			
Antiques—Fine Art				
Coin Collection				
Stamp Collection				
Total	$65,000			$3,576

antique furniture—you name it, none produces income. All of them require care and insurance, though. Some also need polishing regularly.

Are your collectibles still giving you the satisfaction they once did? Are you holding onto them "for the children"? Are some of them locked away in vaults or safe deposit boxes because our robbery-prone society makes them vulnerable at home?

In a word, are you trapped by possessions?

The younger generation often says: Pare down. Some younger people have no interest in polishing silver or maintaining antiques. If you are holding onto

Worksheet XV: Yours
ASSETS EVALUATION

INCOME-PRODUCING ASSETS CURRENT ASSETS	NET SALE VALUE	ANNUAL INCOME (From Budget)	% YIELD (Income ÷ Market Value)	ANNUAL COST OF OWNERSHIP (From Budget)
Checking Accounts				
Savings Accounts				
Credit Union Accounts				
Money Market Funds				
Certificates of Deposit				
Treasury Bills				
Treasury Notes				
Securities				
Stocks				
Bonds				
Mutual Funds				
Total				
NON-INCOME-PRODUCING				
Personal Residence				
Recreational Property				
Cash Value Life Insurance				
Business Interests				
Home Furnishings				
Automobiles				
Jewelry				
Antiques—Fine Art				
Coin Collection				
Stamp Collection				
Total				

collectibles for your children's sake, the best thing to do is talk it over with them frankly. Find out if they are really interested in something that has sentimental but not intrinsic value. You may be in for a surprise.

Then, after you have discussed it with them, remember that only *you* can decide between the possible income that could be derived from selling your collectibles and investing the money, and the sentimental value of holding on to them.

If you decide to sell, get appraisals. Do your homework. Silver and gold, of course, are not priced as high as they were a few years ago, but don't let that stop you.

(In fact, during the "silver rush" many people accepted the silver content value but failed to get the antique value on items they sold; in their greed over high silver prices, they actually got less than they should have.)

The question of holding things for the children brings up the larger question of what you leave for your heirs.

Who says never invade principal?

As you get into retirement, it is important to remember that *you are responsible for yourself*—for your own interests. There is no reason to feel guilty about how much you are leaving or not leaving to children and grandchildren. What is important now is to maintain your purchasing power in the face of inflation's power to eat away at the value of the dollar.

Many who are currently at retirement age grew up in the school that says it is all right to live off income from investments but the principal should never be touched. Preservation of capital, that's the most impor-

tant thing, they say. But isn't the quality of life you are living just as important as the preservation of capital? What is wrong with using a certain percentage of your capital every year? If you used 3 percent a year, it would take you 33 years to use up a given amount of capital even if the remaining balance were not earning interest over the years.

You should find out your life expectancy from the insurance charts. For the average man of 68, it is 12 years. Suppose you doubled that to 24 years and decided to use a certain percentage of capital each year for 24 years? To many, such thinking is heresy. Yet such changed thinking could help prevent inflation's bite on your retirement income and could improve your basic standard of living.

What is important is to realize that only you know your needs. Do the paperwork. Talk to advisers and make your needs known to them. Be frank with sons and daughters. And, when necessary, shed guilt—as well as gilt. (See Exhibit 18.)

FINANCIAL FITNESS FOR WOMEN ON THEIR OWN

○   ○   ○   ○

"What household bills do I need to pay now?"

"Maybe I should sell the house right away . . ."

"Am I still covered under his medical insurance?"

"Why didn't we ever talk about these things?"

○   ○   ○

The average widow in this country is 56 years old. She is destined to spend 20 years on her own. Eighty percent of all women will live alone at some point in their lives.

Despite these surprising statistics (more like staggering, if you suddenly find that you are one of them), most women have not been involved in family finances. They have handled household money and everyday expenses, yes, but few have a solid grasp of insurance matters, taxes, or pensions, or know the whereabouts of valuable papers or loan agreements. Traditionally women have felt, and been encouraged to feel, that someone will take care of them, make all the decisions, and see that everything turns out all right.

It seldom happens that way. All too frequently, after a divorce or the death of a spouse, a woman finds herself not only in emotional turmoil but faced with sudden and confusing financial responsibilities. Well-meaning friends and family give her advice and, willy-nilly, she often follows.

In fact, just the opposite should happen. Since, on average, women outlive men, they should learn financial responsibility early on—not only the mechanics of paying bills, but how to handle all the decisions that affect their financial security. Many of the decisions made before a woman is living alone will affect her afterward, yet when a husband says, "Sign here, dear," and offers a contract, tax return, or other financial obligation, many a wife obligingly takes pen in hand and never thinks to read or query the document.

Signing anything without bothering to read it is a mistake. When you get a chance to look over an income tax return, study it; you can learn a great deal about your own financial situation. When you sign a contract or agreement, read it thoroughly, for once you have signed it you will be just as liable as your husband for its consequences.

Blame English common law—and Blackstone

How did the system ever get this way? It began with English common law, on which our legal system is based, and with Blackstone, who codified common law. He said, "Husband and wife are one . . . that one is the husband."

Before the Industrial Revolution, women were an integral part of what is now called "cottage industry."

The home was the factory. But all money that was earned was turned over to the husband—it belonged to him. A century or so ago, an early female physician who was owed payments for her services had to have her husband go to court to get the money because legally it belonged to him.

With the Industrial Revolution, the family changed from a unit of production to a unit of consumption. The workplace moved out of the home, leaving most wives behind. A husband who could not support wife and family was considered a failure and only poor and immigrant wives took jobs (at extremely low wages, by the way) to support the family.

The leisure class of women needed to worry about little outside the household. Because financial transactions were considered too complicated for women to manage, husbands arranged for others to take control of their money when they died, on behalf of their wives. Even though money and property came to be in their names, women were usually relieved of the duties and responsibilities of financial transactions.

In fact, it was only as recently as January 1, 1980, that Louisiana husbands were stripped of their status as "head and master" of the household. Up until then, a husband could sell the house or the car, borrow money, or make just about any financial deal without his wife's permission and with money that was, in truth, his wife's as much as his.

The disillusionment of divorce

Chances are that a divorced woman will have to get used to downward mobility, for it is almost impossible for two separate parts of a family to maintain the lifestyle they had when they were one.

If you have taken financial security for granted, never knew what your husband's income was, never handled any finances more complicated than the grocery money and maybe the regular monthly bills, readjustment can be rough. For the first time, you may be confronted with a limited fixed income from alimony or child support and with responsibility for the security of your children and yourself.

As a divorced woman, you must set goals and priorities that are realistic for you and your family. You must budget carefully. If you are returning to work but have young children, you must arrange for child care. If you are working, your employer may provide reasonably good medical coverage through a group plan; if you are not working, you will need your own medical plan.

Use this book to plan your financial situation as a single person. Be realistic about your goals and spending, and look beyond today. Remember that every investment decision is *your* decision.

A widow faces countless questions

The widow who best handles her inheritance is the one who has been involved in family financial matters all along, doing more than just writing checks and handling the household budget. But such financially fit women are in the minority.

Most widows are confronted not only with grief but with financial matters of which they know very little. Questions arise daily: How do I start Social Security payments coming? Where is the key to the safe deposit box? Which bills should I pay now? Should I take the lump-sum payment the insurance company is offering? Should I sell the house right away? How does his pension plan work—and do I get benefits under it? What about medical insurance?

If you are newly widowed, make no financial decisions for at least six months to a year. It takes that long to determine what your needs are going to be. Meantime, hold on to your inheritance. Later, when things settle down, make educated decisions.

How can a woman become financially fit?

Clearly, it is essential for a woman to learn how she will handle money if and when she lives alone. The key to learning is open communication between spouses. However, if a husband has had total control of the finances and is unwilling to let go of the power, this can be a problem.

Here are some important points a couple should discuss and steps they should take.

1. Talk about how the woman will survive if the husband dies.
2. Be sure the wife knows where all important papers are kept.
3. Make a point of having the wife meet the husband's financial advisers and get to know them. (She may ultimately find that they are not the ones she wants to keep, but they should be consulted by a widow before she makes any major decisions.)
4. The wife should open her own checking account. If she is working, her earnings can go into that account and she can take responsibility for certain agreed-upon expenditures. If she is a homemaker, and not working, her husband should give her a certain amount each payday for groceries and other household expenses. The budget worksheets in this book can help determine the right amount. (With her own checkbook and responsibilities, a woman learns what money can and cannot do and, if she manages well, what is left over is hers to blow. As long as there is food on the table and bills are paid, no woman should

have to report to anyone or account for where the money is going.)

5. The wife should also establish her own credit history. This can be difficult, sometimes almost impossible, to do after a divorce or the death of a husband.
6. The wife should also get into the habit of reading the financial pages of the newspaper and the monthly financial magazines.
7. The husband and wife together should attend some classes on financial planning.
8. Both should get involved and older children should be included, too. Finances should be a family matter.

o   o   o

IF MRS. ELDER IS WIDOWED . . .

Gertrude Elder would lose her Social Security payment each month, but would continue to collect her late husband's. She would receive $15,000 from his life insurance policy, and would choose to take it in a lump sum so it could be invested. Each month, she would have:

His Social Security	$950	
Income from investments they made before he died	291	
Income from $15,000 life insurance (invested at 4 percent)	50	
1/2 his pension	188	
Total	$1,479	(or $653 less than the Eders' retirement income before he died)

Except for taking the lump-sum life insurance payment, Gertrude Elder should wait at least six months to a year before making any decisions. During this time, she should consider whether to realign her investments for a higher yield. She might also think about whether to live nearer to town. As one widow said, "If and when I move, I've got to be near public transportation. As I get older, I might not be able to drive."

o   o   o

WHAT IF MARTY MID DIES? . . .

From Mr. Mid's How Much Life Insurance Worksheet on page 104, we know that if Mary Mid is widowed, she will have available income of $53,250. This will cover her needs.

Mary should not use the insurance money to pay off the mortgage. Her monthly payments are small, the interest is deductible on her income tax return, and is only 8 percent—low enough to hold onto these days. She can make more by investing the insurance money. (Of course, many people purchase mortgage insurance through the bank or other lending institution that provided the mortgage, naming them as beneficiary; such insurance pays off the mortgage whether you like it or not.)

With $125,000 of insurance coming to her, she will have to consider whether to take one of the options the company offers or accept the lump sum and invest it. Wisely invested her $125,000 could make a big difference not only now but during her own retirement years.

Mary can work until she is 65, or even beyond that age. When she reaches 65, she can start receiving 100 percent of Marty's Social Security benefits. If she elects to start the benefits earlier, between ages 60 and 65, the amount of each payment will be smaller. She must investigate whether Social Security might pay her more based on her own work record than it pays based on Marty's. Chances are it will not, because Mary's earnings have been less than the maximum earnings level that Social Security uses, as she started work only when her first child went off to college.

Mary will be smart also to check in with Marty's employer to find out if she can receive his pension benefit in a lump sum. If she can, she will then be able to take the money from his 401(k) plan and roll it over into an Individual Retirement Account (IRA), and, if she needs to, start withdrawals when she is 59½. If, however, she does not need it, she can let the account continue to accumulate on a tax-deferred basis until she is 70½. In addition, she has her own 401(k) and IRA. She plans to continue to make contributions to both of them.

The key point is that Mary must know her options—by getting involved—before she comes to a decision. And she must not let anyone rush her.

o   o   o

Women must take on their own financial management. They must seek out information and training, broaden their horizons, and take responsibility for their actions, so they are ready if and when they have to live alone. Chances are great that most women will have to live alone at some time during their adult lives.

It could happen to you.

LET'S FACE IT, WHAT WILL YOU LEAVE BEHIND? YOUR WILL

○   ○   ○   ○

"Should my wife have a will?"

"Just what is 'probate,' anyway?"

"Estate planning? That's for rich people, isn't it?"

"How can I be sure people will get what I want them to get?"

○   ○   ○

The purpose of a will is to make certain that your property goes where you want it to go after you die. It is your means of making decisions, putting them on paper, and seeing to it that the paper becomes a legal document that no one can argue with.

If you die without a will, you will be said to have died "intestate." In that case, the state in which you lived immediately before death becomes responsible for deciding who gets your property. Its decisions may or may not fit the ideas you had, but only those left behind will know that. Most likely, it will not agree with what you had thought should be done, for the possibilities of inequities are great.

Just as this book has been created to give you control over your money, your will gives you control over not only who gets what, but how and when. It conserves and distributes your estate the way you want it done. It

names guardians for any minor children you leave behind. (Nothing is worse than a family squabble over who is to take care of children; often a split occurs, with elderly grandparents taking charge and with the children enduring still another turnaround when the grandparents die.)

"Estate" is another of those bugaboo words. It simply means everything you own: your money, your house and land, all your worldly possessions. Estate planning is planning for what becomes of it all. It is really nothing more than caring for those who will survive you. If you have followed this book's instructions, you are well on your way to estate planning already, because:

- You have your papers and records in order.
- You know your assets and who owns what.
- You understand income and expenses.
- You know how much life insurance you have —and need.
- You know about your Social Security benefits and pension benefits.

Your will should be reviewed regularly, at least every five years. Here are some of the reasons a will may need to be updated:

- the birth of a child
- the death of a beneficiary or of the executor (the person you have chosen to handle the details of the will when you die)
- marriage or divorce
- a move to a different state, where the laws may be different
- a major change in your financial circumstances
- new laws affecting estates

Do women need wills?
Yes. Women have property of their own. If nothing else, they usually have personal property, such as jewelry and heirlooms, that they want to pass on to a child or a grandchild. In addition, they usually inherit property from their husbands.

If a woman does not have her own will at the time when her husband dies, she should immediately make one. Obviously this is a difficult chore just after the death of a husband, though. It is much better to make a will when your husband makes his, and then to make changes, as needed, six months or more after his death.

There is another important aspect to a wife's will: It should name the same guardians for the children as the husband's will names. This will avoid a custody fight if husband and wife die at the same time.

Consult a lawyer
Even if you think you don't have enough worldly goods to justify making a will, take a look around you. Insurance policies, company benefits, your home, investments, household furnishings—all may add up to more of an estate than you may have thought you had.

You should have an attorney draw up your will. A good lawyer will know your state's laws, and will avoid problems that you might create by making your own homemade will. To save his or her time, and your money:

- Have ready a list of your assets (from your Net Worth Statement).
- Choose an executor, a friend or relative whom you trust. This person will be fully responsible for seeing your will through probate and making sure your estate is disposed of. This person should live nearby. If he or she dies, you must revise your will to name another.
- Choose a guardian for minor children. Guardians must provide proper care as well as manage money for the children.

Caution: Do not get into the embarrassing or awkward position of naming a guardian without first approaching the candidate on the subject.

- Decide how you want your estate distributed (that is, who gets what).

Finally, ask your attorney to keep the original signed copies of your will, and your spouse's, in his safe. Keep copies in your files at home.

Another dreaded word: probate
Your estate is either of two types: probate and/or taxable. If an asset is jointly owned and does not go through the probate process, it may nevertheless be part of the taxable estate. Since federal estate and gift tax laws frequently change, and since state laws vary greatly, you should ask your lawyer to discuss and explain what happens to a taxable estate where you live.

The function of probate court is to authorize and supervise the payment of funeral expenses, taxes, and debts owed by the person who dies, and to authorize the cost of administering the estate (usually your executor is paid for handling your estate). The court then sees that any remaining property is distributed to the beneficiaries or to those who are entitled to it.

The executor works under the court's supervision and scrutiny. If you do not have a will, the court—acting for the state—will name an administrator.

The probate procedure includes:

1. Probating the will. Application is made for probate of the will, which is filed with the court and declared valid. The court approves the executor named in the will, or names an administrator.
2. Posting of a bond by the executor or administrator (unless your will waives the requirement). The amount of the bond will depend on the size of the estate.
3. Inventory of all assets that are owned in your name *alone*. This is needed to determine whether your estate is solvent. Assets must be evaluated. Appraisers will be called in to judge the value of real estate and certain collectibles such as coins, jewelry, and so on. An up-to-date Net Worth Statement can be a great aid at this point.
4. Advertising for claims against the estate. This is in case any unknown debts are "out there" somewhere. The notice will specify that all claims must be submitted within a stated period of time, otherwise they need not be honored. At the same time all recent and outstanding bills, such as funeral or medical expenses, are paid.
5. Filing of state and federal tax forms, as required by various laws, and payment of the taxes.

6. Final accounting and distribution of the remaining estate to those named in the will.

That, in simple terms, is the probate procedure. It involves certain time limits set by state law (the inventory, for example, must be completed within a certain time). The entire procedure can take anywhere from nine months to two or three years, depending on the complexity of the will, size of the estate, and number of beneficiaries.

> *Note*: Once a will has been probated, it is a matter of public record. For this reason, many people prefer to establish trusts; they are not made public.

What about jointly held property?

Any property that is jointly held is not included in the probate procedure. While jointly held property used to entail decided disadvantages, the Economic Recovery Tax Act of 1981 changed the law so that for federal estate tax purposes it does not make much difference today whether or not property is jointly held. A spouse may leave the surviving spouse an unlimited amount of property without its being taxed. It will be taxed only when the surviving spouse dies, but as the taxable amount decreases each year, fewer and fewer people are being affected.

State inheritance tax laws are different. No two states seem to be alike. Many have neglected to make changes that coincide with the federal law.

Jointly held property has certain advantages, including:

- It passes immediately to the survivor, staying out of probate.
- It is easy to set up.
- It assures an inheritance for a spouse with no funds of his or her own, because jointly held property cannot be sold without the permission of the other spouse.
- It can eliminate ancillary probate (that is, probate in another state). This is important, for instance, if you have a vacation home in another state. Be sure the place is jointly held, in order to avoid probate fees.
- Creditors may not be able to seize jointly held property, unless the surviving spouse assumed liability. Again, each state has different laws.

There are some disadvantages to jointly held property, too:

- Signatures of both spouses are needed in order to sell property. This can be a problem in a divorce situation or if one is absent and has not given a power of attorney to the other.
- Either spouse can clean out a joint bank account.
- Property cannot be willed. Neither spouse has any say in how the surviving spouse will dispose of property.
- It may be subject to gift taxes.
- In a large estate, when one spouse dies, jointly held property added to the surviving spouse's estate may swell it to too large a size, making it tax prone. By careful planning while both spouses are living, wills can be drawn to pass certain property directly to the children or grandchildren.
- Accounts can be frozen by banks, preventing the survivor from using the money.

○   ○   ○

THE ELDERS CONCERNED ABOUT INCAPACITY AND ILLNESS . . .

They have decided to see a lawyer about a Power of Attorney (POA), and they have been advised to make sure their POAs "survive incompetency." In most states, this is called a "durable Power of Attorney." If you have it, it empowers another person, whom you have designated, to act on your behalf. In the Elders' case, they have decided to give Marty Mid this durable POA. It means that Marty can handle their affairs from the time the POA is signed, and continue should either one of the Elders become incapacitated. The POA will stay in effect as long as the Elders are alive or until, for some reason, they decide to revoke it. The POA can be set up to limit the powers to certain transactions. For example, the POA might allow Marty to take care of all bank accounts but limit his ability to sell their home.

○   ○   ○

Setting up a "Living Will"

Many states now recognize your right to make a declaration that, in the event you are in a terminal condition and cannot participate in decisions about your treatment, you do not want your life prolonged by the use of any artificial life-support systems.

Laws passed by such states contain suggested declaration forms, and permit you to add personalized directions. You might wish, for example, to consider listing particular treatments to be withheld or withdrawn—for example, "I do not want surgery, antibiotics, mechanical assistance in breathing, cardiopulmonary resuscitation." Some people are opposed to being artificially fed if they are in a terminal condition. Some want to name a "proxy"—someone who can be trusted to make decisions they would make for themselves if they could.

Some want to emphasize their desire to be kept comfortable and free of pain even if it shortens their lives.

Your declaration must be signed in the presence of two witnesses. Usually there are no restrictions as to who may serve as witnesses.

It is important that your family and physician understand and support your wishes about terminal care. Statutes in some states provide immunity from liability to the physician or medical facility personnel who withdraw life support from a dying patient in accordance with the patient's declared wishes, *if the physician has also obtained the informed consent of the patient's next of kin or legal guardian*.

Talk with your physician about your declaration. Give him or her a copy and ask that it be put in your medical records. If you change doctors, make sure the new doctor gets a copy. And talk with family members about it—or with anyone else who might someday have to make decisions about treatment for you. Give them copies, too. Keep your original declaration at home and easily available with your personal papers—not in your safe deposit box.

Unless or until you revoke it, your declaration will stay in effect. But your own, expressed wishes will always supersede it.

For more information, or for the declaration that is authorized in your state, write to the Society for the Right to Die, 250 West 57 Street, New York, New York 10107.

YOUR OWN
BALANCE SHEET

○   ○   ○   ○

Reading this book and doing these exercises should have put you well along the road to financial fitness. Now it is important to maintain your fit condition.

Don't forget how difficult, overwhelming, and unattainable it may have seemed when you set out. And remember, if you are now where you want to be in handling your money matters, you can stay within that framework yet indulge yourself now and then when it is necessary or seems important to do so. What's important is to watch the dollars and cents just as you would watch the calories.

Some readers may find that they must wage a continual war—winning a skirmish here, losing a tactical fight there, but always striving to keep the upper hand. If you are one of those, you may have to do the equivalent of imposing a crash diet after a period of gorging on too many desserts.

You alone

In the first chapter, I said only you can do it. This guidebook is designed to help *you* and to be adaptable to your needs. But only *you* can take charge.

It's somewhat like exercise class. The instructor can show you which exercises will flatten out the tummy —but it is your tummy—and only you can do the exercises and get the results. The same is true of your diet. You write it down, you count the calories, you make your resolutions and line up your intentions—but you must be the one who says "no" when the dessert cart comes rolling by. This book gives you the program to follow, but it can't stop you from overspending.

Staying in good shape

Once you are in good shape, you *can* stay that way. You will have learned to take charge of your financial life— without anxiety and, in fact, enjoying the occasional binge when you know things are under control. What you have now, and can maintain, is a nice freedom of choice about what you are going to do with your money.

Let's review some of the key points of your financial fitness program. Remember that the exercises may be a little different for each person, just as the exercises in a physical fitness program are a little different for each body's needs.

The following is a summary of what you need to continue doing in order to stay in shape. Don't ever forget that a diet or a physical fitness program is built step by step, one on top of another. Nobody ever ran in a marathon, at least not for very far, without at least some stretching exercises, jogging, and short runs. So every phase counts toward your total fitness.

1. Did you establish your goals?

Are they realistic? You wouldn't expect to shed 10 pounds within a week after starting your physical fitness program—and you can't expect to get money matters under control in a matter of days, either. But just as it can be realistic to take off 10 pounds in a month or so without starving to death, it is also possible to reach your financial goals given sufficient time.

(Idea: You might even think about combining physical and financial goals. What if you decided to take off 10 pounds by a certain date and at the same time to save a certain amount to buy a new outfit by that date?)

2. Did you get your records in order?
Before you go on a diet, it's a good idea to clear all those fattening foods out of the kitchen cabinets. Before starting your exercise program, it's vital to have the right running shoes and/or whatever other equipment you may need. Before getting your financial house in order, it is equally important to toss those useless slips of paper into the trash and set up a sound record system that will help you keep track of where things are—and where you are.

3. Did you use the financial worksheets?
Remember, I said your initial Net Worth Statement is the key to knowing where you stand. It's like weighing and measuring yourself before you start your physical fitness program. Where do you stand now?

Your budget is like keeping track of where your diet is going. It is the mirror that reveals *your* bulges. If there comes a moment of truth—when your pants are still too tight—then you have to decide how you can reduce further.

4. Is credit a problem?
Some people manage to continue to binge despite their diets. "I'll buy that irresistible suit now, then lose weight. By three months from now, the suit will look great on me." But a year later the suit is still in the closet with its price tag still attached.

Have credit cards enabled you to stay on a binge? Is your budget bulging with credit payments, month in, month out, so you have little left to spend on other items? If you have decided to kick the habit and get into shape, you will have to go on a really strict diet. As outlined in the chapter on credit, you may even have to go cold turkey—like taking doctor's orders to get in shape and lose weight fast before you get into deep trouble. Heart attack, diabetes—a rough time awaits those who overextend their physical credit. Bankruptcy awaits those who overextend financial credit.

5. What about Social Security and pension plans?
This is a little like assembling the ingredients and the cookbooks that will help you make a healthy and tasty meal even though you are on a diet. Find out what you will be receiving from Social Security and your company pension plan, if there is one. Know now what your financial benefits will be. After all, you wouldn't start a physical fitness program without knowing what the expected benefits were.

6. Have you checked out your assets?
Assets vary at different stages of life. Evaluating them every so often as you go along is like keeping up with your weight control and changing physical exercise needs at different stages of life. No one follows the same program at 45 or 55 that they followed at 25. And no one's assets are the same, or have the same uses, at those different ages. Use asset evaluation as a measuring tool. Know what it is costing you to own those assets and how much income you are receiving from them at any one time.

7. Determine insurance and retirement needs
Should I realign my assets to produce more income? Should I swim five more laps just to stay in the shape I'm now in? Should I establish an IRA? Good questions to ask yourself and to answer regularly.

Whatever its purpose—covering your life, your home, your medical bills or your automobile—your insurance must fit your individual needs. This is like doing specific exercises for the part of your own body that is most out of shape. Don't forget that having too little insurance could be like losing too much weight: It's unhealthy. But paying more than you need to in premiums when you can't justify the coverage can be equally bad.

Also remember that insurance needs change. Adequate coverage today may not be enough tomorrow, when your family has grown or you're earning more or the expensive college years for the kids are at hand. Assess your risks frankly. List them and add them up. Then figure out what insurance you need in order to handle them. Whatever you do, don't be guided by what insurance your neighbor is buying, any more than you would blindly follow your neighbor's physical fitness program.

8. Be ready to live alone
Your Financial Fitness Program must help you prepare for the time when you will have to live alone for some period. So be aware that if someone else has always cooked the meals and handled your diet, you might very well go off on a binge the first time you are alone in the kitchen. Learn your financial fitness habits while you have your spouse with you. Cook them up side by side and get plenty of practice at handling them alone.

Keep this book as your reference and guide. Don't ever hesitate to go back and reread or redo the exercises you need most. Above all, keep control now that you are in charge. Being in charge of your money will not and must not be an activity that brings you uneasiness, worry, or fear. It's just the opposite, in fact. Taking charge, making the handling of money a regular daily activity, will put you in a continuing state of sound financial fitness, which in turn will give you peace of mind.

INDEX

○ ○ ○